Appcelerator Titanium Application Development by Example Beginner's Guide

Over 30 interesting recipes to help you create cross-platform apps with Titanium, and explore the new features in Titanium 3

Darren Cope

BIRMINGHAM - MUMBAI

Appcelerator Titanium Application Development by Example Beginner's Guide

First published: April 2013

Production Reference: 1120413

Published by Packt Publishing Ltd.
Livery Place
35 Livery Street
Birmingham B3 2PB, UK.

ISBN 978-1-84969-500-8

www.packtpub.com

Cover Image by J. Blaminsky (milak6@wp.pl)

Credits

Author

Darren Cope

Reviewers

Steve Dawes

Stephen Feather

Imraan Jhetam

Acquisition Editor

James Jones

Lead Technical Editor

Neeshma Ramakrishnan

Technical Editors

Chirag Jani

Devdutt Kulkarni

Project Coordinator

Arshad Sopariwala

Proofreaders

Maria Gould

Aaron Nash

Paul Hindle

Indexer

Monica Ajmera Mehta

Graphics

Aditi Gajjar

Production Coordinator

Manu Joseph

Cover Work

Manu Joseph

About the Author

Darren Cope is an experienced Titanium developer having seen the light and the potential of what could be done with Titanium back in early 2011. Since 2011 he has released several cross-platform apps using the technology. He holds TCAD and TCMD certifications and along with creating apps, he has developed modules for the Appcelerator Marketplace. He attended the inaugural CODESTRONG conference in San Francisco in October 2011 and continues to preach the benefits of coding with Titanium through the Appcelerator Titans program. He is very eager to hear from other Titanium developers in the north of England and is trying to start a user group for them. He can be contacted either through his personal website at `http://darren.cope.name` or by e-mail on `mail@darren.cope.name`.

I'd like to thank Tracey for her love, support, and encouragement during the writing of this book, and thank the writers of NCIS who have provided the background noise for most of the time I was writing this book. I would also like to thank Steve Dawes who reached out to me with an opportunity to develop an app in early 2011 and in doing so started the process that got me here.

About the Reviewers

Steve Dawes is a delivery-focused IT consultant with senior management experience in global corporations and director level experience in SMEs.

Steve's experience includes end-to-end delivery of software and infrastructure projects, product development, and strategic roadmap formulation and business change in a variety of sectors including transport, retail, finance, construction, postal, and services with implementations of systems developed in e-commerce, the cloud, the Web, mobile, and SOA architectures.

Steve is a member of the BCS and APM and specializes in interim project management and business transformation projects. Steve works through his company Rockwave Consulting Ltd, www.rockwaveconsulting.co.uk.

Stephen Feather is an Appcelerator Titanium titan, holding TCMD and TCAD certifications. He is a frequent speaker on mobile strategies for small business and non-profit organizations. In 1994 he started his own consulting firm working directly with communications companies such as Netscape, Microsoft, and Oracle in the early days of the Internet. In 1996 he wrote *JavaScript by Example, Que Publishing*, one of the first publications on the then new scripting language. Over the next 17 years, his firm would grow to become a widely recognized vendor of multimedia software for language learning, providing support to colleges and universities throughout the southeastern United States.

In 2009, he co-founded Feather Direct, recognizing a need for quality mobile app development, reputation management, and SEO services for smaller organizations. He volunteers time to assist and train a new generation of mobile app developers through online forums and local user groups.

Imraan Jhetam is a medical doctor and entrepreneur living in England with an equal love for both medical law and technology. He earned his medical degree from the University of Natal in 1983, his MBA from the University of Witwatersrand, and a Master's degree in Law from Cardiff University.

Imraan has been fascinated by computers since his youth and taught himself the basics of programming during his university years. He has been writing programs since the mid 1970s in various languages and for different platforms and has fond memories of his first Apple//e with its then impressive 64 KB RAM.

When he is not busy seeing patients or writing medico-legal reports, he spends his time developing applications and developed Snappa, a social sharing game that is the better way to draw something for friends. This was written using the incredible Titanium Studio tools and Appcelerator Cloud Services and is now in the Apple and Android app stores. He was also third prize winner at the first Codestrong Hackathon with two e-payment apps, *PayBill* and *PayPad*, that also included social media, geo-location, photos, and barcodes, and which were developed in a restricted and short time using Appcelerator Titanium Studio.

You can contact Imraan via `www.snappa.mobi` or via Twitter `@The__i`.

www.PacktPub.com

Support files, eBooks, discount offers and more

You might want to visit www.PacktPub.com for support files and downloads related to your book.

Did you know that Packt offers eBook versions of every book published, with PDF and ePub files available? You can upgrade to the eBook version at www.PacktPub.com and as a print book customer, you are entitled to a discount on the eBook copy. Get in touch with us at service@packtpub.com for more details.

At www.PacktPub.com, you can also read a collection of free technical articles, sign up for a range of free newsletters and receive exclusive discounts and offers on Packt books and eBooks.

http://PacktLib.PacktPub.com

Do you need instant solutions to your IT questions? PacktLib is Packt's online digital book library. Here, you can access, read and search across Packt's entire library of books.

Why Subscribe?

- Fully searchable across every book published by Packt
- Copy and paste, print and bookmark content
- On demand and accessible via web browser

Free Access for Packt account holders

If you have an account with Packt at www.PacktPub.com, you can use this to access PacktLib today and view nine entirely free books. Simply use your login credentials for immediate access.

For Tracey and Emily.
And for Chris, gone but not forgotten.

Table of Contents

Preface

It's fair to say that while Steve Jobs didn't necessarily start a smartphone revolution with the iPhone and iPad he certainly championed it and in doing so created beautifully designed devices that rightfully became both massively popular and highly desired.

Not long after the introduction of these seductive devices came another masterstroke, the App Store. Apple generated massive developer interest by promoting the dream of becoming a rock-star developer by creating apps for this new platform. It was a massive success; a new breed of indie developers flocked to the platform pushing new apps into the App Store hoping their app would be the one to make it big.

The App Store opened in June 2008 with only 500 apps. By October 2011 there were over half a million apps, and it continues to grow with over 500 new apps published everyday. There will soon be 1 million apps available which has resulted in an ecosystem that has paid out over six billion dollars in royalties. Thanks to a lucrative payment strategy whereby Apple gets 30 percent of revenue from every sale, they have become one of the biggest companies in history.

Success of that size doesn't go unnoticed or unchallenged. The monopoly didn't last long and soon after Google came along with Android and its own Android marketplace. While initial take-up was slower than Apple, it has gained ground and by late 2012 both stores had equal number of apps available.

Now the app market has two major players. You can create an app for iOS or Android, but unfortunately there are no common compilers for the two systems, so if you want to write a native app for iOS, you have to use objective-C and Java for Android.

Jeff Haynie and Nolan Wright (the founders of Appcelerator) were ahead of all of this; they already had a way of creating native apps for iOS using JavaScript, and it just so happened that the methodology they used in their Titanium tool would also work for Android. Titanium was launched in 2009 and since then it has attracted over 400,000 registered developers.

Titanium allows you to create native apps that will run on both iOS and Android. A Titanium app can be run on both platforms without changing a single line of code. Over 50,000 apps have been released using the technology; this book will help you to add your app to that list.

The book will guide you through the process of creating a cross-platform app, an app that can be released to both Android and iOS app stores.

The book has been written in a relaxed and friendly manner with carefully selected examples that highlight the core concepts of the chapter. All examples, unless specifically stated, are written so that they may be run on both platforms.

The chapters have been ordered to reflect the order in which I believe the tool should be learned. The initial chapters will provide guidance on how to install and configure the tool before moving on to how to create apps using Titanium. The book then looks in detail at how to design and structure apps. This is the content that will be invaluable later when your apps become larger and more complex. Being able to easily modify and extend your apps because they have been designed with a well-defined structure will be a significant advantage.

The next few chapters then focus on some of the core components of apps with chapters on the cloud, phone gadgets, and data. After this we move on to an important area, interface design, and how to create apps that will run and look good on phones and tablets from both iOS and Android.

Next, the book has a couple of chapters that look into a few optional extras such as social media integration and push notifications, before moving on to the final phase of testing and deploying your app to the app store.

The final two chapters focus on areas that are often considered by developers after an app has gone live, namely analytics and making money from your app.

What this book covers

Chapter 1, How to Get Up and Running with Titanium, guides you through the process of installing Titanium and setting up the Android and iOS SDKs. It then shows you how to create your first, simple cross-platform app and explains the core components of all Titanium apps.

Chapter 2, How to Make an Interface, introduces the tools that are available for making an interface and shows how you can design apps that make use of platform specific features. The next two chapters provide guidance on how to design and structure a Titanium application. Furthermore, they explain how a Titanium app is connected and how the use of best practices will result in more manageable code.

Chapter 3, How to Design Titanium Apps, delves into the detail of how to structure a Titanium app, and how the use of best design practices results in more manageable, stable, and reusable code. It also explains the Model View Controller (MVC) design methodology and touches on Alloy, the latest in design models for Titanium.

Chapter 4, Gluing Your App Together With Events, Variables, and Callbacks, explains how different parts of your app communicate with one another, for example, how a slider indicates its value to a label. It gives a thorough examination of events and also explains some of the problems of defining global variables and how to avoid creating them.

Chapter 5, It's All About Data, describes how to communicate with external sources using HTTP requests. It also covers how to store data locally in files, databases, or properties. Finally, it provides a worked example of how to show foreign exchange prices using Yahoo Query Language (YQL).

Chapter 6, Cloud-enabling Your Apps, looks at how to integrate cloud services into your app and how they can be used to store and retrieve data. It shows examples of Appcelerator Cloud Services and shows the principles of integrating any REST based service.

Chapter 7, Putting the Phone Gadgets to Good Use, describes how to integrate phone gadgets into your app. It provides examples of the camera, compass, geolocation, maps, directions, and accelerometer. It also shows how these gadgets can be combined together to produce an Augmented Reality (AR) experience.

Chapter 8, Creating Beautiful Interfaces, details how to build interfaces that work on both platforms and how the same interface can be altered to produce a different layout for phones and tablets. It also looks into how to break down a complex screen into smaller views and how to handle and control orientation.

Chapter 9, Spread the Word with Social Media, shows how your can integrate Facebook and Twitter into your application. It also shows an alternative way of sharing information on Android using intents.

Chapter 10, Sending Notifications, shows how to add push notification support into your app. It details the full workflow for push notifications from registering with a provider to acting on the notification from within your app.

Chapter 11, Testing and Deploying, examines how to test your app on devices and includes detail on creating certificates and provisioning profiles. It also guides you through the process of successfully deploying your app to iOS and Android stores.

Chapter 12, Analytics, provides examples of how to integrate three analytic providers, namely, Appcelerator Analytics, Flurry, and Google Analytics into your app, and shows the benefits of gathering analytic information.

Chapter 13, Making Money from Your App, provides examples of how to make money from your app. It focuses on integrating adverts from suppliers such as Google AdMob and how you can use in-app purchases to add premium paid functionality into your app.

Appendix A, Git Integration, discusses the integration of Titanium Studio with the cloud-based GitHub source control system.

Appendix B, Glossary, contains the list of terminologies used in the book.

What you need for this book

You can install Titanium onto a PC or Mac running Windows, OS X, or Ubuntu. Apple only supplies iOS development tools for the OS X environment so if you are planning to deploy your app onto iOS, you will need access to OS X. If you have a Mac, you can develop apps for both iOS and Android. Full details of compatibility can be found at `http://docs.appcelerator.com/titanium/3.0/#!/guide/Titanium_Compatibility_Matrix`.

You also need to sign up for an iOS or Google developer account depending on the platforms you are developing for.

Who this book is for

The primary purpose of this book is to provide developers with a guide to creating apps that can be released for both iOS and Android. The book will be particularly well suited to developers with experience of creating web-based content.

It is assumed that the reader already has a working knowledge of JavaScript as well as some of the key standards, such as XML.

Conventions

In this book, you will find several headings appearing frequently.

To give clear instructions of how to complete a procedure or task, we use:

Time for action – heading

1. Action 1
2. Action 2
3. Action 3

Instructions often need some extra explanation so that they make sense, so they are followed with:

What just happened?

This heading explains the working of tasks or instructions that you have just completed.

You will also find some other learning aids in the book, including:

Pop quiz – heading

These are short multiple-choice questions intended to help you test your own understanding.

Have a go hero – heading

These practical challenges will give you ideas for experimenting with what you have learned.

You will also find a number of styles of text that distinguish between different kinds of information. Here are some examples of these styles, and an explanation of their meaning.

Code words in text, database table names, folder names, filenames, file extensions, pathnames, dummy URLs, user input, and Twitter handles are shown as follows: "KS_nav_ui.png and KS_nav_views.png are the two icons that appear at the bottom of the screen on the tabs."

A block of code is set as follows:

```
# * Fine Tuning
#
key_buffer = 16M
key_buffer_size = 32M
max_allowed_packet = 16M
thread_stack = 512K
thread_cache_size = 8
max_connections = 300
```

When we wish to draw your attention to a particular part of a code block, the relevant lines or items are set in bold:

```
# * Fine Tuning
#
key_buffer = 16M
key_buffer_size = 32M
max_allowed_packet = 16M
thread_stack = 512K
thread_cache_size = 8
max_connections = 300
```

Any command-line input or output is written as follows:

```
cd /ProgramData/Propeople
rm -r Drush
git clone --branch master http://git.drupal.org/project/drush.git
```

New terms and **important words** are shown in bold. Words that you see on the screen, in menus or dialog boxes for example, appear in the text like this: "On the **Select Destination Location** screen, click on **Next** to accept the default destination."

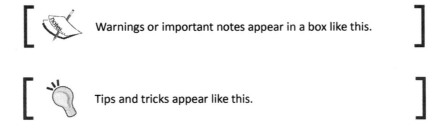

Warnings or important notes appear in a box like this.

Tips and tricks appear like this.

Reader feedback

Feedback from our readers is always welcome. Let us know what you think about this book—what you liked or may have disliked. Reader feedback is important for us to develop titles that you really get the most out of.

To send us general feedback, simply send an e-mail to feedback@packtpub.com, and mention the book title through the subject of your message.

If there is a topic that you have expertise in and you are interested in either writing or contributing to a book, see our author guide on www.packtpub.com/authors.

Customer support

Now that you are the proud owner of a Packt book, we have a number of things to help you to get the most from your purchase.

Downloading the example code

You can download the example code files for all Packt books you have purchased from your account at `http://www.packtpub.com`. If you purchased this book elsewhere, you can visit `http://www.packtpub.com/support` and register to have the files e-mailed directly to you.

Errata

Although we have taken every care to ensure the accuracy of our content, mistakes do happen. If you find a mistake in one of our books—maybe a mistake in the text or the code—we would be grateful if you would report this to us. By doing so, you can save other readers from frustration and help us improve subsequent versions of this book. If you find any errata, please report them by visiting `http://www.packtpub.com/submit-errata`, selecting your book, clicking on the **errata submission form** link, and entering the details of your errata. Once your errata are verified, your submission will be accepted and the errata will be uploaded to our website, or added to any list of existing errata, under the Errata section of that title.

Piracy

Piracy of copyright material on the Internet is an ongoing problem across all media. At Packt, we take the protection of our copyright and licenses very seriously. If you come across any illegal copies of our works, in any form, on the Internet, please provide us with the location address or website name immediately so that we can pursue a remedy.

Please contact us at `copyright@packtpub.com` with a link to the suspected pirated material.

We appreciate your help in protecting our authors, and our ability to bring you valuable content.

Questions

You can contact us at `questions@packtpub.com` if you are having a problem with any aspect of the book, and we will do our best to address it.

1
How to Get Up and Running with Titanium

This first chapter covers the installation of Titanium and associated tools needed to create and test cross-platform apps. By the end of this chapter you will have created a simple app that will run without modification on iOS and Android phones, and tablets.

Congratulations! Give yourself a pat on the back; you have taken a big step towards creating great apps that work on both iOS and Android. You have made a very wise choice. The Titanium application from Appcelerator allows you to design native apps, apps that run on the device itself and not via a browser or over the Internet. Furthermore, a Titanium app is written in JavaScript, which if you have not used before, is a really nice, flexible language to write code in. It's certainly not just a language for making small scripts in a browser which is what it is commonly known for.

You will be using tried and tested functionality. Appcelerator started releasing apps to the Apple App Store in 2009. Since then over 50,000 apps have been deployed to both iOS and Android stores including flagship apps from eBay and NBC. The company has attracted over $50 million of funding from venture capitalists who have seen the potential. You will be supported by both the company and an ever-growing group of nearly 500,000 registered developers. With support for HTML5 web apps and plans to support both Blackberry 10 and Windows 8 later this year, the case for success becomes stronger and stronger.

You have shown an interest in the best tool for creating cross-platform native apps; apps that can make use of the features of the dominant smartphone and tablet platforms. This book will take you from the initial installation of the tool right through to the publishing of a polished app.

By the end of this book you should be able to publish quality apps through both the Android and iOS stores. This book will not teach you to program in JavaScript, but that should not concern you. If you have programmed in other programming languages, then JavaScript will not be alien to you. Some of the more specific language elements such as events and callbacks will be covered in the book. Should you need a reference, I would highly recommend you to look at some of the articles written by the godfather of JavaScript, Douglas Crockford (http://javascript.crockford.com/). Be aware that most Titanium apps can be programmed using only a small subset of the features provided by the language.

This first chapter covers the following:

◆ The installation of Titanium Studio
◆ The installation of Android and iOS SDKs
◆ Creating your first Titanium app
◆ A look into the configuration of apps

System requirements and restrictions

You can run Titanium on Mac, Windows PC, or Linux. Great; however, your choice of operating system may restrict the types of app you can develop, as not all emulators are available on all operating systems. Apple only releases the SDK for iOS on its operating system.

If you don't have a Mac but would like to release your code on iOS, then you can rent a Mac from MacinCloud (http://www.macincloud.com/). You can install Titanium Studio with the Apple SDK. It is slower than having a Mac of your own, but cheaper if you only need a short-term solution.

The following table shows what is available on which operating system:

Operating system	Android emulator	iOS emulator
Mac OS X	Yes	Yes
Windows	Yes	No
Linux	Yes	No

The Appcelerator site states that the minimum memory required to run Titanium is 2 GB. It is advisable to have at least 4 GB of memory, especially if you plan to run the Android emulator.

 You do not need a Google developer account to install and use Titanium within the emulator, but if you plan to release code or run the app on a device, then you do. If you are serious about writing an app, it's a good idea to get an account. You cannot download the iOS SDK without purchasing the iOS developer program membership, so you will need it before beginning to write apps for iOS.

Installing Titanium

Assuming that you meet the preceding requirements, you are ready to install Titanium.

Time for action – installing Titanium Studio

Titanium comprises of Titanium Studio and the SDK. Titanium Studio is the development environment that is built on top of the Eclipse tool. Previous users of Eclipse should find Titanium Studio familiar. The SDK comprises of the *magic* of Titanium where your JavaScript source code is compiled into native code. To install Titanium perform the following steps:

1. Navigate to the Appcelerator site http://www.appcelerator.com and create an account.

2. Then follow the link to **Download Titanium Studio**, selecting the appropriate file for your operating system.

3. Open the downloaded file to install Titanium Studio.

What just happened?

You have downloaded and installed Titanium Studio. There will be a link to **Titanium Studio** either on the **Start** menu (Windows installation) or within the Applications folder (Mac). You have made the first big step towards creating cross-platform native applications.

Setting up Titanium Studio

Now it's time to set up and configure Titanium Studio.

Time for action – setting up Titanium Studio

Open Titanium Studio to begin the process of setting up the tool and perform the following steps:

1. Select the location for your workplace. This will be the base directory for your apps. All of your Titanium projects, and therefore apps, will be stored in directories below this.

> The workspace location should be free of spaces and punctuation characters as it can affect the compilation and deployment of your apps.

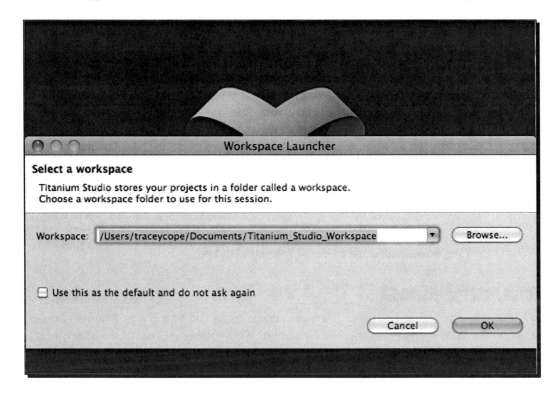

2. Enter your Appcelerator account details and click on **Next**. After a short delay you will be presented with the Titanium welcome screen.

What just happened?

Titanium Studio was opened and a base workspace directory was specified. That completes the installation and initial configuration of Titanium Studio. If you have not already downloaded and installed the platform SDKs you wish to use, you should do this next so you can run code in the simulator. Titanium handles this installation beautifully.

Installing the Android SDK

If you plan to release your app for the Android platform or to just merely evaluate how it looks in the emulator, then you need to install the Android SDK.

If you have a question mark against the Android SDKs on the welcome screen icon, then Titanium cannot find the Android SDK on your system. Click on the icon to start the installation.

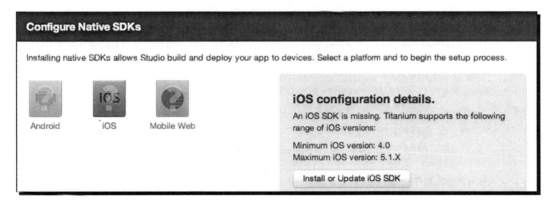

Time for action – configuring the Android SDK

To configure the Android SDK, perform the following steps:

1. Select the installation directory. Note that this does not need to be your Titanium workspace directory, as shown in the following screenshot:

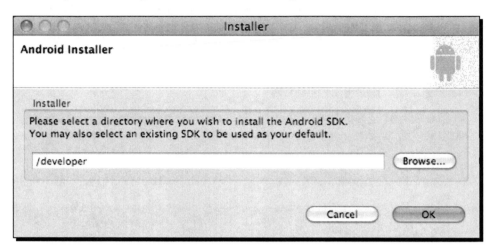

2. Wait while the Android SDKs are downloaded and installed—this will take some time, there is a lot of content to install.

3. Configure the versions of SDKs you wish to use. Make sure that you include Android 2.2 as this is required by Titanium. You can install as many as you like and including 2.2, it just takes extra time to install. If you are not sure which Android device you are targeting, then just install the latest version and Android 2.2 for now. You can always add others later:

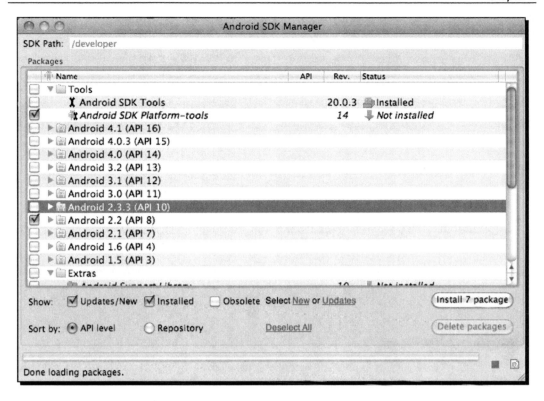

4. Wait while the selected APIs are downloaded and installed. This may take some time if you have selected several SDK versions.

5. Once the installation process completes, the SDK installer will exit and you will be returned to the Titanium dashboard where the question mark will have been cleared from the Android SDK. The Android emulator is now installed and configured for use with Titanium.

What just happened?

The Android SDK was downloaded and you had the opportunity to install specific versions of Android emulator you wish to test against. Titanium Studio took note of the installation directory and stored it in its preferences so that it can communicate with the emulator.

Installing the iOS SDK

If you have a Mac, then the chances are that the SDK that you will want the most is the iOS SDK. It's faster to load and less strict compared to the Android SDK.

Time for action – configuring the iOS SDK

To configure the Android SDK perform the following steps:

1. If the Titanium dashboard shows a question mark against the iOS SDK, it means Titanium cannot locate a suitable iOS SDK. Click on the icon to begin the process of installation.

2. Depending on your version of iOS the App store will be launched with the Xcode application. Install the application.

3. Once the installation process completes, the Titanium dashboard will be updated and the question mark will be cleared from the iOS SDK. The iOS emulator is now ready for use.

What just happened?

The latest iOS SDK was downloaded and installed. Titanium Studio took note of the installation directory so that it can call the emulator and display the logs on the console.

Installation problems – did something go wrong?

This is by no means an exhaustive reference of all the problems that you might encounter. For issues beyond this section you should refer to the developer documentation at `docs.appcelerator.com`, the Question & Answers section of the Appcelerator website `https://developer.appcelerator.com/questions/newest` or Appcelerator support.

If you have a problem with the installation of any of the SDKs, you can investigate the settings by selecting **Preferences** from the Titanium Studio menu. From there navigate to **Titanium Studio | Titanium**, which will result in the following screen:

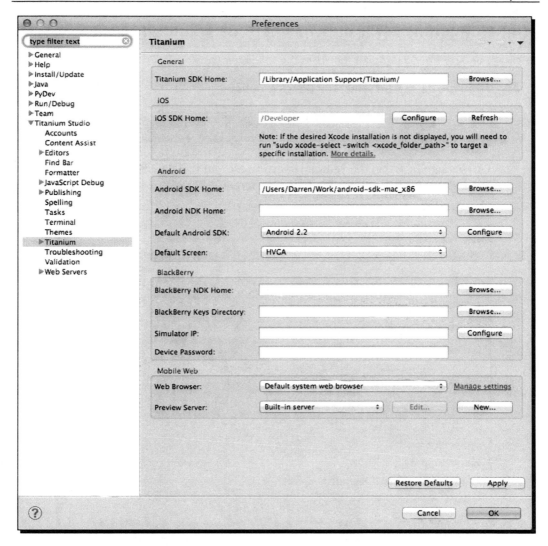

From this screen you can select the location of the Titanium SDK home and Android SDK home, and investigate the location of the iOS SDK.

Your first cross-platform app

Now that Titanium Studio and the mobile SDKs have been installed, it's time to create your first cross-platform app.

Time for action – creating an app from a template

To create an app from a template perform the following steps:

1. From the dashboard select the **Develop** option:

2. On this screen within the **Template** section click on the **New Project** button and on the **Default Project** option. The following screen will appear:

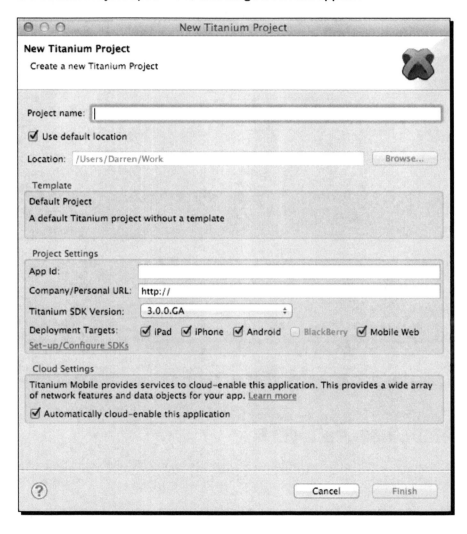

An explanation of the options shown on the **New Titanium Project** screen is given in the following table:

Value	Optional/required	Description
Project Name	Required	This contains the name of the project. This will be the name that appears in the **Project Navigator** window, and will also be the name of the base director of the app. It will probably be the intended name of the app when you release it although it doesn't have to be. You can release the app under a different name.
App Id	Required	This contains the unique identifier for the app. The convention is to use the reverse domain name such as com.domain.project. The minimum requirement is to have an app ID of xxx.x (meaning you must have a dot and something after it). Also note that the app ID does not have to relate to a real domain nor to a domain that you own, although you would be wise to choose a domain you own.
Company URL	Optional	This contains the URL of the company that owns the app. This is optional and will not be shown on the app store.
Titanium SDK Version	Required	This contains the version of the Titanium SDK used to build your app. This can be changed later.
Deployment Targets	Required	This contains a list of checkboxes of device types that you intend to release the app on. This can be changed later. Leaving them all checked as the default setting is not an issue and will not get in your way.
Automatically Cloud enable this application	Required	Do you want to connect to the cloud for this application? This should be left unchecked for this first app. We will cover the cloud enabling of apps later in this book.

For this app the settings used are shown in the following screenshot:

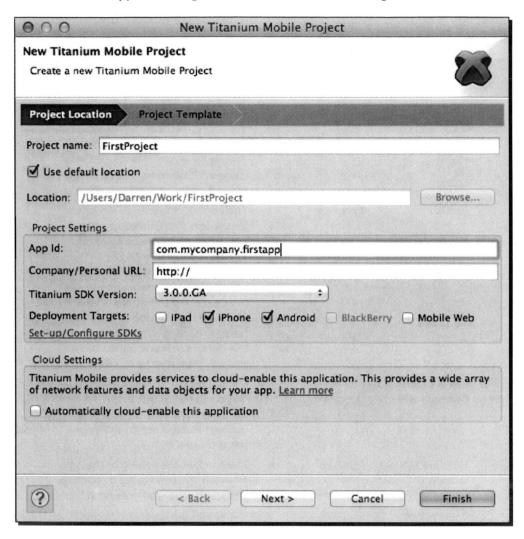

3. Click on **Finish**. The project will be created and you will be presented with the following screen:

4. The screen is a summary of the contents of the `tiapp.xml` file. This file contains the project settings and customizations. It's a file you will become familiar with and refer to often when creating Appcelerator apps. We will take a closer look at the contents of this file later in the chapter, but first let's get straight to business and run our first cross-platform app, using the code that was just generated.

What just happened?

We created our first Titanium app. Titanium will have created the project files and directories required to support the development of the app. The main configuration files will have been configured based on the entries specified on the **New Titanium Mobile Project** screen.

The blank template has created an app with a small amount of code in it. Enough for us to run it to see what we have done. Everything is in place. You have a project, you have configured your emulators, what are you waiting for? Let's run the app!

Time for action – running an app in the emulator

You can run an app from either the run menu or from the navigator window, as shown in the following screenshot:

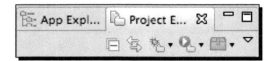

The buttons from left to right are as follows:

Button	Text
Collapse All	Collapse all items in the navigator
Link	Highlight in the navigator the current file in the main editor window
Debug	Run the app using the debugger
Run	Run the app in the emulator or on a connected device (phone or tablet connected to the computer)
Distribute	Package the app for release to an Android or iOS app store

To run the app in the emulator click on the **Run** button on the navigator window and select your chosen emulator from the list. If you are using a Mac, you can really exploit the power of Titanium by running the app on both Android and iOS at the same time. Otherwise, you will have to content yourself with only running the Android version of the app.

The Android emulator can take a long time to start. It certainly takes much longer than the iOS emulator. On some Android emulator devices, you need to unlock the screen display to allow the app to start.

The Android emulator will generate a lot of console messages (colored white), warnings (yellow), and the occasional error (red). This is normal; however, you may need to keep an eye on the errors to see if anything significant is going wrong.

What just happened?

If you have chosen to run the app on both Android and iOS, you will have two emulators running the Titanium application at the same time, as shown in the following screenshot:

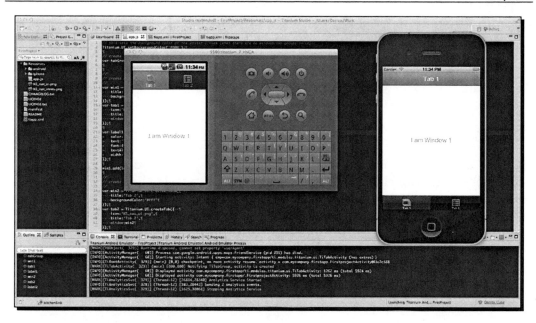

Take a moment to congratulate yourself. By getting to this point you have installed Titanium, configured the emulators, and created your first app. You have come a long way, and have all the tools you need installed and at your disposal. All that remains in this book is to teach you how to make better apps than this.

Did the app fail to run?

Did the following message appear on the console?

```
"[DEBUG] Session could not be started: Error Domain=DTiPhoneSimulatorErro
rDomain Code=2 "Simulator session timed out."
```

It is fairly common to see the timeout error message the first time a new app is run. Titanium has to go through some extra stages running the app for the first time, or the fist time the app is run after a project clean.

Try running it again.

Still didn't run? It's always worth rebuilding the project from a clean build, as this can clear many problems up. First clear down the existing build by clicking on **Project | Clean...** and then try re-running.

A review of the first app

For this next section, we will review what has been created on this first app. A number of files were created and you will need to be aware of some of them. These are the core files that are created for all apps, even this most basic one.

tiapp.xml

This file lives in the base directory of your project and contains your global project settings and compile-time customizations. Titanium Studio provides a clean, simple overview interface to the main settings listed in the file, as shown in the screenshot under step 3 of the *Time for action – creating an app from a template* section. From the overview screen you can:

◆ Add new external modules to your project such as a Twitter or PayPal module extension

◆ Add Appcelerator cloud services

◆ Change the Titanium SDK used to compile your app

◆ Enable deployment targets for supported platforms

◆ Change app version, description, and publisher details

When you open the tiapp.xml file you will notice that along with the overview there is a set of tabs at the bottom of the screen, which allows you to switch between the overview and the raw XML. There are a number of things that you can only change from the raw XML view of the file, for example allowed orientations, so it's worth getting familiar with it. The table given next provides a list of most configurable items within the file. You don't need to examine and learn the options now, in fact it doesn't make for great reading; you can refer to it when you need it. We will look at the effects of some of the settings later in the book.

tiapp XML structure explained

XML	Description
`<?xml version="1.0" encoding="UTF-8"?>` `<ti:app xmlns:ti="http://ti.appcelerator.org">`	This is the standard XML header.

XML	Description
``` <deployment-targets> <target device="mobileweb">false</target> <target device="iphone">true</target> <target device="ipad">false</target> <target device="android">true</target> <target device="blackberry">false</target> </deployment-targets> ```	This is the list of supported devices. This can be changed from the overview screen.
``` <sdk-version>3.0.0.GA</sdk-version> <id>com.mycompany.firstapp</id> <name>FirstProject</name> <version>1.0</version> <publisher>Darren</publisher> <url>http://</url> <description>not specified</description> <copyright>2012 by Darren</copyright> <icon>appicon.png</icon> ```	These settings can be changed from the overview screen.
`<persistent-wifi>false</persistent-wifi>`	Does your app require a persistent Wi-Fi connection, or is the default that turns off after a period of inactivity ok?
`<prerendered-icon>false</prerendered-icon>`	This controls the shine/gloss effect that is added to icons on iOS. Setting this to `true` will prevent the gloss being added.
`<statusbar-style>default</statusbar-style>`	This is the status bar style. See `Titanium.UI.iPhone.StatusBar` in the API documentation to see allowable values.

XML	Description
`<statusbar-hidden>false</statusbar-hidden>`	Should the status bar be hidden?
`<fullscreen>false</fullscreen>`	Should the app start up using the full screen?
`<navbar-hidden>false</navbar-hidden>`	Should the navigation bar be hidden?
`<analytics>true</analytics>`	Do you want to gather analytic information about the app that will be automatically uploaded to the Appcelerator site?
`<guid>d047116f-4ddb-4007-a24f-8702df42e59e</guid>`	This is the unique internal identifier of your app. It is used with the analytics services. Do not change this value.

`<property name="ti.ui.defaultunit">system</property>`
`<iphone>`
`<orientations device="iphone">`
`<orientation>Ti.UI.PORTRAIT</orientation>`
`</orientations>`
`<orientations device="ipad">`
`<orientation>Ti.UI.PORTRAIT</orientation>`
`<orientation>Ti.UI.UPSIDE_PORTRAIT</orientation>`
`<orientation>Ti.UI.LANDSCAPE_LEFT</orientation>`
`<orientation>Ti.UI.LANDSCAPE_RIGHT</orientation>`
`</orientations>`
`</iphone>`
	This lists the allowed orientations for the iOS devices you support. The options shown to the left restrict any displays on an iPhone to portrait (that is with the button at the bottom of the phone). All orientations will be supported by the iPad.

`<android xmlns:android=`
`"http://schemas.android.com/apk/res/`
`android"/>`
	This lists compile-time directives for the Android generator if any. This is also where any `AndroidManifest` overrides are listed.

XML	Description
``` <mobileweb> <precache/> <splash> <enabled>true</enabled> <inline-css-images>true </inline-css-images> </splash> <theme>default</theme> </mobileweb> ```	These are the settings and controls for the generation of a mobile web app.
``` <modules/> ```	Any external modules added to the project will be listed here. This can all be done from the overview screen.
``` </ti:app> ```	This is the closing XML line.

The good news is that for this chapter you don't have to change any of these settings.

Other files in the base directory

There are several other files that were generated when the project was created.

The other files in the project root directory are all text files that do not affect the operation of the app. They will be bundled with your app when it is released. You can update them if you feel the need.

The Resources directory

The other main element created at project inception is the `Resources` directory that looks as follows:

It contains one important file, `app.js`.

app.js

`app.js` is the entry point of any Titanium project—the first line of code that is executed. It can be freely edited as you wish. We will look at the contents of this file in later chapters. For now just accept the contents of the file that have been generated.

KS_nav_ui.png and KS_nav_views.png

`KS_nav_ui.png` and `KS_nav_views.png` are the two icons that appear at the bottom of the screen on the tabs. They are needed for this app but are not important elements of other apps. They can be deleted if they are not used.

The Android and iPhone directories

The `android` and `iphone` directories under the `Resources` folder contain the app icons and splash screens for many different iOS and Android devices supported by your app. We will look in more detail at the contents of these directories in *Chapter 11, Testing and Deploying*.

Pop quiz - Titanium installation and configuration

Q 1. You want to develop apps on your windows PC using Titanium. What platforms can you test on the machine?

1. iOS

2. Android

3. Symbian

Q 2. You will often need to refer to the app configuration file to change settings. Where can you find it?

1. `<project base directory>/manifest`

2. `<project base directory>/resources/app.json`

3. `<project base directory>/tiapp.xml`

4. `<project base directory>/app.js`

Q 3. What is the name of the source code file that is first run when an app starts?

1. `<project base directory>/app.js`

2. `<project base directory>/resources/app.js`

3. `<project base directory>/init.js`

4. `<project base directory>/build/start.exe`

Summary

A lot has been achieved in this chapter without a single line of code being written. You have installed Titanium, downloaded and configured the Android and iOS emulator, created a simple app, and run the app in the emulator.

The rest of the book will redress the code imbalance by concentrating on the tools and commands Titanium provides to help you design and distribute beautiful apps.

2
How to Make an Interface

We achieved a lot in the last chapter. Not only did we install Titanium and the emulators but we also created an app! Now that everything is set up we can start to explore the tools that are available to make cross-platform apps.

This chapter will explore the tools that are available in Titanium for building great, engaging, native cross-platform apps. By the end of the chapter we will have moved far beyond our first app by coding windows, views, buttons, and table views, and establishing principles that can be applied to the other controls in the toolkit. We will also touch on how to handle events triggered by the user, which will provide an insight into some of the techniques that we will cover in more detail in *Chapter 4, Gluing Your App Together with Events, Variables, and Callbacks*.

Expect to read about the following:

- Windows
- Views
- Table views
- Navigation groups and tabs
- Labels and buttons
- Debugging
- Android menus
- iOS style buttons

What's in the toolkit?

Broadly speaking you can split the tools in the Titanium SDK into three categories; tools for laying out information on the screen, tools for getting user input, and tools for showing information. Some tools cross these boundaries and lie outside them, but the following list shows the core tools that you will use most of the time:

Category	Tool
Creating a layout	Ti.UI.Window
	Ti.UI.View
	Ti.UI.TableView
	Ti.UI.ScrollView
	Ti.UI.ScrollableView
Getting input	Ti.UI.Button
	Ti.UI.TextField
	Ti.UI.TextArea
	Ti.UI.Switch
	Ti.UI.Slider
	Ti.UI.Picker
Showing information	Ti.UI.ProgressBar
	Ti.UI.ImageView
	Ti.UI.ActivityIndicator
	Ti.UI.Label
	Ti.UI.TableView
	Ti.UI.AlertDialog
	Ti.UI.WebView

A recap

Before we move on to other tools in the toolkit let's take a moment to examine and understand the code that was generated for us in the last chapter. Even though the app was small, it included several key elements that will be used by most apps.

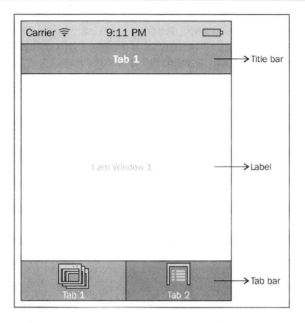

We will now cover the core items in the app. First and most importantly, the window.

Window

A window, or as it is named in the code, `Titanium.UI.Window`, is the canvas on which all other elements are attached. Without a window there can be no sliders, no buttons, nothing. All app elements are attached (or to use the Titanium terminology, added) to a window using the `add` command. An app requires at least one window to function and that window must be called from within the `app.js` file. The following code sample shows how a label is created and added to a window.

```
var win1 = Titanium.UI.createWindow({
    title:'Tab 1',
    backgroundColor:'#fff'
});
var label1 = Titanium.UI.createLabel({
    color:'#999',
    text:'I am Window 1',
    font:{fontSize:20,fontFamily:'Helvetica Neue'},
    textAlign:'center',
    width:'auto'
});

win1.add(label1);
```

A reference to `Titanium.UI.createWindow` is the same as `Ti.UI.createWindow`. Ti is a useful shortcut that is built into Titanium that will be used throughout the book.

In the app created in the last chapter there are two windows, one window per tab (we will cover tabs in a moment). A window will cover the entire available screen unless you specify otherwise, which in this case is the white area between the title bar and the tab bar. Also, you can have modal windows that require user interaction before they can return to operating the parent application.

Tab group and tabs

A tab group is a container for a group of tabs. It is displayed at the top of the screen on Android and the bottom on iOS, and allows the user to move between different screens on your app.

Tab groups are very well integrated and well suited to iOS apps and in particular iPhone apps, where they are commonly found on lots of apps; but it doesn't always look good on Android. As is shown in the next image, a tab group on a low resolution Android device takes up a lot of valuable screen estate. Think carefully about how your app will look on Android before committing to creating your app with it.

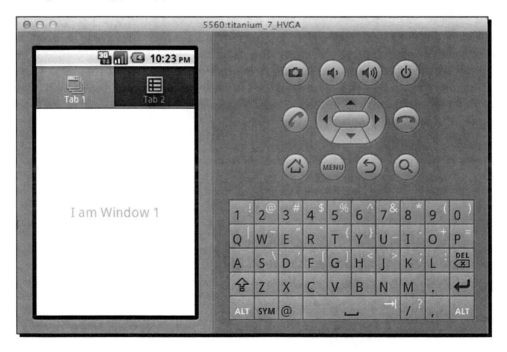

Tab groups may be on the way out in Android. Titanium 3.0 now creates Android action bars instead of tab groups if you set the Android SDK to higher than 11 in `tiapp.xml`. See `http://developer.appcelerator.com/blog/2012/12/breaking-changes-in-titanium-sdk-3-0.html`.

Creating a tab group

Tab groups are created by calling `Titanium.UI.createTabGroup()`. Tabs are added to tab groups. A tab will be associated with the window that should be shown when the tab is selected.

 Be aware that although you can add as many tabs as you wish to a tab group, only a certain amount can be displayed across the screen. They will not shrink to fit in more. The limit on iOS is five before things start to look ugly.

Creating a tab

The following code shows how to create a tab and associate the tab with a window.

```
// create tab group
var tabGroup = Titanium.UI.createTabGroup();


//
// create base UI tab and root window
//
var win1 = Titanium.UI.createWindow({
    title:'Tab 1',
    backgroundColor:'#fff'
});
var tab1 = Titanium.UI.createTab({
    icon:'KS_nav_views.png',
    title:'Tab 1',
    window:win1
});
```

Note the following key attributes of a tab.

Attribute	Description
icon	The icon to display on the tab.
title	The text to display on the tab bar for the tab.
window	The window to associate with the tab. This will be displayed when the tab is selected.

 A tab has many more properties and methods than shown in the previous table. For a complete reference, refer to the API documentation at http://docs.appcelerator.com/titanium.

Labels

Labels are used to display text. Here is an example call to create a label.

```
var label1 = Titanium.UI.createLabel({
    color:'#999',
    text:'I am Window 1',
    font:{fontSize:20,fontFamily:'Helvetica Neue'},
    textAlign:'center',
    width:Ti.UI.FILL,
});
```

The properties are explained in the following table:

Attribute	Description
color	The color of the label text. This can be specified as a predefined color name ('green') or hex triplet; for example, '#FFF' refers to white and '#999' refers to light gray.
text	The text to display.

Attribute	Description
font	The font properties. Note that the font properties are specified in JSON format. Even if you are only defining the fontName property, it should still be JSON formatted otherwise it will be ignored. JSON is discussed in *Chapter 3, How to Design Titanium Apps*.
	Properties that can be specified are: ◆ fontFamily ◆ fontSize ◆ fontStyle ◆ fontWeight
textAlign	The justification of the text within the defined size of the label.
width	The width of the label.

 You may see in some older code the width and height of items shows as 'auto'. The keyword auto has been depreciated! Either specify an explicit value or use the constants Ti.UI.SIZE or Ti.UI.FILL. See *Chapter 8, Creating Beautiful Interfaces* for more information on these constants.

Now that we have an understanding of the contents of the app, it's time to get your hands dirty and make some changes, but first there is one more important but unspectacular element that we should discuss.

Views

Views are an empty drawing surface onto which other items are added. They are the building blocks of a layout. Their beauty is that they allow you to format a section of the screen within the view without having to worry about the other parts of the screen.

What's the difference between a view and a table view?

A table view is used to lay out a vertical list of information such as a list of countries. A view is a container of objects. They are used to help lay out other objects. For example, you could use a view to make a horizontal row of buttons. Views are best thought of as a way to lay out an area of the screen.

Before I attempt to explain how views are used we should add one to the app.

Time for action – adding a view to a window

In the `app.js` file add the following code that will add a view to the second tab:

```
var view = Ti.UI.createView({
    top:20,
    bottom:'50%',
    left:20,
    right:'50%',
    backgroundColor:'red'
});

win2.add(view);
```

What just happened?

A red box has been added to the top left of the second tab as shown in the following screenshot:

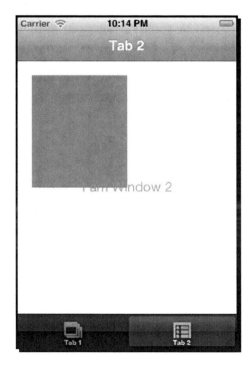

The beauty of views is that they act as containers for anything you add to them. So, if you add a button to a view and give the button details of where you want it positioned, for example, 10 pixels from the top and 10 pixels from the left, it will be positioned 10 pixels from the top of the view. Thus a view becomes a small drawing area independent of the window. If you add something to a view, its position is not relative to the window, but relative to the view. So if we add a button with a specific position to our view, the button will be positioned within the view not relative to the window, as we shall now see.

Time for action – adding a button to a view

In `app.js` add the following code to add the button to the view:

```
var button1 = Titanium.UI.createButton({
    title:'Button in View',
    top:10,
    left:10
});

view.add(button1);
```

 The text on the button is specified by the title argument. Other objects such as a `label` or `textfield` use the text argument to specify the displayed content. See the Appcelerator documentation `http://docs.appcelerator.com/titanium/3.0/#` for the appropriate argument for your object.

What just happened?

A button has been added within the view. Note that the position of the button of 10 pixels from the top and 10 pixels from the left is relative to the view and not the window. This is an important and very useful feature of views. You lay out the view within a window, like drawing a picture in a paint package that occupies only part of your display.

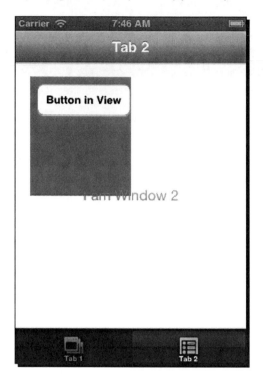

Notice how the button butts up against the top-right edge of the view. We didn't specify a size for the button via the width property, so Titanium made some size judgments for us. Titanium will make a button width as wide as its enclosing object, in this case the view, unless you specify otherwise. This layout information is explained in more detail in *Chapter 8, Creating Beautiful Interfaces* and also at `http://docs.appcelerator.com/titanium/3.0/#!/guide/Transitioning_to_the_New_UI_Layout_System-section-30088148_TransitioningtotheNewUILayoutSystem-ViewTypesandDefaultLayoutBehavior`.

We couldn't add a button without showing you how to make something happen when it is pressed. This next small example will show an alert when the button is pressed.

Time for action – making something happen when the button is pressed

Perform the following steps to make something happen when the button is pressed:

1. Add an event listener to the button. This event listener will respond when the user clicks on the button.

```
button1.addEventListener('click', function(e) {alert('You clicked
me!')})
```

2. Run the app and click on the button!

What just happened?

You added an event listener to the button so that when the button is clicked, an alert box is displayed. The Appcelerator documentation lists the events that are applicable for an object. You will use event listeners frequently in Titanium. They are explained in more detail in *Chapter 4, Gluing Your App Together with Events, Variables, and Callbacks*.

Adding a settings screen – a TableView masterclass

Views really come into their own when they are added to other controls, which we will see later in this chapter. We will also see them being used to control the layout of other elements. However, first of all, it's time to make something simple but useful with our app.

In this example we are going to use a table view to create a setting screen for the app. It's just one of the many uses there are for a table view. It's a versatile item that crops up in many places such as your contact list and your e-mail inbox. It is a very useful tool. We will now create a settings screen similar to that shown in the previous example.

Time for action – adding a new window

Perform the following steps to add a new window:

1. Add a new window and create a tab for it in the same way as in the earlier example from this chapter:

```
var winSettings = Ti.UI.createWindow({
});

var tabSettings = Titanium.UI.createTab({
    icon:'KS_nav_views.png',
```

```
            title:'Settings',
            window:winSettings
       });
```

2. Add the new tab to the tab group:

```
tabGroup.addTab(tabSettings);
```

3. In an attempt to keep the app.js file tidy we will place the code to create the settings layout in a function at the top of the file:

```
function setupSettings() {

}
```

4. The setupSettings function will create a settings layout that will be built on a view. The view will be returned from the function. Make changes to the function code by adding the following code:

```
function setupSettings() {

    var view = Ti.UI.createView({});
    return view;
}
```

5. This view can be added to the winSettings window by adding the code highlighted in the folowing code. The code adds the return value, which is a view, from the executed function to the window:

```
var winSettings = Ti.UI.createWindow({
});

var tabSettings = Titanium.UI.createTab({
    icon:'KS_nav_views.png',
    title:'Settings',
    window:winSettings
});

winSettings.add(setupSettings());
```

6. Run the app. What happens? Nothing! The app looks just as it did before. We have added a view to a window, but the view has nothing added to it and has no display properties specified. It's a transparent container. Still it proves that the code compiles. Let's move on and create a layout.

7. Add the following code that will create a `TableView` container object.

```
var tableView = Ti.UI.createTableView({
style:        Ti.UI.iPhone.TableViewStyle.GROUPED,
scrollable:   true
});
```

> Note the style attribute of `Ti.UI.iPhone.TableViewStyle.GROUPED`. This allows us to split the table view into sections instead of one long block. The style attribute has two options, `GROUPED` or `PLAIN`. .

8. Add a section to the table view. Note that table view sections are only applicable to grouped table views.

```
var firstSection = Ti.UI.createTableViewSection({
headerTitle: 'First',
footerTitle: 'Lots of contextual information'
});
```

9. Add `TableViewRow` object:

```
var firstRow = Ti.UI.createTableViewRow({
title: 'A setting',
hasChild: true
});
```

10. Link it all together by adding `TableViewRow` to `TableViewSection`, `TableViewSection` to `TableView`, and `TableView` to `View`:

```
firstSection.add(firstRow);
tableView.setData([firstSection]);
view.add(tableView);
```

11. Run the app. The screen will look as follows:

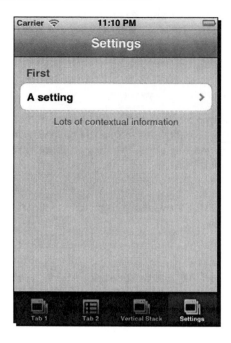

What just happened?

Several things were added to the view to create this screen:

- A `TableViewRow` object with a title and the `hasChild` property. The `hasChild` property results in the > option addition to the right of the settings box.
- A `TableViewSection` object with header and footer information.
- A `TableView` object with a style property of `Ti.UI.iPhone.TableViewStyle.GROUPED`.

> When you run the app on Android you may notice a warning in the console output:
>
> ```
> [ERROR] [TiAPI    (   293)]  !!!
> [ERROR] [TiAPI    (   293)]  !!! WARNING : Use of
> unsupported constant Ti.UI.iPhone.TableViewStyle.
> GROUPED !!!
> [ERROR] [TiAPI    (   293)]  !!!
> ```
>
> The app will still run, but it's a reminder that not everything in the toolkit can be applied to both platforms.

A `TableViewRow` object can have a simple layout with just a title, or it can contain several child elements. Let's add to our example by creating a row with a more complex layout.

 If you do create it as a table view layout that is complex and has a number of rows, then you can get into performance problems. But don't worry, help is at hand! If the same layout is repeated across rows then use the `className` attribute to tell Titanium that the rows belong to the same class. That way Titanium does not have to create a layout for each row.

Time for action – adding a styled TableViewRow object

With a few simple additions and some changes to fonts we can make a more complex table view layout. This example will add a `TableViewRow` object that is similar in appearance to the mailbox e-mail listing. Perform the following steps to add a styled TableViewRow object:

1. Add an empty `TableViewRow` object:

```
var secondRow = Ti.UI.createTableViewRow({});
```

2. Add a title to the new row:

```
var theTitle = Ti.UI.createLabel({
        text: 'The title',
        font:{fontSize:'16',fontWeight:'bold'},
        minimumFontSize:'12',
        textAlign:'left',
        top:'2',
        left:'10',
        height:'20'
    });
```

3. Add another label with context information:

```
var theSnippet =  Titanium.UI.createLabel({
        text:'Lorem ipsum dolor sit amet, consectetuer adipiscing
elit. Aenean commodo ligula eget dolor',
        font:{fontSize:'11',fontWeight:'normal'},
            textAlign:'left',
        color:'#666',
        bottom:'0',
        left:'10',
        height:'26'
    });
```

4. Link the new row to the existing section:

```
firstSection.add(firstRow);
firstSection.add(secondRow);
tableView.setData([firstSection]);
view.add(tableView);
```

5. Run the app.

What just happened?

With a couple of lines of code we have created a cross-platform settings screen! Here is how the results look on iOS and Android:

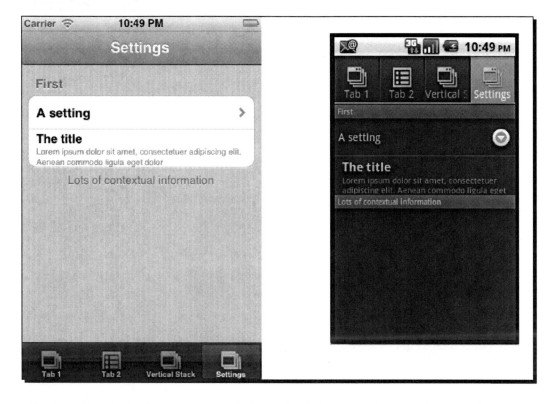

Notice how the display looks better on iOS than Android? Don't be downhearted about this, you can create layouts that are just as good as iOS on Android, we just need to look into ways to display data that work as well on Android. We will look into this and more in *Chapter 8, Creating Beautiful Interfaces*.

Platform-specific tools

There are many fundamental differences between Android and iOS. Android has the menu, iOS has a back button. Titanium respects this and has elements for individual operating systems.

For the final set of examples in this chapter, we will look at some of the platform-specific tools available in Titanium. It may seem incongruous to have platform-specific controls but it is an absolutely necessary part of the toolkit for creating native applications that embrace the identifying features of the platform. If it is a significant feature of an operating system that is not cross-platform it will be included in Titanium. A great example of this is the menu button on Android. It's a fundamental part of the Android design and something that the user will expect to be available yet there is no equivalent in iOS. Your Android app should make use of it.

Adding an Android menu

In the next example we will add an Android menu to our app.

Time for action – adding an Android menu

Perform the following steps for adding an Android menu:

1. Add a function that will define the pop-up menu:

```
function addMenu(win) {
    var activity = win.activity;

    activity.onCreateOptionsMenu = function(e){

    var firstItem = e.menu.add({ title: 'First Item' });
    firstItem.addEventListener("click", function(e) {Ti.API.
debug('First Item'); });

    var secondItem = e.menu.add({ title: 'Second Item'});
    secondItem.addEventListener("click", function(e) {Ti.API.
warn('Second Item'); });

    var thirdItem = e.menu.add({ title: 'Third Item'});
    thirdItem.addEventListener("click", function(e) {alert('Third
Item'); });
    };
}
```

2. Further down `app.js` where the windows are defined, add the highlighted code to call the function:

```
win1.add(label1);
addMenu(win1);
```

3. Run the app using the Android emulator.

What just happened?

A pop-up menu was created that is activated by pressing the menu key when **Tab 1** is selected. The pop-up menu has three items and each of the three items has a different debug action. Selecting the menu item will either send a message to the console or raise an alert.

Time for action – running the Android menu changes on iOS

If you are running on a Mac and have the iOS SDK installed, try running the app on the iOS emulator.

What just happened?

The app will fail to run. The red screen of death that will become familiar as you code your apps will be displayed.

Why did this fail?

The line that caused the error is as follows:

```
var activity = win.activity;
```

An iOS window has no concept of an activity. The activity property will not be available on iOS. The Appcelerator documentation is clear in this respect; the documentation shows that the activity property only exists on Android as shown in the following image:

You have to handle this platform-specific code yourself. Fortunately, it's not hard to do and if you are developing a cross-platform app it is a concept you will use often.

Isolating platform-specific code

When you have platform-specific code you have to have some way of avoiding executing it on the wrong platform. This usually means wrapping the code in an if statement. You can use the `Ti.Platform.name` property to determine the platform you are on. It will return one of the following values regardless of the code being run in the emulator or on a device:

♦ android

♦ mobileweb

♦ iPhone OS

Time for action – add an iOS fix for the Android menu

Here is how to fix the Android menu problem on iOS:

1. Add the following function to `app.js`:

```
function isAndroid() {
    return (Ti.Platform.name == 'android');
}
```

2. Wrap the `addMenu` function where our platform-specific code lies with this code:

```
function addMenu(win) {

    if (isAndroid()) {
    var activity = win.activity;

    activity.onCreateOptionsMenu = function(e){

    var firstItem = e.menu.add({ title: 'First Item' });
    firstItem.addEventListener("click", function(e) {Ti.API.
debug('First Item'); });

    var secondItem = e.menu.add({ title: 'Second Item'});
        secondItem.addEventListener("click", function(e) {Ti.API.
warn('Second Item'); });

    var thirdItem = e.menu.add({ title: 'Third Item'});
        thirdItem.addEventListener("click", function(e) {alert('Third
Item'); });
    }
};
}
```

3. Run the app on the iOS emulator.

What just happened?

An `if` statement was added that ensured that if the app was run on iOS, a menu would not be added to the window. The code now runs on iOS and Android.

The previous example added debug messages to the code. As an aside we will take a moment to take a look at writing debug messages.

Capturing debug messages

There are a few helper functions that are available to enable you to send out debug messages from the app.

Function	Description

`Ti.API.debug('text')`
Or
`console.debug('text')`
	Write a message to the console at the debug level.

`Ti.API.warn('text')`
Or
`console.warn('text')`
	Write a message to the console at the warn level. These messages are colored yellow.

`alert('text')`	Displays an alert box with the text and a single **OK** button.

Debugging code should be removed from your code or disabled before you go live. They are unlikely to result in your app submission being rejected, but the same messages that appear on the console in Titanium will be logged to the log files on your device. You don't want a clever developer snooping on your debug messages when the app is live.

Note that by default debug messages will not appear on the console. The default log level is to record errors and warnings. This can be altered by navigating to the **Run | Run Configurations** menu item. From the dialog box presented, select the appropriate level from the **Log Level** drop-down box. Trace provides a lot of information.

Coding iOS specific elements

In this iOS specific example we shall add a stylized button to the navigation bar.

Time for action – adding an info button to the navigation bar

Perform the following steps to add an info button to the navigation bar:

1. Add a new function to the top of `app.js`:

    ```
    function rightButton(win) {
        if (!isAndroid()) {

            var right = Ti.UI.createButton({
                systemButton:Ti.UI.iPhone.SystemButton.INFO_LIGHT
            });
            right.addEventListener('click',function()
            {
                alert('button clicked!');
            });
            win.setRightNavButton(right);
        }
    }
    ```

2. Add a call to the function from the main body of `app.js`:

    ```
    rightButton(win1);
    ```

3. Run the App in the iOS emulator.

What just happened?

A couple of iOS-specific properties were used in the `rightButton` function.
The `systemButton` property allows a predefined iOS icon to be applied to your
button. There are several styles available (see documentation for `Titanium.UI.`
`iPhone.SystemButton`). Then an iOS specific window method `setRightNavButton`
was used to place this button on the right-hand side of the navigation bar.

Summary

That's enough for this chapter. Yes, there are plenty of other elements in the toolkit that we have not covered. I could show you how to add a slider, or a switch, but I see little value in adding several examples when the principle is very similar to adding a button. Don't take my word for it; have a look at the examples from the code snippets. The main difference is the name of the control.

This chapter has taught you the principles you need to employ for adding any of the items in the toolkit. I urge you to go away and play with the `app.js` code and add sliders, switches, text areas, or any other control. Go ahead and enjoy yourself, it doesn't matter if you break the code, we will be throwing it away after this chapter anyway. It's a good time to move on from this app; it's served us well but it's getting a bit messy and disorganized.

If playing and editing with the code is not your thing, have a look around the Kitchensink app (which can be installed from the Titanium dashboard) and explore the code behind the controls, or look at the API reference on the Appcelerator website (`http://docs.appcelerator.com`).

This chapter has taught the principles of how to add controls to an app, however, in doing so, the code became messy and unstructured. We will address these issues in the next few chapters where we will add some structure to the code, as we look into the design methodologies that result in cleaner and more manageable code.

3
How to Design Titanium Apps

In the last chapter we created an app based on a single file. We also introduced the concept of splitting the executing path of the code to handle platform differences using the Ti.Platform.name *property. This worked for the small app but would be no way to design something larger. The single file approach would get very messy and the code would get more and more complex when new platforms were added. It was a good start but what we need to do now is to lay down the proper principles of Titanium design that will enable us to create complex apps that support many devices without the code getting tied up in knots.*

Towards the end of the chapter we will be touching on the very latest in Titanium design trends. This may be a step too far for a first time Titanium user. If you find it's a bit heavy, skip it; it's not a problem, you can revisit that part of the chapter at a later date.

Expect to read about the following in this chapter:

- How to pass data cleanly through your app using JSON
- How to split code over many files
- How to include and use Appcelerator marketplace libraries
- CommonJS
- Alloy

The majority of this chapter will concentrate on methods to improve the design of your app by making your code more modular. But before we start doing this we should take a moment to examine a fantastic feature that will be used extensively throughout your apps. It is flexible, readily extendible, easy to use, and intuitive. I could go on. It's JSON; it is used throughout Titanium and I love it.

JSON

JavaScript Object Notation (JSON) is a human readable data interchange format. It's very flexible, fast, and easy to use and understand and is included in the core of Titanium. It's used throughout the examples on the Appcelerator website, and it should also be used throughout your code. You are likely to use it whenever you pass data around in Titanium, including function parameters, as well as variables and a host of other areas.

I will highlight the flexibility it provides with an example. Should you want a reference guide then go to `http://json.org/`.

JSON is created using the `{ }` constructor. It consists of a set of name/value pairs. It's best explained using an example. Here is a list of sample JSON definitions in a format that can be used in Titanium:

JSON	Description
`var myJSON = {};`	Empty JSON variable
`var myJSON = {aNum : 1};`	Number attribute

`var myJSON = {`
`  Array : ['elem1', 'elem2',`
`'elem3']};`
	An array within JSON

`setWindowProperties = ({top :`
`0, bottom: 0, backgroundColor:`
`'#000'});`
	Multiple properties in a single JSON variable

`var label1 = Titanium.`
`UI.createLabel({`
`    color:'#999',`
`    text:'I am Window 1',`
`    font:{fontSize:20,fontFamily:`
`'Helvetica Neue'},`
`    textAlign:'center',`
`    width:'auto'`
`});`
	This example from the code generated in *Chapter 1, How to Get Up and Running with Titanium* has a JSON parameter for the font, which is itself an attribute of the parameter to the `createLabel` function

Taking the `setWindowProperties` function call example from the previous table, what would the function definition for `setWindowProperties` look like?

```
Function setWindowProperties(properties) {
  Win1.backgroundColor = properties.backgroundColor;
};
```

Simple; and of course this being JavaScript there is no need to specify the data type as it is determined at runtime. And if you wanted to add another element to the parameter just add it to the call, no need to change the function definition. This makes JSON very flexible and very handy.

> Titanium includes two methods for converting JSON data. You do not need these methods when you are passing JSON around inside your app as it will remain formatted. They are used when you communicate with external data sources such as a database or web service where the data is sent as a string.
>
> ◆ `JSON.stringify`: Takes a JSON formatted string and returns a serialized string that can be sent as text.
>
> ◆ `JSON.parse`: The reverse of `JSON.stringify`. Parse takes a string representation of JSON and returns a JSON formatted object.

Extending your app over multiple files

So far all of the code has been contained in a single `app.js` file. However, this soon becomes cluttered, unstructured, messy, and unmanageable. No language worth its salt expects you to write the full application in a single file. Titanium is no exception and exposes several methods to manage your code over several files.

The simplest and most basic method is `Ti.include`.

Titanium.include

`Titanium.include` allows you to attach source code from another file. It is analogous to `#include` in C, `xsd:include` in XML, and similar to `import` in Java. It allows you to break your code out into files of a manageable size.

> While `Ti.include` makes it easy to split your code over files, it is not the preferred method. Using commons and the require keyword shown later in the chapter should be used where possible.

Time for action – creating an activity indicator

The following example will create a small app with an extra file that contains code to display an activity indicator. Perform the following steps to do so:

1. Create a new blank mobile project without a template.

2. Open app.js. Clear all of the existing code and replace it with the following, which will create a blank window:

```
var win1 = Titanium.UI.createWindow({
    backgroundColor:'#fff'
});

win1.open();
```

3. Create a new file by navigating to **File | New | File**, placing the new file in the resources directory. Call the new file activity.js as it will contain the code to create the activity indicator. The file will automatically be opened in the editor when it is created.

4. activity.js will contain code to return an activity indicator. Add the following code to the new file:

```
function activityIndicator(args) {
        var actInd = Ti.UI.createActivityIndicator({height:50,wid
th:10});
        if (Ti.Platform.osname != 'android') actInd.style=Titanium.
UI.iPhone.ActivityIndicatorStyle.DARK;

        actInd.message = args.message || null;
        if (Ti.Platform.name = 'iPhone OS') args.win.add(actInd);
        return actInd;
    };
```

 There are a few different styles of activity indicator for iOS. See the Titanium API documentation for a full listing. The dark one has been chosen for this example as it contrasts nicely with the white background.

This code creates a function that when called will return the activity indicator to the calling code. The function takes a single JSON parameter and acts on the `message` and `win` attributes. The text in the `message` attribute will be added to the activity indicator to describe the activity to the user. The `win` attribute is needed when the code is run on iOS. An activity indicator can simply be shown on the screen on Android, but on iOS it is attached to a window and hence this needs to be specified. Doing this in this function means that the caller of the function does not need to be aware of this platform idiosyncrasy, the caller simply shows the indicator.

5. Back in `app.js`, add the following code to the top of the file to link the `activity.js` contents to `app.js`:

```
Ti.include('activity.js');
```

 Both `app.js` and `activity.js` files live in the resources directory, so no directory prefix is required for this call. Also note that the full filename needs to be specified for a call to `Ti.include`.

The call to `Ti.include` has effectively added the contents of `activity.js` to `app.js`, so anything declared in `activity.js` can now be called from `app.js`.

6. Create an activity indicator by calling the function defined in `activity.js`. Add the following to the bottom of `app.js`:

```
var act = activityIndicator({message: 'How long do you want to wait?', win: win1});
```

7. Finally, add the following code that shows the activity indicator:

```
act.show();
```

8. Run the app. You will get an activity indicator as shown in the following figure as seen when run on Android.

How long do you want to wait?

What just happened?

The code to create an activity indicator that was defined in `activity.js` was referenced from `app.js` using `Ti.Include`.

`Ti.include` helps to manage code by splitting it into more manageable and organized groups. Common routines can be held in a file for inclusion where necessary. For example you could have a file containing common debugging functionality that can be included when required. This is good but there is a better solution.

The other command supplied to split content into multiple files is `require`. This command imposes more restrictions than `Ti.include` but we get so much more back from using it. Using `require` results in better designed and more modular code. It will be the basis of the code that is used throughout the rest of this chapter.

Require

`require` is a very useful command. It can be used to load a Titanium native compiled module such as the one from the Appcelerator marketplace, `http://www.appcelerator.com/marketplace`, or it can load a commonJS source file. Both uses of `require` correspond to good Titanium design. Let's examine both uses.

Require – loading a marketplace module

The Appcelerator marketplace exists to provide modules for times when you either need functionality that cannot be coded using the Titanium API, or for saving you time by giving you functionality that would take valuable time to code yourself. There are some great modules in the marketplace, some of which are free. We will take advantage of one of the free offerings in the next example when we add a bit of color to the app.

Time for action – adding an Appcelerator marketplace module

Perform the following steps to add an Appcelerator marketplace module:

1. Create a new app by navigating to **File | New | Titanium Project**. From the dialog select **Titanium Classic** then **Default Project** and click on **Next**.

2. Enter the app details on the **New Titanium Project** window.

3. Download the free paint module from the Appcelerator marketplace at `https://marketplace.appcelerator.com/apps/807?1818796952`.

4. Copy the ZIP file into the project root directory.

5. Extract the module ZIP file, `ti.paint-iphone-1.2-android-2.0.1.zip`.

6. Refresh the project by right-clicking on the project name in the navigator list and selecting **refresh** (or more simply by pressing *F5*). Notice the new **Modules** directory in the project navigator window.

7. Open `tiapp.xml` and click on the green plus button on the right-hand side of the **Modules** section.

8. Click on **OK**. The `ti.paint` module is now linked to the app and ready for inclusion in your code. The modules section should look as follows:

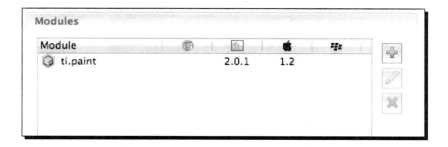

 You may need to clean your project (by navigating to **Project | Clean...**) and recompile the app if the module cannot be found when you next run the app.

9. To activate the module within your app, add the next few lines to `app.js`:

```
var Paint = require('ti.paint');

var paintView = Paint.createPaintView({
    top:0, right:0, bottom:80, left:0,
    // strokeWidth (float), strokeColor (string), strokeAlpha
(int, 0-255)
    strokeColor:'#0f0', strokeAlpha:255, strokeWidth:10,
    eraseMode:false,
    image:'default.png'
});
win1.add(paintView);
```

10. Run the app. You should get something like the following which shows screenshots from the app running in the iOS Simulator and Android emulators (don't judge me on the drawing):

On iOS simulator:

On Android emulator:

Have a go hero - enhancing the paint app

The white space at the bottom of the screen can be filled with buttons that control the drawing surface. The paint module includes example code that can be found in the `modules/iPhone/ ti.paint/1.2/example` directory. Why not implement some of the features shown in the sample code for the module in your app.

You should examine the documentation of any Appcelerator library you download. It's your only reference to the functions and parameters the library expects.

Require – promoting commonJS compliant code

The other use of the `require` command is to create a commonJS compliant structure.

CommonJS adds modularity to your code that `Ti.include` cannot provide. It allows you to create a basic API to your code files providing a basic and reduced implementation of public and private methods of classes in Java or packages in other languages.

When you require a file, it automatically gains two global variables, `exports` and `module`. Assigning variables and functions to the `exports` variable is equivalent to making them public (in Java parlance).

The only methods that can be called from a commonJS file are those that are assigned to the `exports` variable. So, for example:

```
var myPrivateVar = 0;
var myPublicVar = 'Can be seen';
var myPrivateFunc = function();
var myPublicFunc = function();
-- this is where the items are made publically accessible
exports.myPublicVar = myPublicVar; -- variable is now public
exports.myPublicFunc = myPublicFunc; -- function is now public
```

When this source code file is "required" then `myPublicVar` and `myPublicFunc` can be called. The other functions are private.

 For more information on commonJS see `http://wiki.commonjs.org/wiki/Modules/1.1`, or the Appcelerator guide showing the best practice of using commonJS at `https://wiki.appcelerator.org/display/guides/CommonJS+Modules+in+Titanium`.

MVC

Titanium allows you to build an app that runs with native controls on a range of devices, from small screen Android devices to the latest iPads. This is both a tremendous advantage and also a responsibility. Your users will expect the same engaging familiar experience regardless of the format. If you deploy to all supported formats—iOS, Android, and mobile web (I know I have not mentioned this before, but you can create web apps using Titanium but by using MVC it gets easier)—you will have users who are accessing your content on screens with resolutions ranging from 320 x 240 to 1024 x 768 pixel and possibly even higher. These devices range from small phones through the latest hi-res tablets and even to browsers in high-end desktop systems. It is clear that you cannot have the same layout for all devices; it would look ridiculous. That is why it is particularly important when using Titanium to separate your code, especially the UI elements. You have different layouts for different devices and platforms and try to keep our business logic common. You will still retain a big advantage over native app developers, as all of your source code is in one place and one language.

The first app in the first chapter of this book showed that your app could look different depending on the platform it is run on. The solution in that case was to use `Ti.platform.name` to determine what to display based on the platform. This worked fine for an isolated example but will not scale very well for an entire app.

The **Model View Controller (MVC)** methodology is the solution. This splits your code into three areas of functionality:

Function	Description
Model	This is where the data structures and storage elements of your app are defined. This code should be the same regardless of the platform your code runs on.
Controller	The controller is the main business logic of the app. It defines what is done based on the inputs from the UI.
	This can also serve as an interface between the model and the view, although this isn't fixed and model elements can be called directly from the view layer.
	This code should be mostly platform independent.
View	The view layer contains code that is relevant to displaying content. This layer will have the most differences between platforms and should be split off from the other common code.

The advantage in splitting your code into these three areas is that it promotes code reusability, which, unless you are a fan of hard work, is a good thing. In fact surely one of the key advantages of Titanium is that it permits code reuse between mobile platforms that could not be achieved using the native tools. MVC within Appcelerator should be seen as the cherry on the cake.

Most of the examples on the Titanium website and within the remaining chapters of this book are based on the MVC design.

> The Kitchensink app has never been and probably never will be MVC based. It works across platforms and is an example of what can be done with Titanium. It works and is a great advert for what can be achieved using Titanium but should not be regarded as the vanguard of great design.

Time for action – creating a better designed app using MVC

This example will put all of the good practices discussed in this chapter into action. It can be argued that the example is not purely MVC-based and that is probably true. To that I would argue that MVC is a design goal and not a restriction. The app does what we need it to; it keeps the platform-specific areas away from the common business logic. What it does highlight is how a good design pays dividends when creating apps for phones and tablets. This is good stuff; let's get going.

1. Create a new app by navigating to **File | New | Titanium Project**. From the dialog select **Titanium Classic** then **Master/Detail Application** and click on **Next**.

2. Enter the app details on the **New Titanium Project** window. Keep all of the deployment targets checked. The advantage of an MVC methodology is that it is easier to deploy to many targets. Remove the check against the **Cloud settings** option, as it's not relevant for this example. Click on **Finish** to create the app framework.

3. Run the app. You can run the app on any of your supported platforms.

What just happened?

Well this is exciting. The app has layout files that produce different layouts depending on the platform you are on—iPad, Android, and mobile web.

The following screenshot shows the app running on iPhone:

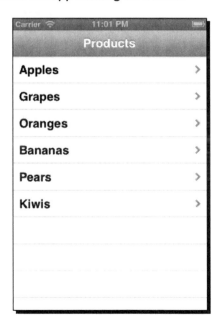

The following screenshot shows the app running on iPad:

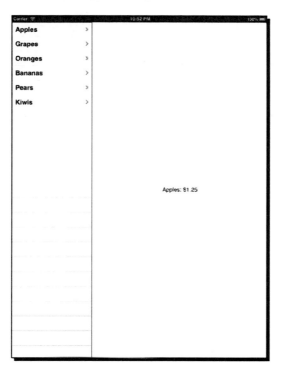

The following screenshot shows the app running on Android:

The following screenshot shows the app running on mobile web:

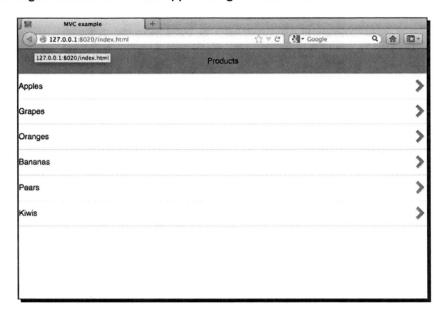

Behind the scenes – a look at the code

Take a moment to examine the directory structure of the new app. The code is now spread over several directories. The code is distributed as shown in the following table:

Directory	Content
resources/app.js	The app.js file and nothing else
resources/ui/common	Common code across all platforms for business logic
resources/ui/handheld/android	Android phone specific layout code
resources/ui/handheld/ios	iPhone-specific layout code
resources/ui/handheld/mobileweb	Browser-based HTML5 specific layout code
resources/ui/tablet	Android and iOS tablet layout

 Given the differences between Android and iOS tablets it can be a good idea to have separate tablet layouts.

This is not a full MVC implementation; that will come in the next example on Alloy but it does show how to split out code for different platforms. Splitting the common business logic from the presentation logic is the first step towards MVC. As there is no storage in this app, there is no need for the model component anyway. It's a good stepping stone and perfectly suitable for this example.

Examine the code in `app.js`. It looks different to the code in any of the previous examples. Let's have a look at what it is doing.

The first thing to notice is the comment:

```
// This is a single context application with mutliple windows in a
stack
```

What does this mean?

Every time you open up a new window with the URL parameter specified, Titanium opens up a new context. Think of these contexts as a new thread or process. These contexts take resources. The example in the first chapter created two windows using the URL parameter and hence had two contexts. This example has one. It is good practice to use a single context for your app where possible to conserve resources. Remember that your apps will be run on battery powered phones that are still relatively low powered. Resources are precious on these devices. An app that is wasteful with resources will run slowly and drain the battery.

There is one unnamed function within `app.js` that executes itself:

```
(function() {
...
})();
```

The `()` on the last line tells JavaScript to execute the function, and therefore to start the app.

The function reads a few properties such as the platform name and display constraints and, based on the values, determines the correct layout file to run.

That's it. It just starts the app and calls the appropriate layout. The layout code and business logic have been split off into the relevant areas.

Before we move on, take time to notice how the layouts are defined. The appropriate layout is read using the `require` command. A window object is returned which is then opened.

An example of require

Open up the `applicationWindow.js` file in the tablet directory (this is the simplest version of the layout files as a tablet can display the entire app on a single window). The file contains an `ApplicationWindow` function that is assigned to the `module.exports` variable at the end of the file.

What is `module.exports`?

This is new. Within a commonJS file you can assign functions and variables to the `exports` variable to make them public.

What you can also do is assign an object to `module.exports` as the single item to return from the file as an object (in this case the return object is a function).

See `http://www.hacksparrow.com/node-js-exports-vs-module-exports.html` for a great post about the differences between `exports` and `module.exports`.

Now examine the call in `app.js`:

```
Window = require('ui/handheld/android/ApplicationWindow');
...
new Window().open();
```

What is going on here?

1. The `Window` variable is being assigned the return variable from the `require` command. In this case it will be assigned the `ApplicationWindow` function.

2. The new command creates a new object of a given type, in this case, a new function (Window's type is a function).

3. The function is executed and returns `Ti.UI.Window`.

4. The open method of the window is executed.

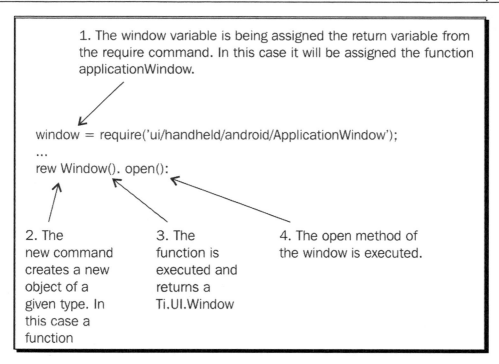

1. The window variable is being assigned the return variable from the require command. In this case it will be assigned the function applicationWindow.

```
window = require('ui/handheld/android/ApplicationWindow');
...
rew Window(). open():
```

2. The new command creates a new object of a given type. In this case a function

3. The function is executed and returns a Ti.UI.Window

4. The open method of the window is executed.

The remainder of the `ApplicationWindow` file contains Titanium code to create windows and views that define the layout. The statements at the bottom of the file concerning `NavigationGroups` and events will be explained in the next chapter as will the code within the `DetailView.js` and `MasterView.js` files.

The beauty of this app is that the design provides a great base to develop on:

- `app.js` is clean and complete. It is just a bootstrap.
- The layout files have been split into different directories.
- `app.js` has logic to call the appropriate layout code for the platform.
- There is a directory for common code.

Alloy

Not for the faint hearted, and very much at the bleeding edge of Titanium, Alloy is an MVC framework for Titanium. It takes a different approach to the MVC design discussed in the last example of adding CSS files and XML definitions. It is included in this chapter because it is the appropriate place to discuss it, but it is a step above what has been discussed so far. It's aimed at people who are experienced in programming with Titanium. Don't feel you have to read this now; you can come back to it later. The remainder of the book does not refer to it.

Are you still reading? Still interested? Not skipped off to the next chapter? Good, I'll let you into a secret. For some of you, Alloy will be a very natural way to program in Titanium. It is especially suited to people coming from a web development background. Even if you are not then it still is a very fast way to create apps. If you are a web developer, the MVC solution from the previous example possibly didn't feel quite right; it didn't quite fit with the MVC methodology. The view code had some of the layout elements such as the width, but it also defined the buttons, the event listeners, the windows, and so on. They are elements that surely belong in the controller. If this was web development, the view code would be in CSS files where only elements of the layout and font sizes and so on are listed and the separation between layout and text is clear. If this is you then you are in for a treat.

Alloy uses a format that is much like CSS for layouts and clearly separates the model, view, and controller elements. It makes a lot of sense once you get the hang of it.

We will make a copy of the previous fruit-based app from the MVC section, but this time using Alloy.

 Alloy is integrated into Titanium 3. If you are having problems running Alloy apps then you may be missing a pre-requisite. Please refer to `http://docs.appcelerator.com/titanium/3.0/#!/ guide/Alloy_Quick_Start` for manual installation instructions.

Time for action – creating an Alloy app

Perform the following steps to create an Alloy app:

1. Create a new blank mobile app by navigating to **File | New | Titanium Project.** From the list of templates select **Alloy** and then **Default Alloy Project**. Click on **Next**.

2. Enter your project name, app ID, and any other configuration details and then click on **Finish**. The app will be created from the template.

3. Run the app to check that the initial creation worked. You should get a simple **Hello World** message displayed.

4. Examine the directory structure that was created by Alloy (you may have to refresh the project in Titanium Studio to see this):

Directory	What goes in there
app/assets	All images, app icons, splash screens, and user content can be put here. These files will be copied to the resources directory by the Alloy compile process and so can be referenced in your code without the app/assets directory prefix.
app/ controllers	The controller files. This is where the business logic of the app will live.
app/models	The model files.
app/styles	The CSS styling of views.
app/views	The user interface definitions.
plugins	This contains the Alloy compiler elements. The contents of this directory are internal to Alloy so there is no need to look or change things in this directory.

Alloy has generated a set of directories with the MVC code segregation.

Do not put any code, images, or any file at all in the resources folder if you are using Alloy. The contents will be deleted when alloy creates the source code from your framework. Use the app directory as your code base.

The app is set up and configured. It's now time to mould it into the fruit app from the previous MVC example.

5. The first customization is to get the product list populated and onto the screen. The MVC fruit app initial screen consists of a window and a table view where the products are listed. This can be replicated in index.xml quite easily. Remove the label definition from index.xml and replace it with a table view. index.xml should look as follows:

```
<Alloy>
    <Window class="container">
        <TableView id="MasterTable"></TableView>
    </Window>
</Alloy>
```

This definition describes an initial window that contains one table view.

6. The code to populate the table belongs in the associated controller file named `index.js`.

> Controllers, models, views, and styles are linked by the filename. So, in this example `index.xml` is associated with `index.js` and `index.tss`.

The `index.js` file is in the controller directory (in case you had not guessed). It contains all of JavaScript business logic related to the initial window. We will copy the code to populate the table from the MVC example, and add it to the table view defined in `index.xml`. `index.js` will look as follows:

```
//some dummy data for our table view
var tableData = [
    {title:'Apples', price:'1.25', hasChild:true, color: '#000'},
    {title:'Grapes', price:'1.50', hasChild:true, color: '#000'},
    {title:'Oranges', price:'2.50', hasChild:true, color: '#000'},
    {title:'Bananas', price:'1.50', hasChild:true, color: '#000'},
    {title:'Pears', price:'1.40', hasChild:true, color: '#000'},
    {title:'Kiwis', price:'1.00', hasChild:true, color: '#000'}
];


$.MasterTable.setData(tableData);


$.index.open();
```

The `$` keyword is used to identify components in the associated view definition. The component is named by the ID attribute in the `index.xml` file. In this case we have:

Component	Identifier
Window	Not specified, there is no ID attribute. As this is the top level component in the view definition, it will be defaulted to the name of the controller which in this case is `index`.
Table view	`MasterTable` as specified by the ID attribute.

Run the app. The product list is displayed. How easy was that?

The next step is to add a detailed view and define a way to pass the fruit selected when a row is clicked. This information is shown on a `detail` window. A new window means a new controller is required.

7. From the command line, enter the following to create a new controller called `detail`:

```
alloy generate controller detail
```

This command will create a view, style, and controller definitions.

8. The `detail` window merely has a window and a label. The edited contents of the `detail.js` file are included in the following code, although you can probably guess for yourself what it looks like:

```
<Alloy>
    <Window class="container">
        <Label id="result"/>
    </Window>
</Alloy>
```

The file defines a window that will be given a default identifier of `detail` and `Label`, referred to as `result`.

9. The `detail` window label shows the price of the selected item of fruit. It needs to be passed this information. Just as in the MVC example we will use an event listener to do this. There is no other functionality in the `detail` window so the controller code in `detail.js` looks as follows:

```
Ti.App.addEventListener('MVC:tab:itemSelected', function(e) {
    $.result.text = e.name+': $'+e.price;
});
```

10. Modify `index.xml`, adding code to trigger the event listener when a row in the table is clicked. Adding an event listener can be done by the traditional manual method in JavaScript by defining it in the controller file but Alloy provides a neat alternative. Add the highlighted code to the table definition in `index.html` to add a click event handler to the table view.

```
<TableView id="MasterTable" onClick="doClick"></TableView>
```

The highlighted code adds a click event handler to the table view that calls the `doClick` function when triggered.

11. In the `index.js` controller file add the `doClick` function that acts on the event:

```
function doClick(e) {

    Ti.App.fireEvent('MVC:tab:itemSelected', {
            name:e.rowData.title,
            price:e.rowData.price
    });
}
```

Almost everything is in place. You could run the app now and when the row is clicked, the event will be fired and the label updated. However, there is no code to display the detail view so all the code amounts to nothing on the display. The final piece of the jigsaw is the code to display the `detail` window when the row is clicked.

First, we need to briefly touch on something that will be covered in more detail in *Chapter 8, Creating Beautiful Interfaces.* A stack of windows is created differently on Android and iOS. On Android a window stack can be created by opening a new window that opens up in front of the existing window. The native Android back button is used to close the new window and navigate back to the lower window in the stack. iOS doesn't have this back button functionality. The single button is used to minimize the app. There is no hardware button to remove a window from the stack. Instead iOS has the concept of a `NavigationGroup` that adds a back button to the status bar for a stack of windows. You can see examples of this on the iOS settings screen.

The next steps control how the windows are opened on both iOS and Android.

12. In `index.xml`, add `NavigationGroup` that is included if the platform is iOS. Add the highlighted code to the file:

```
<Alloy>
    <Window class="container">
        <NavigationGroup id="navgroup" platform="ios,mobileweb">
            <Window title="Window 1" id="MasterWindow">
                <TableView id="MasterTable" onClick="doClick"></
TableView>
            </Window>
        </NavigationGroup>
    </Window>
</Alloy>
```

 The platform attribute is used to conditionally include elements based on the operating system.

13. Moving to the `index.js` controller. Add code to open the `detail` window when the row is clicked. Add the highlighted code to the existing function:

```
function doClick(e) {

    if (OS_IOS || OS_MOBILEWEB) {
        $.navgroup.open(Alloy.createController('detail').
getView());
    } else {
        Alloy.createController('detail').getView().open();
```

```
        }
        Ti.App.fireEvent('MVC:tab:itemSelected', {
                name:e.rowData.title,
                price:e.rowData.price
        });
}
```

Notice the OS_IOS and OS_MOBILE_WEB keywords. They are a shorthand way in Alloy of conditionally executing the code. In this case they direct us to only open a navigation group if the app is running on the mobile web or iOS.

There are several useful shortcuts in Alloy.

Shortcut	Description
OS_IOS	True if the app is running on iOS
OS_ANDROID	True if the app is running on Android
OS_MOBILEWEB	True if the app is running in mobile web
ENV_DEV	True if the app is running in the simulator
ENV_TEST	True if the app is running on a device
ENV_PRODUCTION	True if the app has been built for distribution

14. Run the App. The result is the same app as the previous MVC example!

What just happened?

Congratulations; you have created an app in Alloy.

Pop quiz - Titanium design

Q 1. You have designed your app using Alloy and now wish to add a new file to the project. Which directory can you not use?

1. resources
2. modules
3. app

Q 2. You have created a file in commonJS format and now wish to make the variable posX public. Which command is correct?

1. var public posX;
2. return posX;

3. `exports.posX = posX;`

4. `posX.export;`

Q 3. Advanced: What other command can you use to make the variable public?

1. `module.exports.posX = posX;`

2. `posX.module.export;`

3. `var posX.export;`

4. `return posX.export;`

Summary

If you should take one piece of information from this chapter, I would hope that it is this:

"Organize your Titanium code into manageable chunks along functional boundaries"

You will get into a horrible mess at some point in the future if your app's initial design is poor. Having to re-factor thousands of lines of code when you need to release a version of your previously iPhone only app for an Android tablet is no one's idea of fun. Remember that Titanium allows you to create apps for a wide range of devices on differing platforms that may affect your layouts and require platform-specific code. It doesn't matter if you use Alloy, MVC, Coffeescript, Kranium, or anything new that comes along, just be clear with your design and code separation. You can thank me for the advice later.

The chapter first introduced the `Ti.include` command for merging content from multiple files before going on to discuss the more modular `require` and commonJS framework.

Later in the chapter, the concept of MVC was introduced which separated the code into model, view, and controller elements. Admittedly, there was not a lot of code showing model but that will come in *Chapter 5, It's All About Data*.

Following on from MVC we looked at the cutting edge of Titanium design with an example of how to program using Alloy. This improves the MVC framework, adding in CSS styling and further code segregation. This promises to be a very productive way to code Titanium apps.

In the next chapter we will move away from the high level view of how Titanium apps should be structured and the placement of code and examine the interdependencies within an app. We'll also learn how apps are structured and hang together at the component level.

4

Gluing Your App Together with Events, Variables, and Callbacks

The last chapter showed how proper design methodologies could improve the structure of an app, how code reuse could be maximized by using an MVC framework, and how layouts for different platforms could be accommodated. For this chapter we move our focus back to the code level and look at how elements of an app fit together and communicate with each other. We will see how, for example, a picker will indicate the selected value to a label, or how you update a progress bar. We will dive into learning principles of events and callbacks that will be used extensively throughout the remainder of the book.

This chapter exposes the glue that holds your Titanium apps together. This will help you move on from small example apps with single buttons and alert boxes that have been shown in the book so far to more complex, interconnected, engaging apps. We will also continue to focus on code quality by showing how to avoid trouble (and in the longer term, how to avoid poor user reviews when your app is live) by using good design principles.

The topics that will be presented are:

- Sharing data and a few best practices
- Events and listeners
- Sending and capturing messages
- Global variables
- Namespaces

Sharing data

A common issue in Titanium is that of sharing data between windows. Fortunately, if you follow the few best practices, this need not be a problem for you. The issue usually manifests through a situation where the developer of the app wants to pass some information between two windows, but he/she cannot do it. The other window just doesn't see the information on the first window. What is the problem? It's most likely to be a problem of execution context.

Execution context

When your app starts up, it will create an execution context to execute your code. Don't worry about the term *execution context*; it's just your little view of the world in which your app runs. When the app first starts there is a single context and so all of your libraries and global data can be seen throughout your app.

Suppose you then create a window using the `url` parameter:

```
Ti.UI.createWindow({
  url:'picturePicker.js'
});
```

This will then create a separate context for this window. Nothing from your original context will be shared or accessible; your window will execute with a clean slate. In some circumstances this can be useful but most of the time it causes problems. If in doubt, do not open windows using this method, as you will divorce yourself from the data for the rest of the app. All of the examples provided by Appcelerator use a single execution context, including the ones with several windows over multiple tabs.

See the example at `http://docs.appcelerator.com/titanium/3.0/#!/api/Titanium.UI.Window`.

Check out the best practices at `http://docs.appcelerator.com/titanium/3.0/#!/guide/Coding_Strategies`.

Global variables

Global variables are very easy to create in Titanium. We have already seen many of them in the book so far. Any variable that is not enclosed within a function is likely to be a global variable, so many of the variables defined in `app.js` will be global. Variables need to be enclosed in a function or a closure in order for them to be constrained. Global variables will exist for as long as your app runs, which can use valuable resources. An example of a closure is shown in the first example in this chapter.

What is the right way to share data?

There are a couple of methods for sharing data:

Method	Advantages	Disadvantages
Global variable	It is easy to define.	Cannot be garbage collected. The data can hang around for as long as the app is open.
Creating an application property using `Ti.App.Properties`	It is persistent.	Slow and unpractical for anything other than small amounts of data. Slower than the global variable method.
Filesystem	It is persistent.	Only practical for large amounts of data.
Events	It is easy to define, can be removed and garbage collected.	You have to remove the event listener to garbage collect it when you are finished with it.
Modifying the window object	The information will be garbage collected with the window. It is a neat solution.	None.

We will show the best ways to share data in the remainder of the chapter. The first example shows how to pass information between windows by modifying the `window` object. This will exploit the loose typing that exists in JavaScript. This method can be applied to other elements of the Titanium SDK, such as views, buttons, sliders, and so on. The second method is events. You will use events a lot in Titanium so we will cover them in detail later in this chapter.

For the first example we will show how to share data between elements by modifying the object. We will do this by creating a tea strength selection app. The app will allow the user to select their favorite strength of tea.

Time for action – sharing information between windows

To share information between windows perform the following steps:

1. Create a new blank mobile app by clicking on **File | New | Titanium Project**. Don't use a template as it will just generate code that gets in the way.

2. This application will be a single window app, so remove all of the code from `app.js`, replacing it with a single, self-executing function. This is a chapter about good code design so we are including it in this example. With the self-executing function in `app.js`, we can be sure that all variables within the app are enclosed within a function.

> **What is a self-generating function?**
>
> It's a function that executes as soon as it is defined. Notice in the following example that the function is enclosed in brackets and then has () to execute the function after the function definition. It is not necessary to enclose the function in brackets; it's just a good convention. These brackets at the end of the function definition cause the function to self execute. The good thing about this is that all of the variables are defined within the function and so can be cleared when the function completes.

```
(function() {
  var win1 = Titanium.UI.createWindow({
      title:'Select Color',
      backgroundColor:'#fff'
  });
  // open window
  win1.open();
})();
```

3. Create the simple layout for the window, which will consist of a set of colors shown using a table view representing tea strength. Add the following code snippet to `app.js`:

```
var Teas = ['#F5F5DC', '#FFE4B5', '#FFE4C4', '#D2B48C',
'#C3B091', '#C3B091', '#926F5B', '#804000', '#654321',
'#3D2B1F'];

allRows = [];
var theColours = Ti.UI.createTableView({});

for (var i=0; i<Teas.length; i++) {
```

```
theRow = Ti.UI.createTableViewRow({backgroundColor:
Teas[i], height:50, TeaColour:Teas[i]});
allRows.push(theRow);
}

theColours.setData(allRows);
win1.add(theColours);
```

 TableViewRow has a TeaColour attribute. JavaScript is loosely typed so we can create a custom attribute to objects without invalidating them. In this case we will pass information about TableViewRow using the attribute in much the same way as we will pass information to a window. It's perfectly safe and acceptable and another great feature of JavaScript.

4. Create a function to return the verdict of the supplied tea color. The function will return a string based on the color hex code.

```
function getVerdict(colour) {
   var indicator = colour.charAt(1);
   var msg;
   // Make a crude decision on the strength of the tea based
   on the 2nd character of the hex color
   switch(indicator) {
      case 'F': msg = 'Milky'; break;
      case 'D': msg = 'Nice'; break;
      case 'C': msg = 'Perfect'; break;
      case '9': msg = 'A bit strong'; break;
      case '8': msg = 'Builders tea'; break;
      case '6': msg = 'Send it back'; break;
      case '3': msg = 'No milk here'; break;
   }
   return msg;
};
```

5. Next, create a function to display a result window showing the verdict of your tea selection. Admittedly, this is not the best use of a modification to a window object, but it does prove a point.

```
function showTeaVerdict(_args) {
   var teaVerdict = Ti.UI.createWindow({layout:'vertical'});

   teaVerdict.backgroundColor = _args;
   teaVerdict.msg = getVerdict(_args);
```

```
var judgement = Ti.UI.createLabel
({text:teaVerdict.msg, top:'50%'});
var close = Ti.UI.createButton
({title:'Choose again', top:'25%'});
close.addEventListener('click', function(e)
  {teaVerdict.close();
  // release the resources
  teaVerdict = null;
  });

teaVerdict.add(judgement);
teaVerdict.add(close);
teaVerdict.open();
}
```

6. Finally, add the event listener that will show the result window when the user clicks on a row on the table. The selected color is determined by using the `source` attribute that is automatically passed with other information with the `click` event. The `source` attribute contains a reference to `TableViewRow` that fired the event. In our example we use this to access our custom attribute `TeaColour`. There will be more on these event attributes later in this chapter, or alternatively you can visit `http://docs.appcelerator.com/titanium/3.0/#!/api/Titanium. UI.TableView-event-click`. Add the following lines of code:

```
theColours.addEventListener('click', function(e)
{showTeaVerdict(e.source.TeaColour)});
```

7. Run the app!

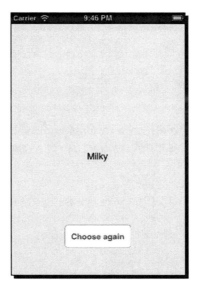

What just happened?

You were able to pass information from a table view to a window by creating a custom attribute to both a window and `TableViewRow`. This custom attribute is a very useful way of sending information between objects. An even better way is using events.

Events

Events are the messages that are created through the use of your app. Smartphones and tablets are full of gadgets and things to touch and drag, and so there are the following events happening all the time:

- Buttons pressed
- Touch gestures
- View scrolling
- Location changes

You need a way to handle these inputs and react to them. This is done with events.

Events are very common in Titanium; you will include them in probably every app that you write. They are hard to avoid and have appeared in examples from earlier chapters. In *Chapter 2, How to Make an Interface*, where an iOS button was put on the taskbar, we saw the following code:

```
function rightButton(win){
    if (!isAndroid()) {

        var right=Ti.UI.createButton({
            systemButton:Ti.UI.iPhone.SystemButton.INFO_LIGHT
        });
        right.addEventListener('click',function()
        {
            alert('button clicked!');
        });
        win.setRightNavButton(right);
    }
}
```

And in *Chapter 3, How to Design Titanium Apps*, we saw the following code:

```
table.addEventListener('click', function(e) {
self.fireEvent('itemSelected', {
```

```
        name:e.rowData.title,
        price:e.rowData.price
  });
  });
```

This is event handling and firing and will be explored in detail.

The button definition is perfectly standard:

```
var right=Ti.UI.createButton({
        systemButton:Ti.UI.iPhone.SystemButton.INFO_LIGHT
    });
```

The next command adds an event listener that determines what happens when the button is clicked:

```
right.addEventListener('click',function()
    {
        alert('button clicked!');
    });
```

The following table shows the breakdown of the `addEventListener` command:

Code	Description
`right`	This is the item the event listener is attached to. This defines the scope of the event. In this case the event is associated with a button.
`addEventListener`	This is the method to add a listener to an item. You can add event listeners to pretty much everything in Titanium.
`'click'`	This is the first parameter of the `addEventListener` method and specifies the event to respond to. There are many standard events such as `click`, `touch`, `scroll`, `close`, and `open`. The events that are applicable to an object are listed in the SDK documentation on the Appcelerator website, for example a close event is appropriate and may be triggered for a window but not for a button.
	You can specify any text as this parameter if you wish to define your own event. We will see more on this later.

Code	Description
```function ()``` ```{alert ('button``` ```clicked!');``` ```});```	This is the code to run when the event is caught. This can be a function declared inline as in the example to the left or any function that is in scope.
	A standard event such as `'click'` will have a set of properties automatically passed to it. All you need to do is define a parameter to your function and the parameter will receive the following properties: ◆ `rowData` ◆ `source` ◆ `type` ◆ `x` and `y` We will explore these properties later in this chapter.

Event scope

Event listeners can either have a local or global scope. For the purposes of this section we will refer to them as either local or global event listeners. A local event listener is defined and associated with an object. For example, to create a local event listener for a button, you would write:

```
var right=Ti.UI.createButton({
        systemButton:Ti.UI.iPhone.SystemButton.INFO_LIGHT
    });
right.addEventListener('click',function()
```

This is an example of a local event listener. The code will be executed only when a `'click'` event is triggered or fired on the button. For this event to execute, the user must either press the button on the screen or the `click` event must be fired on the button:

```
right.fireEvent ('click');
```

 In Titanium 3.0 you can now make your `click` events bubble up to the parent view or window. It's the same principle as was used on a table view where the event listener was defined against the table view but handled clicks from any row. Similarly, you can handle events from child items of the view by having the `click` event bubble to the parent view. For more information visit `http://docs.appcelerator.com/titanium/3.0/#!/guide/Event_Handling`.

Global events are defined against `Ti.App` and are visible throughout your app. As they are not associated with an object, they will not respond to any event fired on an object such as `touchstart`, `click`, or `close`. They are user-defined events that must be fired from within code. Here is an example from the last chapter. Notice that the event listener is defined before the code to fire it. The listener must exist if it is to catch the event!

```
Ti.App.addEventListener('MVC:tab:itemSelected', function(e) {
  $.result.text = e.name+': $'+e.price;
});

Ti.App.fireEvent('MVC:tab:itemSelected', {
    name:e.rowData.title,
    price:e.rowData.price
  });
```

Event properties

When a standard event such as `click` is triggered, Titanium creates a set of properties that are passed along with the event. This allows you to access context information on the event that was fired, for example to find the x and y coordinates when a `touch` event was triggered on a window.

A great example of the property passing is the MVC example in the previous chapter, which contained this piece of code that accessed the properties of `TableViewRow` that was clicked. This was how the fruit name and price were sent to the other window.

```
table.addEventListener('click', function(e) {
  self.fireEvent('itemSelected', {
    name:e.rowData.title,
    price:e.rowData.price
  });
});
```

In this case the `title` and `price` properties of the row that was clicked are accessed using the `rowData` property, which is automatically passed.

There are a number of standard properties. These properties are passed to all event listeners for system events (they are not passed to events with user-defined names):

Property	Description
source	A reference to the parent object
x	The x coordinate when the event was fired
y	The y coordinate when the event was fired

Property	Description
`type`	The type of event fired; for example, this will return click in a `click` event

There are properties that are applicable to only certain objects, for example:

Property	Object	Description
`rowData`	Table	You can access the properties of the row that triggered the event.
`direction`	View	In a `swipe` event on a view, this indicates the direction of the swipe.
`value`	Text field	In a `change` event against a text field this contains the new value. This also applies to the `change` event on a slider.
`success`	E-mail dialog	This is an indicator of the successful sending of an e-mail.

There are many more properties that are specific to events on objects. The Titanium API documentation should be your guide and reference.

Making something happen – fireEvent

`fireEvent` is used when you want to signal an action or when you want to make something happen. You can fire custom named events to a matching handler or you could even simulate a system event such as a button press by firing a `'click'` event on the button.

You can fire an event on an object or globally.

The MVC example in the last chapter contained a good example of event handling and firing. `MasterView.js` contained the following code:

```
function MasterView() {
  var self = Ti.UI.createView({
    backgroundColor:'white'
  });
...
  var table = Ti.UI.createTableView({
    data:tableData
  });
  self.add(table);
```

```
//add behavior
table.addEventListener('click', function(e) {
  self.fireEvent('itemSelected', {
    name:e.rowData.title,
    price:e.rowData.price
  });
});
```

The highlighted lines of code signify the following:

◆ A variable called `self` is created and we assigned a view to it.

◆ A variable called `table` is created, which is a table view.

◆ An event listener is added to the table to catch the `click` event. Whenever the table is clicked, the `click` event is caught and a function is run. The function fires an `'itemSelected'` event on the view object. This event passes the `price` and `title` properties of the clicked `TableViewRow` along with the event.

The Alloy example achieved the same using a global event handler.

When the table view is clicked, the following code is executed:

```
Ti.App.fireEvent('MVC:tab:itemSelected', {
    name:e.rowData.title,
    price:e.rowData.price
});
```

The following is the corresponding event listener in `detail.js`:

```
Ti.App.addEventListener('MVC:tab:itemSelected', function(e) {
  $.result.text = e.name+': $'+e.price;
});
```

> Notice the name of the event handler. It's a good idea to prefix the name of your global event handlers with a prefix that identifies your app. Conflicts can occur with global event listeners just as they can with global variables.

Let's put this event logic to the test in the next example where we show standard and custom event handlers in action.

Time for action – creating a progress bar game

In this next example a progress bar will be used for a very simple game. The idea of the game is that you have to press a button fast enough to push the progress bar back to the start. The progress bar will slowly advance towards the end and you have to constantly keep trying to move the bar back by touching a view that keeps moving around. Will you be fast enough to beat the progress bar? Perform the following steps to create a progress bar game:

1. Create a new blank mobile app by clicking on **File | New | Titanium Project**. Don't use a template as it will just generate code that gets in the way.

2. This application will be a single window app, so remove all of the code from `app.js` and replace it with the following:

```
var win1 = Titanium.UI.createWindow({
    title:'Tab 1',
    backgroundColor:'#fff'
});

// open window
win1.open();
```

3. Add a progress bar to the window. Add the following creation command to the top of the file:

```
var progress = Ti.UI.createProgressBar({
  min:0,
  max:100,
  value:30,
  message:'Can you stop progress?',
  width:'70%'
});
```

Then add the highlighted commands to the end of the file to add the progress bar to the window and show it:

```
win1.add(progress);
progress.show();
// open window
win1.open();
```

If you now run the app, you will see a static progress bar on the screen:

 The progress bar is partly filled when the app starts because `value` is set to `30` in the definition.

The progress bar will advance based on a timer. This timer will call a function to move the progress bar every second. The next few steps will set up the timer.

4. Create an event listener on the progress bar that will listen for `'update'` events and move the bar along. Add the following code after the definition of the progress bar:

```
progress.addEventListener('update', function(e){
  progress.value = progress.value + e.value;
});
```

5. We now need code that will move the progress bar along until it reaches the end when a message is sent out telling the user that he/she has lost. This will be done by creating a function which will be added at the top of `app.js`:

```
function increment(e) {
  if (progress.value < 95) {
```

```
     // I know its contrived. You could just set the value of the
progress bar here
        progress.fireEvent('update', {value:10});
    }
    else {
      alert('No you cant');
    }
};
```

6. Create a timer that will call the `increment` function every second. Add the next command after the `increment` function is declared in the previous step:

```
var progTimer = setInterval(increment, 1000);
```

This line creates a timer using the Titanium keyword `setInterval`. The first parameter is the function to call and the second the interval in milliseconds.

Now run the app. The progress bar should move along sedately with progress being regularly triggered by the interval timer. An alert box will be repeatedly shown when the progress bar gets to the end. You will need to exit the Simulator to stop the app. This untidy finish needs to be cleaned up, which leads on to the next step.

7. The maximum value for the progress bar, and hence the end of the game, is 100. If this value is reached, we have some cleaning up to do. The timer needs to be cleared away and the progress bar should be removed. We will do this with another custom event listener that will wait for a complete event before cleaning up. Add the following code:

```
Ti.App.addEventListener('complete', function(e) {
  progress.hide();
  clearInterval(progTimer);
});
```

8. This `'complete'` event needs to be triggered when the progress bar moves to the end. Make the highlighted change to the `increment` function to fire the event:

```
function increment(e) {
   if (progress.value < 95) {
      // I know its contrived. You could just set the value of the
progress bar here
        progress.fireEvent('update', {value:10});
    }
    else {
      Ti.App.fireEvent('complete');
      alert('No you cant');
    }
};
```

The progress bar incrementing logic is now in place. The next steps create the randomly placed view that when touched will move the progress bar back.

9. Create a new view as follows:

```
var randomPosView = Ti.UI.createView({
  width:'10%',
  height:'10%',
  backgroundColor:'green',
  borderColor:'black',
});
```

10. Add a function to move the progress bar back when the view is pressed or if the progress bar is next to the start popup, a congratulatory message.

```
function decrement(e) {
  if (progress.value <= 5) {
    Ti.App.fireEvent('complete');
    alert('Well Done!');
  } else {
    progress.fireEvent('update', {value:-15});
  }
};
```

11. Add an event listener to the view that will call the `decrement` function when the user touches the view:

```
randomPosView.addEventListener('touchstart', decrement);
```

12. Add the code that moves the view to a new position. Add the following highlighted code to the `increment` function that moves the view to a random position on the screen when the timer fires:

```
function increment(e) {
  if (progress.value < 95) {
    // I know its contrived. You could just set the value of the
progress bar here
    progress.fireEvent('update', {value:10});
    randomPosView.left = Math.random() *
    Ti.Platform.displayCaps.platformWidth;
    randomPosView.top = Math.random() *
    Ti.Platform.displayCaps.platformHeight;
  }
  else {
    Ti.App.fireEvent('complete');
    alert('No you cant');
  }
};
```

13. Finally, add the moveable view to the window:

```
win1.add(randomPosView);
```

14. Run the app!

The example project is available to download into Titanium Studio from GitHub (`https://github.com/myleftboot/stopProgress.git`).

What just happened?

This app is a great example of event handlers. There are the object-based event handlers such as the one associated with the view `randomPosView.addEventListener('touchstart', decrement);` and global event listeners `Ti.App.addEventListener('complete'.`

The difference between the two event listeners is their scope. The `Ti.App` object is globally accessible whereas `randomPosView` is associated and constrained to and by the view.

The trade-off with the globally available object is that there is nothing to automatically clear the event listener up. If the view is removed and cleared up, the `touchstart` event listener automatically gets cleared away with it. The global event listener added in step 7 should be removed if possible. This is not done for tidiness, as we will show next.

Global event listeners and garbage collection

Event listeners defined using `Ti.App.addEventListener` are globally accessible throughout your app. This is a very useful bit of functionality but on the other hand you need to take care while using it. The `Ti.App` object lasts for the duration of your app and is not garbage collected. This is important; if the event listener is not garbage collected, neither is anything that is referenced from within the code. Suppose the global `'complete'` event listener in the previous example looked like the following code snippet:

```
Ti.App.addEventListener('complete', function(e) {
  progress.hide();
  clearInterval(progTimer);
});
```

The event listener hides the progress bar when the event is fired. The progress bar is not needed and should be removed from the display, and its resources cleared ready to be garbage collected.

There are two reasons why it will not be garbage collected:

- The event listener still exists and references the progress bar. While the event listener exists, the progress bar will not be garbage collected.

- The progress bar object is still linked to the `progress` variable and will only be garbage collected when the variable moves out of scope. As the variable is defined in `app.js`, this will not happen. To remove the reference you should nullify the reference to the object `progress = null;`.

So our correct event listener code becomes the following:

```
Ti.App.addEventListener('complete', function(e) {
  clearInterval(progTimer);
  progress.hide();
  progress := null;
  randomPosView.hide();
  randomPosView := null;
});
```

A progress bar and view will not consume too much memory but this will become an issue when you are referencing larger objects such as images, videos, windows, cameras, and so on. Your app will consume more resources and slowly grind to a halt or crash if you do not manage your resources. Do the right thing!

- Be aware of the lifespan of your object.
- Nullify references to objects when they are not needed. It's not enough to just close, remove, or hide an object; it will still hang around consuming memory.

So if you want to tidy up after you have hidden a view, and removed it from a window, remember to do the final step; nullify the variable. The view can then be garbage collected and release precious resources. Remember these apps are running on phones with limited memory.

 The examples in this book have been designed to be easy to read and short to write. They do not do the right thing by nullifying references, but neither do most of the examples on the Appcelerator Q&A website. Don't let this be an excuse for your code.

Should you wish to read more on this (and you should, it's worth investing 5 minutes of your life on this), then you can find out more from the Appcelerator wiki at `http://docs.appcelerator.com/titanium/3.0/#!/guide/Managing_Memory_and_Finding_Leaks`.

Better event code using callbacks

There is another improvement that can be made to the event listener. This improvement will conserve resources and make the event listener more flexible.

Taking our example from an earlier section in this chapter:

```
Ti.App.addEventListener('complete', function(e) {
  progress.hide();
  clearInterval(progTimer);
});
```

The event listener includes the code that should be run when the event is fired. As we saw from the last section, the problem with this is that the objects referenced from within the event listener cannot be garbage collected while it exists. But what if the items were not listed in the listener? What if instead of the event listener listing what should happen when it is fired, the code that fires the event told the event listener what should happen?

We have the following listener:

```
Ti.App.addEventListener('complete', function(e) {
  progress.hide();
  clearInterval(progTimer);
});
```

And we have the following trigger:

```
Ti.App.fireEvent('complete');
```

What if the `fireEvent` call instead told the event listener what it should do? The code for the event listener becomes:

```
Ti.App.addEventListener('complete', function(e) {
  if (e.code) {
    e.code();
  };
});
```

And the code for the trigger changes to:

```
Ti.App.fireEvent('complete', {code:  function() {
    progress.hide();
    clearInterval(progTimer);
  }
});
```

We can see an example of the flexibility of JavaScript in the preceding code. The function is passed as a variable to the event listener, which then executes it. This is an example of functions being first class objects in JavaScript.

The advantage of this approach is twofold:

♦ The event listener has no references so the view and progress bar from the previous example can be garbage collected while the event listener still exists.

♦ The event listener does not just do one defined thing. `fireEvent` now calls the shots, and it tells the event listener what is done. A single event listener can now do many different things.

Have a go hero - adding callbacks

The advantages of using callbacks for flexibility are clear. Why not change the progress bar game to callbacks?

This section would not exist if it were not for the excellent developer blog entry written by Aaron Saunders, one of the leading lights in Titanium development. You can visit `http://developer.appcelerator.com/blog/2011/10/callbacks-are-your-friend-events-arent-too-bad-either.html` for more information.

Before we move on to the rest of the book, here are a few questions to test your knowledge of good Titanium design.

Pop quiz - events

Q 1. What function do you use to create a global event handler?

1. `Ti.App.createEventListener`
2. `Ti.API.addEventListener`
3. `global.addEventListener`
4. `win.createEventListener`
5. `win.addEventListener`

Q 2. Which command will remove an event listener defined as follows?

```
win.addEventListener('showAlert', function(e) {
  alert(e.message);
});
```

1. `win.removeEventListener`

2. `Ti.API.removeEventListener`

3. `win.deleteEventListener`

Q 3. Assuming that the event listener defined in the following piece of code is the only event hander in the app, what will happen when the fireEvent command is run?

```
var win = Ti.UI.createWindow({});
win.addEventListener('showAlert', function(e) {
  alert(e.message);
});
Ti.API.fireEvent('showAlert', {message: "Something just happened");
```

1. An alert showing the message "Something Just Happened" will appear

2. The program will result in an error

3. Nothing

Summary

The last two chapters represent the heavy rule-based part of the book. Well done for persisting with them. You will reap the rewards when you use the principles you have learned in the last two chapters on your apps.

There are other solutions to the issue of sharing data and context, although you will often see the namespace used as a solution on the Appcelerator Q&A site and on developer blogs. Should you wish to use a more pure method of sharing data, then consider reading the Appcelerator best practices or developer blogs.

A clear, official review of some of the principles laid out in these chapters can be seen in the Appcelerator best practices document at `http://docs.appcelerator.com/titanium/3.0/#!/guide/Coding_Best_Practices`.

This brings us to the end of first part of the book where you will have learned the basics of programming in Titanium. The rest of the book builds on these principles by using some of the other elements of the toolkit to build more complex and better-looking apps.

If you love to code, this is where it starts to get tasty.

5
It's All About Data

If this book was split into two parts, this chapter would have been the start of part two. The first part, representing the first four chapters, was aimed at getting you introduced to Titanium and encouraging you to program using best practices so that you can avoid getting into a mess when you do start to code your own apps. Now the focus changes; there will be more real-world coded examples and it will be assumed that you have some familiarity with the tool. This chapter is all about data – how to retrieve, store, and send data.

Unless you are going to write another flashlight or spirit-level app, the chances are that you will need to manage data. Even the humble spirit-level app will probably need to store the users' default settings of tolerance/sensitivity. What I am trying to say is that it is very likely that you will need to handle data of some form in your app, so you will need to at least be aware of the concepts introduced in this chapter.

The data-based (did you see what I did there?) topics introduced in this chapter are:

- Accessing external data
- Reading and displaying RSS feeds
- File storage for offline use
- Using the SQLite database
- Dipping into YQL

External data

Titanium provides several methods of retrieving external data. Some of which (such as the bonjour service) are platform specific. All of the commands are under `Ti.Network`. Most of the time you will use `Ti.Network.createHTTPClient` to access web services with the GET and POST methods.

You will use this method a lot in your apps, so it is important that you understand how to use it and what it can do. Let's walk through a typical example of a Titanium HTTP data retrieval request. The method for posting data is pretty much the same as getting it. I'll explain the differences in the next section.

Time for action – creating an HTTP request

To create an HTTP request perform the following steps:

1. The first step is to create an `HTTPClient` variable. For this example we will call it `xhr`.

    ```
    var xhr = Titanium.Network.createHTTPClient();
    ```

     There is no return value or response from an HTML call. Unlike all other function calls, for example reading from a file, an HTML request can take quite some time to respond. It will be executed in the background while your app continues to function. You don't want your app to stop and wait for several seconds or more while the data is retrieved; the app should continue to operate while the data is being retrieved in the background. You set the HTML call up, execute the request, and then leave it to Titanium to call your code with the data when the request completes.

2. The `onerror` property defines the code that will be called in the event of something going wrong. This is where you define what you want to happen if the request fails. In this case we are showing an alert, but you can do whatever you like.

    ```
    xhr.onerror = function(e)
    {
          Ti.UI.createAlertDialog({title:'Network Error',
    message:'Unable to retrieve data.'}).show();
    };
    ```

3. When the request completes successfully, the code associated with the `onload` property will be called. In this case all we are going to do is to log the status code returned from the server on the console.

```
xhr.onload = function()
{
        Ti.Api.log(this.status);
};
```

4. If you like to see those progress bars that slowly move to complete as something is downloaded, you will need to know about the `ondatastream` property. This will be triggered at regular intervals as data is downloaded. The `progress` property will have a value from 0 to 1 indicating the percentage of data that has been received. This event will only be called if your server is set up correctly. If your event is not being called, you may need to look at your server setup.

> The `ondatastream` call must be set up before the call to open the HTTP request, otherwise it will not be called. This is a common gotcha.
>
> This event will not be called if you are downloading a small amount of data.
>
> If you are posting information, the equivalent event is `onsendstream`.

```
xhr.ondatastream = function(e)
{
        Ti.API.info('ONDATASTREAM1 - PROGRESS: ' + e.progress);
};
```

5. Initialize the server call with a URL. The GET or POST indicator is also set here. In this case we want to get some data.

```
xhr.open('GET', 'http://news.google.com/?output=rss');
```

6. Execute the HTML request. Either of the `onload` or `onerror` properties will be triggered upon completion.

```
xhr.send();
```

What just happened?

We set up and executed an HTTP request. When the HTML call completes, a response will be sent from the server. This will be passed to the code associated with the `onload` or `onerror` property. There are various bits of information that you can access from within the `onerror` and `onload` events:

Property	Description
`this.responseText`	The data returned from the server in the text format
`this.responseData`	The data returned from the server as `Ti.Blob`
`this.responseXML`	The data returned from the server in the XMLDOM format
`this.status`	The status code returned from the server, for example 200
`this.statusText`	The status description returned

Now it's time to see a real example of an HTTP request. For the first example app in this chapter, we are going to create an RSS feed reader. This will require us to revisit the table view setups first introduced in *Chapter 2, How to Make an Interface*, and show in detail how the `Ti.network.createHTTPClient` command works and how to make the best of it.

An example of posting information to a server using `createHTTPClient` is shown in *Chapter 6, Cloud-enabling Your Apps*, in the Parse example.

RSS reader

The RSS reader will be coded in the CommonJS format, which will allow us to drop the functionality into other apps. The RSS feed chosen will be the BBC business news, but of course you could substitute any well-formed RSS feed in its place.

Not all RSS feeds are valid. Before you question your own code because the feed you have chosen does not display correctly, check the validity of the feed. **World Wide Web Consortium (W3C)** have an excellent and thorough RSS validator at `http://validator.w3.org/feed/`.

Time for action – fetching RSS

To fetch RSS perform the following steps:

1. Create a new blank mobile app by clicking on **File | New | Titanium Project**. Don't use a template, as it will just generate code that gets in the way.

2. This application will be a single window app, so remove all of the code from `app.js` replacing it with the following:

```
var win1 = Titanium.UI.createWindow({
    backgroundColor:'#fff'
});

// open window
win1.open();
```

3. Create a new file by clicking on **File | New | File**. Name the file `rssReader.js`. This file will be the CommonJS format RSS reader.

4. Create a new public function `fetchRSSFeed`, which will return the RSS of a given URL. Write the following code that defines the function and sets up the HTTP request:

```
exports.fetchRSSFeed = function(_args) {
  var xhr = Titanium.Network.createHTTPClient();
  xhr.open('GET', _args.url);
```

5. Add an event to handle what should happen if a request should fail. In this case a function will be called.

```
xhr.onerror = function(e)
  {
       if (_args.error) _args.error();
  };
```

6. Add the event that we want to be fired every time. The `onload` event will receive the XML response, and if something has been returned, it will be logged to the console.

```
xhr.onload = function(e) {
  var xml = this.responseXML;

  if (xml === null || xml.documentElement === null) {
     alert('Error reading RSS feed. Make sure you have a network
connection and try refreshing.');
       if (_args.error) { _args.error(); }
```

```
      return;
    }
    Ti.API.info(this.responseText);
  };
```

7. Finally, add the following command to execute the HTML request:

```
xhr.send();
```

8. Modify `app.js` by adding a call at the end of the function to retrieve the RSS.

```
var rss = require('rssReader');
rss.fetchRSSFeed({url: 'http://feeds.bbci.co.uk/news/business/rss.
xml?edition=uk'});
```

9. Run the app! You will see the RSS returned from the call on the console.

What just happened?

You created an app to fetch an RSS feed and dump its contents to the console. When the app runs, you should see the RSS spooled to the console.

In the next example we will add code to parse the returned RSS and make it presentable.

Time for action – parsing and displaying the RSS

To parse and display the RSS perform the following steps:

1. The RSS fetched in the previous example now needs to be parsed. A new function called `parseRSS` in `rssReader.js` will be created. It will be passed the XML fetched from the Web and the code to be called when it is completed. Here is the function in full. We will go through what is going on later.

```
parseRSS = function(_args) {
  var items = _args.data.documentElement.
  getElementsByTagName("item");
  var data = [];

  for (var i = 0; i<items.length; i++) {
    var item = items.item(i);
    var image;
    try {
      var image = item.getElementsByTagNameNS
      ('http://search.yahoo.com/mrss/', 'thumbnail').
      item(0).getAttribute('url');
    } catch (e) {
      image = '';
    }
```

```
data.push({
  title:        item.getElementsByTagName
  ('title').item(0).text,
  link:         item.getElementsByTagName
  ('link').item(0).text,
  description: item.getElementsByTagName
  ('description').item(0).text,
  pubDate:      item.getElementsByTagName
  ('pubDate').item(0).text,
  image:        image
});
}
if (_args.then) {
  _args.then({data: data});
}
};
```

The function first grabs all the `item` elements in the returned XML from the call to `var items = _args.data.documentElement.getElementsByTagName("item");`.

It then loops through these elements examining one at a time via the call to `var item = items.item(i)`.

This is the XML structure we are going to parse at an item level.

```
<item>
  <title>The title</title>
  <description>More information</description>
  <link>http://www.bbc.co.uk/news/business...</link>
  <guid isPermaLink="false">
  http://www.bbc.co.uk/news/business...</guid>
  <pubDate>Fri, 16 Nov 2012 15:16:15 GMT</pubDate>
  <media:thumbnail width="66" height="49" url=
  "http://news.bbcimg.co.uk/media/images/photo.jpg"/>
  <media:thumbnail width="144" height="81" url=
  "http://news.bbcimg.co.uk/media/images/other_photo.jpg"/>
</item>
```

The elements we are interested in are `title`, `description`, `link` (for reading the detail), and a picture. The picture is stored in the `media:thumbnail` element. This has a namespace of `media` (which is defined as `xmlns:media="http://search.yahoo.com/mrss/"`) so is a little bit harder to parse than the other elements. This is why the code parses this element separately with the `getElementsByTagNameNS` command.

All of the parsed elements are added to the data array. When all elements have been parsed, this array is passed to the function (passed in as the `'then'` property) that will display the data.

2. So we have now fetched the RSS and parsed it. The next step is to display it. This will be done using the flexible table view that was introduced in *Chapter 2, How to Make an Interface*. Add a new file to the project called `rssView.js`. Create a public function (this is CommonJS; public functions are assigned to exports) called RSSView, with the following code snippet:

```
function RSSView() {
  var self = Ti.UI.createView({
    backgroundColor:'#fff'
  });

  var table = Ti.UI.createTableView();
  self.add(table);

  self.refreshRSSTable = function(_args) {

    if (Object.prototype.toString.apply(_args.data) ===
    '[object Array]') {
      var rows = [];
      for (var i = 0; i < _args.data.length; i++) {
        rows.push(createRssRow(_args.data[i]));
      }
      table.setData(rows);
    }
  };

  return self;
}
module.exports = RSSView;
```

This function creates a view and adds a table view to it. A function called refreshRSSTable is added to the view, so it can be called by anything implementing the view. This is a handy trick. We will show how it is called in a later step.

3. Now add the createRssRow function. This function is called from refreshRSSTable and will lay out TableViewRow with a single RSS data item.

```
var createRssRow = function(item) {
  var tablerow = Ti.UI.createTableViewRow({
```

```
    height: 70,
    link: item.link,
    className: 'RSSRow'
  });
  var imageview = Ti.UI.createImageView({
    image: item.image,
    height: 42,
    width: 68,
    left: 5,
    top: 3
  });
  var titleview = Ti.UI.createLabel({
    text: item.title,
    color: '#000',
    height: 70,
    font: {
      fontSize: 16
    },
    left: 83,
    right: 5
  });
  tablerow.add(imageview);
  tablerow.add(titleview);

  return tablerow;
};
```

4. Add code to app.js to add this new view so that it can be displayed.

```
RssView = require('rssView');

var rssView = new RssView();

win.add(rssView);
```

5. Cast your mind back to the end of the last example where the returned RSS was logged to the console. We now have the tools to parse this data, so the fetchRSSFeed function needs to be updated to call the parser. Add the highlighted code to the onload event:

```
xhr.onload = function(e) {
  var xml = this.responseXML;
```

```
      if (xml === null || xml.documentElement === null) {
        alert('Error reading RSS feed. Make sure you have a
        network connection and try refreshing.');
        if (_args.error) { _args.error(); }
        return;
      }

      parseRSS({data: xml, then: _args.success});
    };

    xhr.send();
```

6. Now for the magic; this is the step where we link it all together. Modify the call to `fetchRSSFeed` in `app.js` making the change (as highlighted in the following code snippet):

```
var rss = require('rssReader');
rss.fetchRSSFeed({url: 'http://feeds.bbci.co.uk/news/business/rss.
xml?edition=uk', success: rssView.refreshRSSTable});
```

 The `refreshRSSTable` function will be executed against `rssView`.

Now that all of this code is linked, this is what a successful request will do:

   i.   The request calls `rss.fetchRSSFeed` passing the function that is to be called to display the data, `rssView.refreshRSSTable`.

   ii. `fetchRSSFeed` passes the raw XML returned from the HTTP request to `fetchRSSFeed` and also passes on `rssView.refreshRSSTable`.

   iii. `fetchRSSFeed` parses the data and calls `rssView.refreshRSSTable`, passing an array of the parsed data.

   iv. `rssView.refreshRSSTable` is executed and the table view is populated with the results.

7. Run the app!

What just happened?

This app showed how to code an HTTP client call. It also showed the clever trick of adding functions to an object so that they may be executed against the object in its scope.

The code for this project can be found at `https://github.com/myleftboot/ProfileStorage`.

Appcelerator have produced a similar project with more functionality that can be downloaded from `https://github.com/appcelerator-developer-relations/Sample.RSS`.

Storing data on the device

So you have downloaded the XML and presented it on-screen. What are you going to do with it now? If your user closes the app now and then re-opens it an hour later, would you grab the RSS again? If you were showing the latest news, the user would accept this. But if your RSS was, for example, a major league fixture list or next year's cricket fixtures, it would not be acceptable to refresh the content every time your user accesses the feed. Furthermore, what if the device is offline, outside network coverage, or in airplane mode? What would you do then?

The answer is to store the XML. This means that the users do not have to wait for the list to be refreshed every time they open the screen, and also allows the content to be browsed when the device is offline. It is better to display the content last fetched than to display nothing at all.

There are three different methods for storing data on the device. You can keep it in a file, in a database, or in property files.

Which one should you use; filesystem, database, or properties?

A basic maxim that works quite well for storage is that if it's an image or some other media, it should be a file; if it has lots of repeating things, it's a database; otherwise, it could be a setting. The following table is a better guide to what each storage medium is suited to:

Storage	Usage
Application properties (`Ti.App.Properties`)	This is used when: ◆ The data consists of simple key/value pairs ◆ The data is related to the application rather than the user ◆ The data does not require other data in order to be meaningful or useful ◆ There only needs to be one version of the data stored at any one time It is used for persistent storage of program variables, and settings. You can store JSON data in here, which is a very useful way to store program context.

Storage	Usage
Database (`Ti.Database`)	This is used when: ◆ There are many similar data items ◆ The items of data relate to each other ◆ You require flexibility over how the data will be presented when you retrieve it ◆ The data accumulates over time, such as during transaction, logging, or archiving data An organized set of data such as a product list should be stored here. The select operations offered will make finding items easier and quicker. Do not store media files in a database. While SQLite can store this content, it will be slower to retrieve than the filesystem. In this case, consider having a database of filenames that link to the real files. Logging and transactional data is better put into a database rather than a filesystem as the tools provided by SQL mean that it is easier to retrieve and manage the data than a file. For example, you can write a `delete` statement on the database to remove all transactions over a week old. If, on the other hand, you were writing to a file, you would have to write code to read through the file and remove matching lines.
File (`Ti.Filesystem`)	This is used when: ◆ The data is already provided in the file format ◆ The data is an image, movie, or sound clip Remember that it is your responsibility to manage the files you create. Apple will expect you to mark transactional files to make sure they are not backed up.

Storing data in files

`Titanium.Filesystem.File` contains all of the file operations you would expect to be able to perform, including opening, closing, writing, reading, deleting, moving, and more.

 On iOS you need to set `Ti.Filesystem.File.remoteBackup` against certain files created by your app. iOS backs up data from an iPhone/iPad to iTunes and the cloud, and Apple are quite strict about what should be included in the backup. Any app that creates content that violates Apple's guidelines on what they deem acceptable to be backed up will be rejected. Also be aware that this `remoteBackup` property is only relevant for iOS and will cause errors if your app executes this command on Android. You will need to conditionally exclude this line if running on that platform. Android doesn't have the same backup restrictions for user-generated content.

The following example shows how easy it is to create a new file:

```
var f = Ti.Filesystem.getFile
(Ti.Filesystem.applicationDataDirectory,file);
f.write(xml);
f.setRemoteBackup(false);
```

 The file will be created if it does not exist.

Files in `Ti.Filesystem.applicationDataDirectory` will be backed up on iOS so the `remoteBackup` property needs to be set.

To close a file and release the associated resources, set the file handle to null. The following example shows how we would close the file written in the previous example:

```
f = null;
```

Use the filesystem when other methods of storage are not suitable. If you can, bundle the files with the app when it is released.

Storing data in the database

Database storage on most phones is through the beautifully small yet feature-packed SQLite. Depending on what your definition of a database is, it's the most installed database in the world. It's certainly the most widely installed SQL database given that it is bundled into iOS, Android, Windows 8, and most modern browsers. It's also powerful despite its small size and can manage an impressive number of SQL operations. It's small, fast, and efficient. It should be your first choice when considering local storage.

There are two methods of opening a SQLite database (which is really a file; a SQLite database is a file). The following table indicates what methods to use:

Command	Usage
`Ti.Database.open`	This opens a SQLite database from local storage. Use this when you wish to create a new database from your app.
	If the database file does not exist, this will create a new empty file.
`Ti.Database.install`	If your database is distributed with your app, iOS needs to copy it to local storage before it can be opened.
	The `install` command will copy the file if it does not exist in local storage before opening the database. If the database already exists locally, this command behaves exactly the same way as the `open` command.
	If you have a SQLite database distributed with your app, use `install`; there is no overhead compared to the `open` command.

Once the database is open, you can execute SQL against it, as shown next:

```
var db = Ti.Database.open('emp', 'employees');
db.execute('CREATE TABLE emp (ename VARCHAR2(30), dept VARCHAR2(10));
');
db.execute('INSERT INTO emp (ename, dept) VALUES ("JOHN", "SALES");
');
```

Selecting values back from the table is done as follows:

```
var emps = db.execute('SELECT ename FROM emp;');
while (emps.isValidRow())
{
  Ti.API.info(emps.field(1));
  emps.next();
}
emps.close();
db.close();
```

> Note the highlighted `close` command in the last example. You must close a SQLite database and any rows when you are finished with them to release the resources. They are not automatically cleared and will use up valuable memory otherwise.

Storing settings in Ti.App.Properties

`Ti.App.Properties` should be used for storing application properties. Long string values can be stored as a property, which makes them very useful for storing stringified JSON data.

Strings, integers, doubles, and Boolean values can all be stored and accessed using the appropriate command. In the following example we are going to store a Boolean value for `enabled_preference`. If the property does not exist, it will be automatically created.

```
if(!Ti.App.Properties.hasProperty('enabled_preference')) {
  Ti.App.Properties.setBool('enabled_preference', true);
}
```

The code to retrieve the property is as follows:

```
Ti.App.Properties.getBool('enabled_preference', true);
```

 The second parameter `getBool` is the default value to return if the property does not exist.

Time for action – comparing the speed of database, file, and application properties

In this next example we are going to compare the speed of reading and writing data using the properties, database, and files. The example will count the time it takes to write 1000 records and then read them back again. The results of this comparison are intended to be of interest and should not be a reason to use or avoid a method. It is not fair to compare the performance of writing properties with that of a database as it suits one method far more than the other.

You can grab the source to this project from `https://github.com/myleftboot/ProfileStorage`. Perform the following steps to compare the speed of database, file, and application properties:

1. Create a new blank mobile app by clicking on **File | New | Titanium Project**.
2. Create the usual single window setup in `app.js`.

```
Titanium.UI.setBackgroundColor('#000');

var win1 = Titanium.UI.createWindow({
    title:'Storage Profiler',
```

```
    backgroundColor:'#000'
});

win1.open();
```

3. Create a view to place the controls on. Note the `layout` property of `vertical`. This instructs the view to stack the items placed on it vertically. We will cover this in more detail in *Chapter 8, Creating Beautiful Interfaces*.

```
var vw = Ti.UI.createView({layout: 'vertical'});
win1.add(vw);
```

4. Create a progress bar to indicate the status of the activity. Add the `start` and `end` functions that will compute the start and finish times of the tests. Note that the `end` function will take an object as a parameter and set the `text` attribute of it. In the next step we will see how this use of an object as a parameter results in cleaner code. The `resetPB` function tidies up the progress bar, moving it back to the start to make it ready for the next test.

The `_args.obj.text` variable in the end function can be broken down, as follows:

- `_args` is the parameter. The type is not defined but JSON will be passed.
- `obj` is the attribute of the JSON parameter. In this case the `obj` attribute will be a `label` object.
- `text` is the attribute of the `label` object that will be modified. In this case the time taken to complete the test will be assigned.

The following is the code:

```
var iterations = 1000;
var started;
function start(_args) {
  progressBar.message =
  'Writing '+ iterations + ' '+ _args.message
  started = new Date;
}

function end(_args) {
  var end = new Date;
  _args.obj.text = end - started+ 'ms';
}
```

```
function resetPB(_args) {
  progressBar.setValue = progressBar.getMin();
  progressBar.setMessage(_args.message);
}

var label = Ti.UI.createLabel({text:   'Compare the performance of
Properties, database and files'
                            ,color: '#888'
                            ,height: 40});

var dummySpace = Ti.UI.createView({height:30});

var progressBar = Ti.UI.createProgressBar({
  min:      0,
  max:      1000,
  value:    0,
  color:    '#fff',
  message: 'writing '+ iterations + ' records'
});
```

5. Add a button that when pressed will fire off the `Ti.App.Properties` test. This test will write 1000 properties, then read them back, and record the overall time. The highlighted commands are where the application properties are get and set. Also worth noticing is the parameter to the end function. As set up in the previous step, the `propertiesResult` label object is passed to the end function where the label text is updated.

```
var testProperties = Ti.UI.createButton({
  title:     'Test Properties',
  height:    40,
  width:     150,
  top:      30,
});

testProperties.addEventListener('click', function() {
  start({message: 'properties'});
  for (i=0; i< iterations; i++ ) {
    Ti.App.Properties.setInt('P'+i, i);
    progressBar.setValue(i);
  }
  resetPB({message: 'Reading '+iterations+ ' properties'});
  var result;
```

```
    for (i=0; i< iterations; i++ ) {
      result += Ti.App.Properties.getInt('P'+i, i);
      progressBar.setValue(i);
    }
    end({obj: propertiesResult});
  });

  propertiesResult = Ti.UI.createLabel({
    color: '#fff',
    height: 40
  });
```

 Notice the value of top:30 assigned to the
testProperties button. This is a really easy way
to add space between components in a vertical layout.
The value for top does not mean placing the button
30 pixels away from the top of the view, but in this case
it's 30 pixels from the object above it in the view. The
same effect could be achieved by specifying 30 for the
bottom value of the previous object.

6. Add a button that when pressed will fire off the Ti.Database test.

```
var testDatabase = Ti.UI.createButton({
  title:    'Test Database',
  height:   40,
  width:    150,
});

testDatabase.addEventListener('click', function() {

  start({message: 'database'});

  var db = Ti.Database.open('theProfiler');
      if (Ti.Platform.name == 'iPhone OS')
      db.file.setRemoteBackup(false);
  db.execute('CREATE TABLE IF NOT EXISTS profiler
  (id INTEGER)');
      db.execute('DELETE FROM profiler');
      // insert values
  for (i=0; i< iterations; i++ ) {
    db.execute('INSERT INTO profiler(id) VALUES (?)', i);
```

```
        progressBar.setValue(i);
    }

    resetPB({message: 'Reading '+iterations+ ' database
    entries'});
    var result;
    var rows = db.execute('SELECT SUM(id) FROM profiler');

        if (rows.isValidRow())
        {
            result =  rows.field(0);
        }
        rows.close();
        db.close();
        progressBar.setValue(progressBar.getMax());
    end({obj: databaseResult});
});

databaseResult = Ti.UI.createLabel({
  color: '#fff',
  height: 40
});
```

The database db reference is closed before the row
reference. This is fine as the rows were fetched from
the database and stored in the rows object when the
select statement was executed.

7. Add another button to test the speed of reading and writing files.

```
var testFile = Ti.UI.createButton({
  title:    'Test File',
  height:   40,
  width:    150,
});

testFile.addEventListener('click', function() {
  start({message: 'file'});
  var theFile = Ti.Filesystem.createTempFile();
  var result;
  for (i=0; i< iterations; i++ ) {
```

```
  theFile.write(i+' ', true);
  progressBar.setValue(i);
}

resetPB({message: 'Reading '+iterations+ ' records from
file'});
// Read the contents of the file
// We can only get the whole file as a blob
// so we have a bit of work to do to process it
var contents = new String(theFile.read().toString); // read
file and convert it to a string

var contentsArr = contents.split(' ');
for (i=0; i< contentsArr.length; i++ ) {
  result += contentsArr[i];
  progressBar.setValue(i);
}
end({obj: fileResult});

theFile = null;
})

fileResult = Ti.UI.createLabel({
  color: '#fff',
  height: 40
});
```

8. Add the three buttons and the progress bar to the view (vw). Unlike other components, progress bars are initially hidden, so an extra call is needed to show it after it has been added to the view.

```
vw.add(label);
vw.add(testProperties);
vw.add(propertiesResult);
vw.add(testDatabase);
vw.add(databaseResult);
vw.add(testFile);
vw.add(fileResult);
vw.add(progressBar);
progressBar.show();
```

9. Run the app!

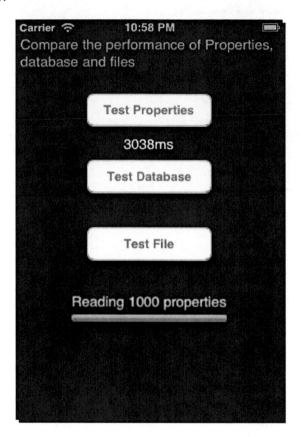

What just happened?

You created an app that compares the speed of writing and reading 1000 numbers to different storage devices. The app has a single window and a vertically arranged view of components. The app shows how to create properties, insert and select from databases, and how to write and read files.

YQL

This last example is a cracker. We have saved the best for last for this chapter. It's a mashup involving the local SQLite database and the SQL database provided by Yahoo! known as YQL. YQL, for those of you who aren't aware, allows you to issue web search queries against the Yahoo! search engine as though it were a SQL database.

YQL is issued from Titanium using the `Ti.Yahoo.yql` command. The structure of the command is simple. The first parameter is the query and the second is the callback code to run when the command completes. See the following example call that gets the weather forecast for Sunnyvale, California:

```
Ti.Yahoo.yql('select * from weather.forecast where woeid=2502265',
function(e) {do_something_with_it(e);});
```

> Notice the structure of the `Ti.Yahoo.yql` command. YQL is executed against the Yahoo! web services in much the same way as the HTTP requests which we saw earlier in this chapter. So, in keeping with the HTTP requests, the second parameter is a callback to execute when the request completes some time later.

The callback is always called, even if the phone is offline. You can examine the return status of the request by examining the object passed to the callback. The object (`e` in the preceding example) has the following two properties:

Property	Usage
`success`	If this is `true`, the request has been completed and the `data` property will contain the returned YQL.
	If this is `false`, it means the command has failed.
`data`	This is the YQL response returned from Yahoo!.

In this example we are going to use YQL to look for foreign exchange prices. The app will consist of a single screen with a picker where you select your desired currency and below that a list of the current currency rates.

> This example creates a SQLite database from the command line. You need to locally install SQLite to do this. You can download SQLite for free from `http://sqlite.org`.

Time for action – creating a foreign exchange list

To create a foreign exchange list perform the following steps:

1. Create a new blank mobile app by clicking on **File | New | Titanium Mobile Project**. Don't use a template as it will just generate code that gets in the way.

2. We are going to create a SQLite database file containing the foreign exchange pairings we are interested in. Pre-populating the file means that it is available when the app starts. Create a new directory in the new project called db under the `resources` directory to house the database file.

3. Navigate to the new db directory using the command line / terminal. Then run `sqlite3`. Notice the parameter to the command that sets the database file.

> If you prefer to work with a nice GUI when editing your SQLite files, then you should use the SQLite browser. It's available for free and for both OSX and Windows at `http://sqlitebrowser.sourceforge.net/`.

The following are the required commands:

```
>sqlite3 currencies.sqlite
SQLite version 3.7.14.1 2012-10-04 19:37:12
Enter ".help" for instructions
Enter SQL statements terminated with a ";"
sqlite>
```

> You may have to add SQLite to your path before you can run it from the db directory.

4. Create the table to house the currency pairs.

```
sqlite> create table if not exists currencies
   ...> (base     varchar2(5) not null
   ...> ,counter  varchar2(5) not null
   ...> ,nickname varchar2(30)
   ...> ,type     varchar2(10) not null);
```

5. Populate the table with the currency pairs.

```
sqlite> insert into currencies(base, counter, nickname, type)
values ('EUR', 'USD', 'Fiber', 'Major');
```

```
sqlite> insert into currencies(base, counter, nickname, type)
values ('USD', 'JPY', 'Yen', 'Major');

sqlite> insert into currencies(base, counter, nickname, type)
values ('GBP', 'USD', 'Cable', 'Major');

sqlite> insert into currencies(base, counter, nickname, type)
values ('AUD', 'USD', 'Aussie', 'Major');

sqlite> insert into currencies(base, counter, nickname, type)
values ('USD', 'CHF', 'Swiss', 'Major');

sqlite> insert into currencies(base, counter, nickname, type)
values ('USD', 'CAD', 'Loonie', 'Major');

sqlite> insert into currencies(base, counter, type) values ('GBP',
'JPY', 'Cross');

sqlite> insert into currencies(base, counter, type) values ('EUR',
'GBP', 'Cross');

sqlite> insert into currencies(base, counter, type) values ('EUR',
'JPY', 'Cross');

sqlite> select count(*) from currencies;

9

sqlite>
```

 In `sqlite`, operations are saved to the file (or committed in other databases) as soon as they complete.

6. We now have all the data we need for this example, so exit SQLite by entering `.quit`.

7. Return to Titanium Studio. Create the usual single window setup in `app.js`.

```
Titanium.UI.setBackgroundColor('#000');

var win1 = Titanium.UI.createWindow({
    title:'Currency Prices',
    backgroundColor:'#000'
});
```

8. Create a function that returns a picker. The picker is populated from the currency values in the SQLite database. As the SQLite database has been created outside of the app, that is, not created from the app code, it needs to be installed and not opened so that the first time `db` is accessed, it is copied to internal storage.

```
function createCurrencyPicker() {
  var currencyPicker = Ti.UI.createPicker(
    {height               :'40%',
```

```
        selectionIndicator : true});

   // populate the picker from the SQLite currencies

   // Database file already exists so we need to use install,
   to copy it to the internal storage
   var db = Ti.Database.install('db/currencies.sqlite',
   'currencies');
   var data = db.execute
   ('SELECT DISTINCT counter FROM currencies;');

   var pickRow = [];  var i = 0;
   while (data.isValidRow()) {
     pickRow[i++] = Ti.UI.createPickerRow
     ({title:data.fieldByName('counter')});
     data.next();
   }

   data.close();
   db.close();

   currencyPicker.add(pickRow);
   return currencyPicker;
};
```

9. Create the layout. The single window display will add the picker to the top of the screen and a table view with the currencies below it. Add the following code to `app.js`:

```
var vertLayout = Ti.UI.createView({layout:'vertical'});


var stockList = Ti.UI.createTableView({});

var picker = createCurrencyPicker();

vertLayout.add(picker);
vertLayout.add(stockList);

win1.add(vertLayout);
win1.open();
```

10. Run the app to check that the picker is displayed and populated.

11. The value selected from the picker will be used to select a list of currency pairs. So for example, if **USD** was selected from the picker, the currencies selected from the database would be **EURUSD**, **AUDUSD**, **GBPUSD**. The following function will create an array of currency pairs from the counter currency passed in:

```
function refreshCurrencies(_args) {
  var db = Ti.Database.install
  ('db/currencies.sqlite', 'currencies');
  var data = db.execute('SELECT base||counter pair FROM
  currencies WHERE counter="'+_args.value+'";');

  var pairs = [];
  var i = 0;
  while (data.isValidRow()) {
    pairs[i++] = data.fieldByName('pair');
    data.next();
  }

  data.close();
  db.close();

};
```

12. Now we need a function to get the currency values using YQL. We will be using the `yahoo.finance.xchange` table that lists the current currency exchange rates. The function will accept a list of currency pairs as a parameter; it will then extract these values from the array and create a comma-separated list. This list of currency pairs will be passed to the YQL. The function will log the returned values to the console using `Ti.API.info`, so we can see the result.

 The YQL developer console (`http://developer.yahoo.com/yql/console/`) is an excellent tool for testing out YQL queries and for browsing the tables that can be selected from.

The following is the code:

```
function fetchValues(_args) {
  // returns a list of prices from an array of stocks

  if (_args.pairings.length > 0) {
    var currencies = new String;
    for (i=0; i< _args.pairings.length; i++) {
      currencies += ',"'+_args.pairings[i]+'"';
```

```
      }
      // lose the first character ','
      currencies = currencies.substr(1);

      var theYql = 'SELECT * from yahoo.finance.xchange WHERE
      pair IN (' + currencies + ')';

      // send the query off to yahoo
      Ti.Yahoo.yql(theYql, function(e) {
        Ti.API.info(e.data);
      });
    }
};
```

13. Now we need to link together the currency picker selection to the YQL query. Add an event listener to the picker to spot when the picker value changes and call `refreshCurrencies` to get a list of the applicable currencies.

```
picker.addEventListener('change', function(e)
{refreshCurrencies({value: e.selectedValue[0]}) });
```

 Make sure you add the event listener after the picker is defined, otherwise you will get an error as the object will not exist.

The `selectedValue` property returns an array as it is possible to select multiple values from a picker. We are only interested in a single selected value so grab the first element, `[0]`.

14. The `refreshCurrencies` function needs to call `fetchValues` to get the new currency values. Add the following highlighted code to the end of the `refreshCurrencies` function:

```
while (data.isValidRow()) {
  pairs[i++] = data.fieldByName('pair');
  data.next();
}

data.close();
db.close();

fetchValues({pairings: pairs});
};
```

15. Run the app. The picker will be displayed at the top. Select a different currency from the list. The console will show the value returned from the YQL query, as shown in the following screenshot:

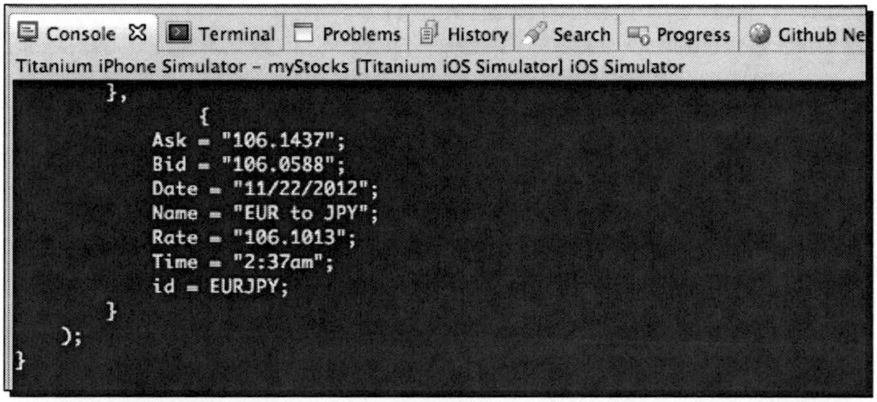

16. The final stage is to display the currency values returned from the YQL call on the table view. Create a function that will populate the table view parsing the results, as shown next:

```
<results>
    <rate id="EURUSD">
        <Name>EUR to USD</Name>
        <Rate>1.2797</Rate>
        <Date>11/20/2012</Date>
        <Time>9:06am</Time>
        <Ask>1.2798</Ask>
        <Bid>1.2795</Bid>
    </rate>
</results>
```

The function extracts the values from the array, creating a `TableViewRow` layout for each currency. This is then applied to the table view declared earlier.

```
function populateTable(_args) {
  var tabRows = [];
  // we need to make single objects returned into an array
  var rates = (_args.JSON.rate instanceof Array) ?
  _args.JSON.rate : [_args.JSON.rate];
  for (var i in rates) {
    var tableRow = Ti.UI.createTableViewRow({
      height: 70,
```

```
            className: 'RSSRow'
        });
        var layout = Ti.UI.createView({});

        var pair = Ti.UI.createLabel({
            text: rates[i].Name,
            color: '#000',
            height: 70,
            font: {
                fontSize: 16
            },
            left: 20
        });

        var value = Ti.UI.createLabel({
            text:   rates[i].Rate,
            color: 'blue',
            height: 70,
            font: {
                fontSize: 16
            },
            right: 20
        });
        layout.add(pair);
        layout.add(value);
        tableRow.add(layout);

        tabRows.push(tableRow);
    }
    stockList.setData(tabRows);
};
```

The function loops through the rates returned from the YQL request. Note that if a single rate is returned, then it is not formatted as an array but a single object. A fix is needed to create an array of the results if the value returned is not one:

```
var rates = (_args.JSON.rate instanceof Array) ? _args.JSON.rate :
[_args.JSON.rate];
```

17. Finally, link the code that fetches the YQL with the code in the last step that displays it. Make the following highlighted changes to the `fetchValues` function:

```
var theYql = 'SELECT * from yahoo.finance.xchange WHERE
pair IN (' + currencies + ')';
```

```
    // send the query off to yahoo
    Ti.Yahoo.yql(theYql, function(e) {
      populateTable({JSON: e.data});
    });
```

18. Run the app!

What just happened?

You created an app that combines the use of the local SQLite database with the database-like YQL service. From here you can access a wealth of information via YQL.

Have a go hero - adding offline storage

Bearing in mind that your application should be able to handle being offline, you could put your database skills learned in this chapter to good use by amending this app to store the prices when they are fetched. Then, if the query to YQL fails because of the device being offline or for some other reason, the historical values can be displayed.

Pop quiz - data handling

Q 1. You issue a YQL query but your phone is in airplane mode and cannot access the Internet. Which one of the following will happen?

1. The error callback will be called
2. The callback will be called with `success: false` **passed**
3. An alert asking the user to go online will be shown to the user
4. The `onerror` event will be fired if it has been declared

Summary

This chapter may not have been very exciting visually, but it did teach the following two elements that will underpin most apps:

- ◆ Local storage
- ◆ HTTP requests

By using HTTP requests you can interface to web servers and from there get and post data to and from your phone. It's your connection to the Internet! Conversely, by using local storage you can store content locally for those times when your phone is offline. These are really useful components of an app that you will use time and time again.

The next chapter moves on from the traditional method of local storage to the new kid in town, the cloud. We will look into how we can interface apps to cloud-based services and look closely at the cloud offering from Appcelerator.

6

Cloud-enabling Your Apps

Cloud computing is already a big thing and it's only going to get bigger as companies embrace the advantages of offsite managed storage and processing. You will probably be aware of some of the early adopters of cloud computing such as Evernote and Dropbox who have created a great position in the market. But the cloud is far more than just storage as we will discover in this chapter. Come with us as we embrace the advantages of the cloud and what it can do for you and your apps.

Suppose that you made a brilliant shoe designer app that allowed users to design their own custom shoes on their phone. Your app allows them to save their designs so they can finish them at a later date and then hopefully buy their custom design by uploading them to your store. Brilliant, people love it and the orders are rolling in. But you are missing a trick. As the designs are stored locally on the users' phones, the user can't continue the design when on a computer, or worse if the phone were lost, the design and that extra purchase is also lost. If the user could store the design away from the phone they could take it with them and share their design with others, or better still collaborate on it. This is one of the big advantages of the cloud. As phone networks continually improve connection speeds and users' appetites for data increase, the use of cloud storage and processing is becoming more and more of a core requirement.

This is how apps such as Evernote have made a killing. Your content travels with you. It doesn't matter if you are accessing the content from your phone or web or even TV, it's all the same. Just as you would expect if you were accessing e-mails or Twitter.

This chapter will show how to integrate with the cloud and will concentrate on how to use some of the storage-based solutions. Specifically you will learn how to:

◆ Integrate with Appcelerator Cloud Services

◆ Interface to a REST-based cloud service

◆ Send and receive data from the cloud

Before the cloud

If this book were written a year ago the content would be very different, and the difference is almost solely down to the emergence of cloud-based solutions. The chapters would still be the same; you would still be looking for beautiful interfaces (*Chapter 8, Creating Beautiful Interfaces*), functioning apps using the gadgets of the phone (*Chapter 10, Sending Notifications*), and spreading the word using social media (*Chapter 9, Spread the Word with Social Media*), but the solutions presented would be different. Back then if you wanted to use social media you would integrate a library, and similarly if you wanted to register for push notifications, you would plug in another interface. Not anymore. Since the introduction of cloud-based services, you can handle all of these requirements and more with one interface. A number of one-stop-shop solutions have come to the market with competitive rates for cloud solutions. Appcelerator have heavily promoted their own cloud offering, but that doesn't mean it's your only option—there are other players in this area.

Which cloud services can you use with Titanium?

Here is a comparison of the services offered by three cloud-based providers who have been proven to work with Titanium:

	Appcelerator Cloud Services	Parse	StackMob
Customizable storage	Yes	Yes	Yes
Push notifications	Yes	Yes	Yes
E-mail	Yes	No	No
Photos	Yes	Yes	Yes
Link with Facebook/ Twitter account	Yes	Yes	Yes
User accounts	Yes	Yes	Yes

The services offered by these three leading contenders are very similar. The main difference is the cost. Which is the best one for you? It depends on your requirements; you will have to do the cost/benefit analysis to work out the best solution for you.

Do you need more functionality than this? No problem, look around for other PaaS providers. The PaaS service offered by RedHat has been proven to integrate with Titanium and offers far more flexibility. There is an example of a Titanium app developed with RedHat Openshift at `https://openshift.redhat.com/community/blogs/developing-mobile-apps-for-the-cloud-with-titanium-studio-and-the-openshift-paas`.

It doesn't stop there; new providers are coming along almost every month with new and grand ideas for web and mobile integration. My advice would be to take the long view. Draw up a list of what you require initially for your app and what you realistically want in the next year. Check this list against the cloud providers. Can they satisfy all your needs at a workable cost? They should do; they should be flexible enough to cover your plans. You should not need to split your solution between providers.

Clouds are everywhere

Cloud-based services offer more than just storage. You will see cloud solutions in most of the remaining chapters of the book which cover social media, push notifications, and analytics. The content of these chapters has been split between the cloud solution and the traditional method of using a tailored web service (such as Urban Airship for push notifications, or Flurry for analytics).

As this is a book on using Titanium, it would seem appropriate to show the Appcelerator Cloud Services for the first example.

Appcelerator Cloud Services

Appcelerator Cloud Services (**ACS**) is well integrated into Titanium. The API includes commands for controlling ACS cloud objects.

In the first example in this chapter we are going to add commentary functionality to the simple forex app created in the last chapter. Forex commentary is an ideal example of the benefits of cloud-based storage where your data is available across all devices.

First, let's cover some foreground to the requirements.

The currency markets are open 24 hours a day, 5 days a week and trading opportunities can present themselves at any point. You will not be in front of your computer all of the time so you will need to be able to access and add commentary when you are on your phone or at home on your PC. This is where the power of the cloud really starts to hit home. We already know that you can create apps for a variety of devices using Appcelerator. This is good; we can access our app from most phones, but now using the cloud we can also access our commentary from anywhere. So, comments written on the train about the EURUSD rate can be seen later when at home looking at the PC.

When we are creating forex commentary, we will store the following:

- The currency pair (that is EURUSD)
- The rate (the current exchange rate)
- The commentary (what we think about the exchange rate)

> We will also store the date and time of the commentary. This is done automatically by ACS. All objects include the date they were created.

ACS allows you to store key value pairs (which is the same as `Ti.App.Properties`), that is `AllowUserToSendEmails: True`, or custom objects. We have several attributes to our commentary post so a key value pair will not suffice. Instead we will be using a custom object.

We are going to add a screen that will be called when a user selects a currency. From this screen a user can enter commentary on the currency.

Time for action – creating ACS custom objects

Perform the following steps to create ACS custom objects:

1. Enable ACS in your existing app. Go to `tiapp.xml` and click on the **Enable...** button on the **Cloud Services** section. Your project will gain a new `Ti.Cloud` module and the ACS authentication keys will be shown:

2. Go to the cloud website, `https://my.appcelerator.com/apps`, find your app, and select **Manage ACS**. Select **Development** from the selection buttons at the top.

3. You need to define a user so your app can log in to ACS. From the **App Management** tab select **Users** from the list on the right. If you have not already created a suitable user, do it now.

4. We will split the functionality in this chapter over two files. The first file will be called `forexCommentary.js` and will contain the cloud functionality, and the second file called `forexCommentaryView.js` will contain the layout code. We are still trying to comply with the MVC design principles laid out in *Chapter 2, How to Make an Interface*. Create the two new files.

5. Before we can do anything with ACS, we need to log in. Create an `init` function in `forexCommentary.js` which will log in the forex user created previously:

```
function init(_args) {
    if (!Cloud.sessionId) {
        Cloud.Users.login({
            login: 'forex',
            password: 'forex'
        }, function (e) {
            if (e.success) {
                _args.success({user : e.users[0]});
            } else {
                _args.error({error: e.error});
            }
        });
    }
};
```

 This is not a secure login, it's not important for this example. If you need greater security, use the `Ti.Cloud.Users.secureLogin` functionality.

6. Create another function to create a new commentary object on ACS. The function will accept a parameter containing the attribute's pair, rate, and commentary and create a new custom object from these. The first highlighted section shows how easy it is to define a custom object. The second highlighted section shows the custom object being passed to the `success` callback when the storage request completes:

```
function addCommentary(_args) {
    // create a new currency commentary
```

```
        Cloud.Objects.create({
            classname: className,
            fields: {
                pair:     _args.pair,
                rate:     _args.rate,
                comment:  _args.commentary
            }
        }, function (e) {
            if (e.success) {
                _args.success(e.forexCommentary[0]);
            } else {
                _args.error({error: e.error});
            }
        });
    }
```

7. Now to the layout. This will be a simple form with a text area where the commentary can be added. The exchange rate and currency pair will be provided from the app's front screen. Create a `TextArea` object and add it to the window. Note `keyboardType` of `Ti.UI.KEYBOARD_ASCII` which will force a full ASCII layout keyboard to be displayed and `returnKeyType` of `Ti.UI.RETURNKEY_DONE` which will add a **done** key used in the next step:

```
var commentary = Ti.UI.createTextArea({
  borderWidth:2,
  borderColour:'blue',
  borderRadius:5,
  keyboardType: Ti.UI.KEYBOARD_ASCII,
  returnKeyType: Ti.UI.RETURNKEY_DONE,
  textAlign: 'left',
  hintText: 'Enter your thoughts on '+thePair,
  width: '90%',
  height : 150
});
mainVw.add(commentary);
```

8. Now add an event listener which will listen for the **done** key being pressed and when triggered will call the function to store the commentary with ACS:

```
commentary.addEventListener('return',
                            function(e) {forex.addCommentary({
                                pair:       thePair,
                                rate:       theRate,
                                commentary: e.value})
                            });
```

9. Finally add the call to log in the ACS user when the window is first opened:

```
var forex = require('forexCommentary');
forex.init();
```

10. Run the app and enter some commentary.

What just happened?

You created functions to send a custom defined object to the server. Commentary entered on the phone is almost immediately available for viewing on the Appcelerator console (`https://my.appcelerator.com/apps`) and therefore available to be viewed by all other devices and formats.

Uploading pictures

Suppose you want to upload a picture, or a screenshot? This next example will show how easy it is to upload a picture to ACS.

Time for action – uploading a photo to the cloud

Perform the following steps to upload a photo to the cloud:

1. Create a new project by navigating to **File | New | Titanium Project**. Select the **Default Project** template.

2. Enable ACS in your existing app. Go to `tiapp.xml` and click on the **Enable...** button in the **Cloud Services** section.

3. Go to the cloud website at `https://my.appcelerator.com/apps` find your new app and select **Manage ACS**. Select **Development** from the selection buttons at the top.

4. You need to define a user so your app can log in to ACS. From the **App Management** tab select **Users** from the list on the right. If you have not already created a suitable user, do it now.

5. We will split the functionality in this chapter over two files, the cloud functionality in `cloud.js` and the usual layout items in `app.js`.

6. First create the layout in `app.js`. This will be a simple button and image view will allow the user to upload a photo from the photo gallery when the button is clicked. The image view will show the selected photo:

```
var win1 = Titanium.UI.createWindow({
    backgroundColor:'#fff'
});

var options = Ti.UI.createView({layout: 'vertical'});

var sendPhoto = Ti.UI.createButton({title: 'Send photo to the
cloud'});

var thePhoto = Ti.UI.createImageView({height: '30%', width:
'30%'});

options.add(sendPhoto);
options.add(thePhoto);
win1.add(options);
win1.open();
```

7. Add a link to the `cloud.js` file where the cloud functionality will be stored. Add these lines to the top of `app.js` file:

```
var upload = require('/cloud');
upload.init();
```

8. Add an event listener to show the photo gallery that will be called when the button is pressed:

```
sendPhoto.addEventListener('click', function(e) {
    Ti.Media.openPhotoGallery({
        autoHide:   true,
        mediaTypes: [Ti.Media.MEDIA_TYPE_PHOTO],
        success:    function(e) {showPhoto(e);
sendPiccyToCloud(e)}
        });
});
```

9. Add the `showPhoto` function to set the image view to the photo returned from the photo gallery:

```
function showPhoto(_args) {
    thePhoto.setImage(_args.media);
}
```

 There is more detail on the photo gallery and gadgets in *Chapter 7, Putting the Phone Gadgets to Good Use.*

10. Add the function that will send the photo to the cloud. This function will first write the photo to a file before uploading as the ACS picture upload function can only work with files and not blob data:

```
function sendPiccyToCloud(_args) {
    // first we need to write out a file of the piccy
    var file = Ti.Filesystem.getFile(Ti.Filesystem.
applicationDataDirectory, 'cloudThis.png');
    file.write(_args.media);
    // then send this file to the Cloud

    upload.sendPiccy(file.name);
    file = null;
}
```

11. Create the `cloud.js` file by navigating to **File | New | File**. Add the following initialization function to the file. This function will log in to the ACS cloud services with the username and password created in step 4:

```
var Cloud = require('Ti.Cloud');

//login as the cloud user....
function init(_args) {
```

```
      if (!Cloud.sessionId) {
          Cloud.Users.login({
              login: 'pic',
              password: 'piccy'
          }, function (e) {
              if (e.success) {
                  _args.success({user : e.users[0]});
              } else {
                  _args.error({error: e.error});
              }
          });
      }
  };
  exports.init = init;
```

12. Now add the function that uploads the picture to ACS. Remember that the picture must be a file:

```
function sendPiccy(_args) {
    // create a new photo

    Cloud.Photos.create({
        photo: Ti.Filesystem.getFile(Ti.Filesystem.
applicationDataDirectory+'/'+_args)
    }, function (e) {
        if (e.success) {
            var photo = e.photos[0];
            alert('Success:\n' +
                'id: ' + photo.id );
        } else {
            alert('Error:\\n' +
                ((e.error && e.message) || JSON.stringify(e)));
        }
    });
}
exports.sendPiccy = sendPiccy;
```

13. Run the app!

What just happened?

You created an app that allows the user to upload a picture from the photo gallery to ACS. When the app is run, you are presented with a screen with a single button. Pressing this button opens up the photo gallery; you then select a picture and it is uploaded to ACS and can be seen from the ACS web interface as shown in the following image:

Photos in cloudScreenshot-development		
Photos ID	**photo**	**filename**
512aa1ba95810f1890000b3b		cloudThis.png

The power of the cloud! Now we move on to the next example where we display the objects we are creating.

> Photos can be downloaded from ACS using the same query functionality as shown in the next example. See `http://docs.appcelerator.com/titanium/3.0/#!/api/Titanium.Cloud.Photos` for an example.

Fetching ACS stored content

For this next example we will return to the forex commentary app that was created earlier in the chapter. It's all well and good storing the commentary, but we also need a way to look at it. This next simple example will show how to create a panel to show the last three commentary entries across all currency pairs.

Time for action – creating a panel to show commentary entries

You need to have completed the last example before starting this example. It's no use trying to fetch ACS content without storing some first. Perform the following steps to create a panel showing commentary entries:

1. Ensure that the following calls are included:

    ```
    var forex = require('forexCommentary');
    forex.init();
    ```

2. We need a function that will get the last three custom objects from ACS. The query command has two parameters. The first defines the query, and the second is where you specify what you want to do with the results that are returned. In the following example, the object returned is called `forexCommentary`:

    ```
    function getLast3Comments(_args) {
        Cloud.Objects.query({
            classname: 'forexCommentary',
            limit:      3,
            order :     '-created_at'
        }, function (e) {
            if (e.success) {
                _args.success(e.forexCommentary);
            } else {
                _args.error({error: e.error});
            }
        });
    };
    ```

     It is very easy to change the query. For example if we only wanted to get the commentary for euros to dollars (EURUSD), we would add:

    ```
    order :     '-created_at',
    where :     {pair : 'EURUSD'}
    ```

3. Now create a table view to display the commentary and add it to the window:

    ```
    var latestCommentary = Ti.UI.createTableView({});

    mainVw.add(latestCommentary);
    ```

4. Create a function that creates the table view layout. This function will parse the `forexCommentary` object returned from ACS, grabbing the elements we wish to use to create a formatted table view object.

The format of the `forexCommentary` object has the following format:

```
{
    comment = "Moving nicely";
    "created_at" = "2012-12-13T23:30:39+0000";
    id = 50ca651f9dc3d1168a04ac96;
    pair = AUDUSD;
    rate = "1.0526";
    "updated_at" = "2012-12-13T23:30:39+0000";
    user =       {
        admin = false;
        "confirmed_at" = "2012-12-10T21:49:41+0000";
        "created_at" = "2012-12-10T21:49:41+0000";
        email = "forex@copeconsultancy.co.uk";
        "external_accounts" =            (
        );
        id = 50c658f5df52405ff4000c0f;
        "updated_at" = "2012-12-17T20:46:10+0000";
        username = forex;
    };
}
```

```
function createCommentaryRows(_args) {
    var tabRows = [];
    var moment = require('moment');

    for (var i in _args) {

        var tableRow = Ti.UI.createTableViewRow({
            height: 70,
            className: 'CommentaryRow',
        });
        /* it's always a good idea to give you tableview rows
a class, especially if the format is common. It helps Titanium to
optimize the display */
        var layout = Ti.UI.createView({layout:'horizontal'});

        var leftPanel = Ti.UI.createView({
            layout: 'vertical',
            width: '30%'
        });

        var pair = Ti.UI.createLabel({
            text: _args[i].pair,
            color: 'black',
```

```
            font: {
                fontSize: 16
            },
        });

        var rate = Ti.UI.createLabel({
            text:   _args[i].rate,
            color:  'black',
            height: 20,
            font: {
                fontSize: 16
            },
        });

        var created = moment(_args[i].created_at);

        var when = Ti.UI.createLabel({
            text:   created.fromNow(),
            color:  'black',
            height: 20,
            font: {
                fontSize: 14
            },
        });
        var comments = Ti.UI.createLabel({
            text:   _args[i].comment,
            color:  'black',
            height: Ti.UI.FILL,
            width:  Ti.UI.FILL,
            font: {
                fontSize: 12
            },
        });

        //layout the left panel
        leftPanel.add(pair);
        leftPanel.add(rate);
        leftPanel.add(when);
        // layout the row
        layout.add(leftPanel);
        layout.add(comments);

        tableRow.add(layout);

        tabRows.push(tableRow);
    }
    latestCommentary.setData(tabRows);
};
```

The highlighted code will transform the value returned from ACS for the created date, which will have a format that is similar to `2012-12-12T23:16:17+0000` to something far more friendly such as `8 hours ago`, or `3 days ago`. This is thanks to the functionality in the excellent `moment.js` library (`http://momentjs.com/`).

5. Add a call to link it all together. This will call the function to get the commentary and pass the results to the table view formatter function defined in the last step.

```
// run this when the form opens
forex.getLast3Comments({success: function(e)
{createCommentaryRows(e)}});
```

6. Run the app!

What just happened?

You created a table view to display the last three currency comments. The content will look as follows:

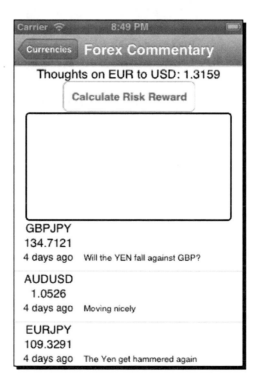

Parse

For the last example, we will show how easy it is to use a different cloud solution. It was said at the start of the chapter that you can integrate cloud solutions from other providers into your project, and this example will prove it.

This example uses Parse, which was chosen for two reasons. Firstly, and most importantly, Parse has a `REST API` so we can see an example of cloud integration using REST, and secondly it has an excellent user interface so you see the results at the end of the example.

Time for action – storing custom objects using Parse

We are going to show how you can store a custom object in the cloud via `REST API` using Parse. We will once again use the forex app for this example. It is a repeat of the last example in that we will be storing the forex commentary again. The only difference is the REST web service used to make the calls. We will store the currency pair, entry price, stop loss, and take profit values.

1. If you have not already done so, sign up for an account with Parse.

2. Create a new application. Each application has its own application and API key application ID and API key that are used to authenticate our REST requests. Navigate to the new app then select **Overview** from the menu bar. The **Application ID** and **REST API key** values will be listed on the left. Stay on this screen, we will be using these key values in a couple of steps' time.

3. Create a new CommonJS-based file in your project root to store our `PARSE REST API` functionality. In this case call it `parseCommentary.js`.

4. Add the following function to the new file. This function will construct the HTML call and then send the request. The highlighted sections show the lines where the application and API keys are specified and also where the custom data object is created:

```
function addCommentary(_args) {
    // create a new currency commentary using Parse
    var url = 'https://api.parse.com/1/classes/forexCommentary';
    var post = Ti.Network.createHTTPClient({

    onload : function(e) {
        console.log("Received text: " + this.responseText);
     },
```

```
    // function called when an error occurs, including a timeout
    onerror : function(e) {
        Ti.API.warn(JSON.stringify(e));
    },
    timeout : 5000  // in milliseconds
    });
 // Prepare the connection
    post.open("POST", url);
    post.setRequestHeader('X-Parse-Application-Id', '** YOUR APP
ID **');
    post.setRequestHeader('X-Parse-REST-API-Key', '** YOUR API ID
**');
    post.setRequestHeader('Content-Type', 'application/json');

    var data = JSON.stringify({
            pair:    _args.pair,
            rate:    _args.rate,
            comment: _args.commentary
        });
    // Send the request.
    post.send(data);
};
exports.addCommentary = addCommentary;
```

5. Return to the `forexCommentaryView.js` file and change the event listener that listens for the **done** key on the forex commentary text field. In the previous example this event listener contained the call to the ACS cloud. Make the change highlighted in the following code so that it now calls the parse interface.

```
var parse = require('parseCommentary');
commentary.addEventListener('return', function(e) {
                    parse.addCommentary({
                        pair:      thePair,
                        rate:      theRate,
                        commentary: e.value});
                });
```

6. Run the app and enter some commentary!

What just happened?

With one small function you created an interface to a REST-based API. Your code is cloud-enabled in six simple steps! When the app is run and commentary is added you will see an entry on the console, such as that shown in the following command line, indicating a successful transfer:

```
[INFO] {"pair":"EURJPY","rate":"109.6969","comment":"Drop back on the h4"}
[INFO] Received text: {"createdAt":"2012-12-14T07:06:03.833Z","objectId":
"18p1tZSYg5"}
```

You can also inspect the objects created from the Parse website as shown in the following screenshot:

StackMob

It is also possible to create the previously mentioned functionality with StackMob. Rather than repeating the examples over again you can look at the Appcelerator blog for an example of how to integrate StackMob into your project at `http://developer.appcelerator.com/blog/2011/11/titanium-appcelerator-quickie-stackmob-api-module-part-one.html`.

Other cloud offerings

Suppose the cloud service that you want to use is not in the list shown at the start of this chapter. Can you use it with Titanium and can you use it for all devices? It's fortunately very easy to work this out.

If the cloud service has either a JavaScript or a REST API, then you can use it with Titanium for cross-platform development. If it only has an iOS or Android SDK (and in that case you would have to question why) then you will need to find a module in the marketplace that will act as an interface or develop your own module.

Choosing your cloud service

This is a rapidly changing area. New players are continually bringing cloud-based solutions to market. Thanks to the success of the cross-platform app development tools such as Titanium, almost all include a JavaScript API, and can therefore be used with Titanium apps. You might think it's simply a matter of choosing the best one for you.

But a word of caution; you need to be aware of the cost of the service. Look beyond the initial developer price. Look at how your app will be funded when it is live. Do the plans you have for your app and the anticipated cost per user match the price you will receive per user from the sale/advertising/other revenue? Do the maths first. Work all this out before you start development. It's too late when your app is live and your platform is costing you more than you are receiving from your app. Imagine how your users would feel when you pulled the Twitter feed and push notifications from your app because you couldn't afford to keep up the hosting prices.

On the other hand, remember the benefits. Please don't let this stop your big idea, just be aware that you will be footing the bill for whatever wonderful service you provide, and that you will be in the same market with other apps that provide wonderful services for free but have considerable resources and a long term view to monetization (or a very bad idea and will bleed cash). If you can't make your wonderful service at a price where your cost received per user is above the cost outlay then you had better change or shelve your idea.

Remember that you are going to be closely linked to your chosen provider. It will be storing lots of important data which will make any changes to the service very hard once the app is live. You need to make the correct decision up front. Also resist the urge to jump on board with a new provider who is offering everything for nothing. Remember they have to fund themselves too. So if they are offering something the others aren't, ask yourself the question, how are they funding it? How will this make them money? You don't want to trust your data to someone who has a high risk business model that results in them going bust in a year's time.

Pop quiz - cloud services

Q 1. You see a great new image recognition service that has an iOS SDK and a JavaScript API. Can you use it with Titanium?

Q 2. Is Appcelerator Cloud Services is the only cloud storage option for Titanium apps?

Summary

Cloud-based services extend the functionality available on mobile phones, providing extra connectivity features and integration. If you are not using these services yet you probably will be in the next couple of years.

In the next chapter we will look at how to make the best use of all the gadgets on your phone. This is the chapter where all of the toys will come out of the box!

7

Putting the Phone Gadgets to Good Use

It's time to have some fun. It's time to lift the lid and look at all of those lovely toys that are within the new breed of smartphones. It's time to play with the accelerometer, camera, compass, and geolocation. If it's a gadget, it's covered here.

Boy, the combination of a few gadgets has certainly focused the imagination of a new breed of developer. From a simple spirit-level app through to augmented reality apps and all manner of apps in between—even the most humble app, which uses a map view to show a location—will use a gadget to give a more immersive experience.

This chapter will delve into:

- ◆ The camera
- ◆ The accelerometer
- ◆ Geolocation
- ◆ Augmented reality
- ◆ Maps (not strictly a gadget, but it fits with geolocation)

The camera

The camera is not only for taking pictures. It can take video, and as we will touch on later in the chapter, it can can be used as the basis for augmented reality apps.

Before that, it's time to get a grip of the basics. This first example will show you how to incorporate the camera into your app and how to show the picture taken by the user.

Time for action – using the camera

Let's get started with the camera. This is a simple demonstration on how you can incorporate the camera into your app.

This example is available for download or browse at `https://github.com/myleftboot/` `Chapter-7-camera`. To use the camera, perform the following steps:

1. Create a new blank mobile app by clicking on **File** | **New** | **Titanium Project**. Don't use a template as it will just generate code that gets in the way.

2. Create the window for the app:

```
var win1 = Titanium.UI.createWindow({
    backgroundColor:'#fff'
});
```

3. The layout for this example will be a button, and below that an image view, which will show the picture taken by the camera. All simple stuff!

```
var options = Ti.UI.createView({layout: 'vertical'});

var showCamera = Ti.UI.createButton({title: 'Show Camera'});

var thePhoto = Ti.UI.createImageView({height: '30%', width:
'30%'});

options.add(showCamera);
options.add(thePhoto);
win1.add(options);
```

4. Add a function to update the image with the photograph. It's not strictly necessary to have a function for this; it just makes the example look tidy:

```
function showPhoto(_args) {
  thePhoto.setImage(_args.media);
}
```

5. Now let's move on to the part that shows the camera. Pressing the button will activate the camera. Add an event listener to the button. An explanation of the parameters used follows after the listing:

```
showCamera.addEventListener('click', function (e) {
Ti.Media.showCamera({animated: true,
                     autoHide: true,
                     saveToPhotoGallery: true,
                     showControls: true,
                     mediaTypes: [Ti.Media.MEDIA_TYPE_PHOTO],
                     success:    function(e) {showPhoto(e)} ,
                     error:      function(e) {alert('There was a
problem accessing the camera')}
                     })
});
```

The `Ti.Media.showCamera` call shows the camera and has a number of parameters. These are shown in the following table:

Parameter	Description
animated	Should the camera just appear and disappear or should it scroll out as it appears? This doesn't apply to all platforms but can be set anyway.
autoHide	When the user takes the picture or cancels the camera, do you want it to disappear? Or will the app control when the camera is removed from the display?
saveToPhotoGallery	Do you want the picture to be saved to the photo gallery? You don't have to save pictures to the gallery.
showControls	Do you want to display the camera controls, such as zoom and flash?
mediaTypes	Do you want to record video and take photos?
success	What do you want to do with the image/video when it has been captured?
error	What do you want to do if there is an error in capturing the photo?

6. Run the app!

What just happened?

You created a small app that will allow you to capture a picture. There is no point in running this app on the simulator as it will return an error when you try to access the camera. The simulator does not try to pretend that it has a camera. You need to run this on a device. You can find instructions on how to do this in *Chapter 9, Spread the Word with Social Media*.

When you take a picture, the image appears on the image view below the button. This is very nice; completely cross-platform, and with very little code. The next example will build on this app and will allow you to choose a photo from the phone gallery and e-mail it.

Time for action – selecting a photo from the photo library

This example is available for download or browse at `https://github.com/myleftboot/Chapter-7-camera/tree/emailFromLibrary`. Perform the following steps to select a photo from the photo library:

1. Open the code from the previous example.

2. Add a button to the existing layout:

   ```
   var emailFromLibrary = Ti.UI.createButton({title: 'Email from
   photo library'});
   options.add(emailFromLibrary);
   ```

3. Add a function that will create a new e-mail with the subject and add the picture as an attachment:

   ```
   function emailPiccy(_args) {

     var toSend = Ti.UI.createEmailDialog({});

     toSend.subject = 'A photo I took earlier';
     toSend.messageBody = 'Thinking of you...';
       toSend.addAttachment(_args.media);
       toSend.open();
   }
   ```

4. Lastly, add an event listener to the button added in an earlier step. This code will open up the photo gallery browser. The `success` attribute defines the code that should be run when a photo is selected. If the user cancels, nothing happens.

   ```
   emailFromLibrary.addEventListener('click', function(e) {
     Ti.Media.openPhotoGallery({
       autoHide: true,
       mediaTypes: [Ti.Media.MEDIA_TYPE_PHOTO],
   ```

```
        success:    function(e) {emailPiccy(e)}
    });
});
```

5. Run the app! While you can run this example on the simulator, and you will get the
   e-mail dialog appearing, it will not send the mail. It only pretends to (it is a simulator
   after all). The following is a screenshot of the app in action on an Android device:

What just happened?

You added code to the app created in the first example to show the photo gallery and then
e-mail the selected picture.

Are there no pictures in your photo gallery to pick from?

How do you get a picture into the simulator photo library?

Open the browser on the simulator. Navigate to a page containing
an image you would like to use. Click on the image and hold the
click until a list of options appears. Select **Save Image**. The image
will now be in your photo library.

Have a go hero - e-mailing a camera photo

Add code to the first example that displays the photo taken on the screen so that the image is e-mailed.

That's enough for the camera for now, although we will be revisiting it later in the chapter when we use it along with a few other gadgets to show how it can be used for augmented reality. But before we do that, we need to introduce some of the other gadgets.

The accelerometer

The accelerometer is used to detect movement of the device. It sends out updates of the device's position on any of the three axes, that is, left/right, up/down, and forward/backward. To use the accelerometer, you define a listener to `Ti.Accelerometer`. Once you have this event listener defined, your code will be called every time the accelerometer detects movement of the device.

 Be kind to your user's phones! Remove the event listener to `Ti.Accelerometer` when you have finished with it. The accelerometer will continue to provide constant updates of the device's position and drain the battery as long as you retain the event listener. Be frugal with the gadget, conserve battery life, and be sure to remove the event listener when you are finished with it by calling `Ti.Accelerometer.removeEventListener`.

In this first example, we will compute the pitch of the device and display it on a slider.

Time for action – showing the accelerometer on a slider

To show the accelerometer on a slider, perform the following steps:

1. Create a new blank mobile app by clicking on **File | New | Titanium Project**. Don't use a template as it will just generate code that gets in the way.

2. Create the window for the app:

   ```
   var win1 = Titanium.UI.createWindow({
       backgroundColor:'#fff'
   });
   ```

3. Create the slider that will display the accelerometer pitch value. Also add a label to show the raw value. Add both of these to the window:

```
var masterVw = Ti.UI.createView({layout: 'vertical'});

var rawSlider = Ti.UI.createSlider({max: 2
                                    ,min:-2});

var rawLabel = Titanium.UI.createLabel({});

layout.add(rawSlider);
layout.add(rawLabel);
win1.add(masterVw);
```

4. Create a function to update the slider and label it with the updated accelerometer value. Notice that the function computes the pitch by using the tangent of the z and y values:

```
updateSliders = function(e)  {
  var raw = Math.atan(e.z/e.y);

  rawLabel.text = 'raw '+parseFloat(raw).toFixed(4);
  rawSlider.value = raw;

};
```

For an explanation on how pitch can be calculated using the tangent, please visit http://en.wikipedia.org/wiki/Tangent.

5. Now add code to connect to the accelerometer. The app needs input from the accelerometer while the window is on screen. If the user moves the app into the background or places another window on top of this, the connection to the accelerometer should be released (unlike those sports apps that track your location where the connection to the GPS is retained even though the app is in the background). In this case, the input from the accelerometer is only used to update a slider on the screen, so we have no interest in it when it's in the background. The connection to the accelerometer should only be active when the window has focus:

```
 win1.addEventListener('focus', function() {Ti.Accelerometer.
addEventListener("update", updateSliders);});
```

 Make sure that a focus event is defined before the window is opened, otherwise it will be ignored.

6. Because we are being kind to our users, add another event listener to disconnect from the accelerometer when the window is removed from the screen. Note that the `blur` event will fire at different times to the `close` event. A `blur` event will fire when the window is closed and also when the window is moved into the background:

```
win1.addEventListener('blur', function() {Ti.Accelerometer.
removeEventListener("update", updateSliders);});
```

7. Run the app!

What just happened?

You created an app that showed the pitch of the phone on a slider.

Did you notice how sensitive the accelerometer is? Even when you are holding the phone still in front of you, the slider is twitching left and right due to all the tiny changes. This is a problem for apps using the accelerometer. It's so sensitive that the small changes keep making things twitch.

A common requirement is to try to smooth the output from the accelerometer. We need something that will preserve the large movements while ignoring the small, involuntary ones. This will be shown in the next example where we try two solutions to this problem. We will try truncating the accelerometer data so that the small movements are ignored, and we will also add a low pass filter algorithm to ignore the small changes.

 A great example of how low pass filters remove noise from data can be found at `http://phrogz.net/js/framerate-independent-low-pass-filter.html`.

Time for action – smoothing the accelerometer response

To smooth the accelerometer response, perform the following steps:

1. Open `app.js` from the previous example.

2. Add the variables given next to `app.js`. These are your tuning variables. They allow you to configure the smallest increment that can be considered a move, and how quickly the formula reacts to a large move. In short, these figures allow you to walk the line between having a slider that is just like the raw one that reacts quickly but is jittery, and one that is more like a supertanker, which reacts to change slowly but with no jitters and makes steady progress:

    ```
    var noiseAttenuation = 3;
    var accelerometerMinStep = 0.02;
    var filterConstant = 0.2;
    ```

3. Now add two more variables. These values are used to store the previous results of the filter and do not need to be modified. They will be managed by the filter code when it is running:

    ```
    var alpha     = 0;
    var lastValue = 0;
    ```

4. Now add the low pass filter code. This comes in two functions. The `clamp` function simply ensures the value does not go outside of the range of 1 to 0. The `lowPassFilter` function is the code to work out the smoothed value of the accelerometer input:

    ```
    clamp = function(val) {
      if (val > 1) return 1
      if (val < 0) return 0;
      return val;
    }

    lowPassFilter = function(val)
    {
        var diff = clamp(Math.abs(lastValue - val) /
        accelerometerMinStep);

        alpha = (1.0 - diff) * filterConstant /
        noiseAttenuation + diff * filterConstant

        lastValue = val * alpha + lastValue * (1.0 - alpha);

        return lastValue;
    }
    ```

5. The smoothed value is going to be shown on extra sliders below the original one. Add the sliders and the labels to the code as highlighted next:

```
var rawSlider = Ti.UI.createSlider({max: 2
                                    ,min:-2});
var lowSlider = Ti.UI.createSlider({max: 2
                                    ,min:-2});
var truncSlider = Ti.UI.createSlider({max: 2
                                    ,min:-2});
var rawLabel = Titanium.UI.createLabel({});
var lowLabel = Titanium.UI.createLabel({});
var truncLabel = Titanium.UI.createLabel({});

masterVw.add(rawSlider);
masterVw.add(rawLabel);
masterVw.add(lowSlider);
masterVw.add(lowLabel);
masterVw.add(truncSlider);
masterVw.add(truncLabel);
```

6. Add the computation of the slider values to the `updateSliders` function as highlighted next:

```
updateSliders = function(e)  {
  var raw = Math.atan(e.z/e.y);
  var low = lowPassFilter(raw);
  rawLabel.text = 'raw '+parseFloat(raw).toFixed(4);
  rawSlider.value = raw;
  lowLabel.text =  'low '+parseFloat(low).toFixed(4);
  lowSlider.value = low;
  truncLabel.text =  'truncated '+parseFloat(raw).toFixed(1);
  truncSlider.value = parseFloat(raw).toFixed(1);
};
```

7. Run the app!

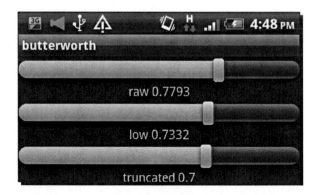

What just happened?

The code for the low pass filter has certainly removed the jittery sliders when the phone is held still, but it does mean the slider is slower at responding compared to the raw slider when you start a large move. It's rather like a large pendulum; it takes time to get going and to stop.

The truncated value solution also removes the jitters when the phone is held still, but makes any large movement rough. It's not a solution to the problem!

Have a go hero - tuning the filer response

It's worth playing around with the values of the variables added in step 2. Higher values tend to produce an effect that reduces the noise when the phone is held still but does mean the slider is slower to respond to real movement. It's the converse for lower values. Have a play and find values that suit you the best.

The compass

Both iOS and Android phones include a compass. We will make use of this in this next simple example, where we will use the compass to show the phone direction and heading.

Time for action – displaying the compass heading

This example is available for download or browse at `https://github.com/myleftboot/ chapter-7-compass`. To display the compass heading, perform the following steps:

1. Create a new blank mobile app by clicking on **File | New | Titanium Project**. Don't use a template as it will just generate code that gets in the way.

2. Create the window for the app:

    ```
    var win1 = Titanium.UI.createWindow({
        backgroundColor:'#fff'
    });
    ```

3. The layout will simply consist of two labels arranged vertically. One will display the compass bearing and the other label displays a summary of your bearing. Add the labels to the window:

    ```
    var vertVw = Ti.UI.createView({layout: 'vertical'});

    var compassHeading = Ti.UI.createLabel({});
    var direction = Ti.UI.createLabel({});
    vertVw.add(compassHeading);
    ```

```
vertVw.add(direction);
win1.add(vertVw);
```

4. Add a function that will update one of the labels with the compass bearing and compute the rough direction, which will be applied to the other label. The function will return a description of the bearing by splitting the compass bearing into eight segments. A bearing of between 338 and 23 degrees is deemed to be north. If it is between 23 and 68, it's north-east, then east, and so on around the compass:

```
function updateLabels(_args) {
  compassHeading.text =
  _args.heading.magneticHeading+ ' degrees';

  var headingText = null;
  var theBearing = _args.heading.magneticHeading;
  switch(true) {
    case (theBearing >= 0 && theBearing < 23):
      headingText = 'North';
      break;
    case (theBearing >= 23 && theBearing < 68):
      headingText = 'North East';
      break;
    case (theBearing >= 68 && theBearing < 113):
      headingText = 'East';
      break;
// I've cut some of the options out to keep this listing short.
This set of cases continues upward until
    case (theBearing >= 338 && theBearing <= 360):
      headingText = 'North';
      break;
        }
  direction.text = 'You are looking '+headingText;
}
```

5. Even if we are just reading the magnetic north value from the compass, the phone will also want to work out the true value for north. In order to work that out it needs to have an estimate of the phone's location. Nothing accurate, just the rough coordinates. If you are going to get the phone's location, you should explain to the user why you need it. This will be explained in more detail in the *Geolocation* section later in this chapter.

6. Add the following line to display the reason you are going to get the phone's location for:

```
Ti.Geolocation.purpose = 'To get the compass bearing';
```

Why do we need to get the location for a compass bearing?

When you get a value from the compass, the value for true north is computed 'for free'. It's not something you can prevent or control. It is determined for you, and in order to compute the value, you need to do some Maths. The calculation of where true north is from the magnetic north reading is dependent on where the phone is. It will be a different offset in Alaska than in Turkey.

7. Hook up to the compass by adding an event listener to `Ti.Geolocation.addEventListener("heading", <<your code to be called>>);`. This is all you need to do to activate the compass, and it will remain active and send updates of any changes to the phones bearing until you remove the event listener. Notice that this example includes code to remove the event listener when it is no longer needed. This is a good practice; these gadgets consume power, so release them when you are finished with them. We need the compass for as long as the window is displayed on screen. It's important to note the difference between the window being active and on screen and being closed. If the user chooses to look at another app and move our app into the background, the window will remain open, but will become inactive. A `blur` event will fire but `close` will not. So if this was hooked up to the `close` event listener, the compass would remain active when the window was put into the background. The `focus` event will be called when the app starts up and the window first opens, and also when it is re-shown after being reactivated:

```
win1.addEventListener('blur', function() {Ti.Geolocation.
removeEventListener("heading", updateLabels);});
win1.addEventListener('focus', function() {Ti.Geolocation.
addEventListener("heading", updateLabels);});
```

8. Run the app! You will need to run this app on a device as there is no compass (not even a simulation of one) on either the Android emulator or iOS Simulator.

What just happened?

You created a small app that converts your phone into a compass! The heading and an approximate direction are shown. The following screenshot shows the app in action on an Android device. Notice how small the font size is. This can happen when no size is specified. Don't worry about this now; we will be addressing this in the next chapter.

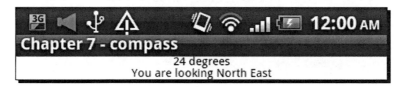

Augmented reality

Augmented reality (AR) is the process of adding computer-generated imagery to a real-world environment. You will see it on TV where images and lines are added to sports coverage showing the distance that a cricket ball has been hit, or in football with an offside line, or American football with a line showing where the next first down will be and the distance to it. In smartphones, it's the process of adding images to the camera viewer.

This will be a simple example of AR. There is plenty more that needs to be done to make a full AR app, such as including inputs from the accelerometer and the GPS. Calculations also need to be made of pitch and distance. This is all possible with Titanium but is beyond the scope of this book. Should you need to look into this further, you should take a look at the excellent Titanium AR book *Augmented Reality using Appcelerator Titanium Starter, Trevor Ward, Packt Publishing*.

 Do not rely on this example for navigation. It is only an example to prove the concept.

Time for action – creating a simple augmented reality app

For this next example, we are going to build an AR viewer into the compass app created in a previous example. The app will add a button that will take the current compass reading as a bearing to follow. The AR view will then be shown and the bearing tracked on the viewer. The bearing will scroll across the view as you move the device through the correct bearing.

Code will be added that will simulate the AR experience when the app is run on the simulator.

This example is available for download or browse at `https://github.com/myleftboot/chapter-7-compass/tree/AR`. To create a simple augmented reality app, perform the following steps:

1. Continuing from the compass example created earlier in this chapter; add a button to the screen that will show the AR viewer when clicked. The `showARView` function will be defined later in this example.

    ```
    ARButton = Ti.UI.createButton({title: 'Follow bearing in AR'});
    ARButton.addEventListener('click', showARView);
    ```

2. Add the button to the front screen, as highlighted next:

    ```
    vertVw.add(direction);
    vertVw.add(ARButton);
    ```

3. Now create the components of the AR display. The bearing will be displayed as a large red label. The AR view itself is a full screen transparent view (note the background color) that acts like a pane of glass for us to draw our AR objects on:

```
var ARView = Ti.UI.createView({layout: 'vertical'
                                ,background: 'transparent'});

var ARBearingLbl = Ti.UI.createLabel({color: 'red',
                                font: {fontSize: '80dp'}
                                });
```

The font properties of the label are `font: {fontSize: '80dp'}`. It's enough to say for now that this will make the label size large on all platforms. Should you need to know more, the font size properties are covered in detail in *Chapter 8, Creating Beautiful Interfaces*.

4. Add a few variables that will be used in the AR computations that will be declared in the next few steps:

```
var viewAngle = 15;
var pixelsPerDegree = Ti.Platform.displayCaps.platformWidth /
viewAngle;
var theBearing;
var lastHeading = 0;
```

Variable	Description
`viewAngle`	This holds an estimation of the number of degrees that are viewable through the camera. So if the phone was pointing north, the right-hand side edge of the screen would be a bearing of (15/2) 7.5 degrees.
`pixelsPerDegree`	This is a function of `viewAngle` and the number of pixels across the screen. As the compass reports headings to the nearest degree, this variable holds the number of pixels the label will move every time the heading changes. It is used to compute the label position.
`theBearing`	This holds the bearing that is displayed.
`lastHeading`	This stores the heading that was last reported. It sets up the value in `theBearing` when the AR screen is first opened.

5. Now create the function that exposes the simplicity of AR. AR at its most basic level is just the camera with a view added on top (like a transparency added to an overhead projector for the older readers), as shown in the next function. The function creates the AR display and sets the bearing and bearing label text. This function will be called when the user presses the button defined in step 1. Note that the functionality differs if the code is run on the simulator as it does not have a camera:

```
function showARView() {
  if (Ti.Platform.model === 'Simulator' ||
  Ti.Platform.model.indexOf('sdk') !== -1 ){
    ARBearingLbl.text = theBearing = 120; // set a value for
    the simulator
    simulatorAR();
  } else {
      theBearing = lastHeading;
    Ti.Media.showCamera({animated:      false,
                  autoHide:      false,
                  showControls:  false,
                  autofocus:     false,
                  overlay:       ARView
              });
      ARBearingLbl.text = theBearing;
    displayBearingOnAR();
  }
}
```

The parameters to the `Ti.Media.showCamera` call are important to get a realistic AR experience. They are shown in the following table:

Parameter		Description
`autoHide:`	`false`	Do not allow the user or the OS to close the camera. The app will control when it is closed.
`showControls:`	`false`	Do not show the camera controls. We just want a full screen camera.
`overlay:`	`ARView`	This is the transparent view that will be used to create the AR experience.

6. Add the `displaybearingOnAR` function. This function will build the AR view. In this case it's simply a matter of adding the bearing to the AR view:

```
function displayBearingOnAR(_args) {

  ARView.add(ARBearingLbl);
};
```

7. To recap what has been defined so far in this example, a functionality has been created to display the camera with an overlay when the AR button is clicked. This AR overlay view has a label added to it. Now it's time for the AR magic. If the bearing is 45 degrees and if the phone is pointed at 45 degrees, we would expect that the bearing label would appear in the center of the screen. If the phone is rotated to the right towards 90 degrees, the label should start to move to the left of the screen before disappearing off the left-hand side edge as the phone rotates further. This screen position needs to be computed and changed when the compass reports a new heading. The following function will do that:

```
function newPosition(_args) {

  var newHeading = _args.heading;
  var newBearing = theBearing;

  // if heading near to N but slightly NE (such as 5 degrees),
  then bearings at 350+ need to be considered
  if ((newHeading <= viewAngle /2) &&
  (360 - theBearing <= viewAngle / 2)) newBearing -= 360;
  // similarly if heading near to N but slightly NW
  (such as 355 degrees), then bearings
  at 5 or less need to be considered
  if ((newHeading >= (360 - viewAngle /2)) &&
  (theBearing <= viewAngle / 2)) newBearing += 360;

  // if the heading with within the confines of the screen i.e.
  less than half a screen from the centre line
  (viewAngle is the middle)
  var isItOnScreen =
  (Math.abs(newHeading - newBearing) <= viewAngle / 2);
  var newPosition = Ti.Platform.displayCaps.platformWidth / 2 +
  ((newBearing - newHeading) * pixelsPerDegree);

  return {X: newPosition, onScreen: isItOnScreen};
}
```

There are four highlighted sections in the code. The first two are to handle the special circumstance where we have a bearing that is very near to north (that is somewhere in the range of 350 to 360 degrees or 0 to 10). If the bearing is slightly to the north-west of north at something like 355 degrees, the bearing should appear on the left of the screen when the phone is pointing slightly north-east at say 5 degrees. It's the same as looking at the outside of a clock from the center and you were looking at 1 o'clock; 11 o'clock would be on your left, and three on your right. The first and second highlighted sections in the middle of the function that adds or subtracts 360 to or from `newBearing` handles this case and creates a wraparound effect.

The third highlighted piece of code determines if the bearing is close enough to the compass heading that it should appear on screen (which is plus or minus half of `viewAngle`).

The last highlighted portion of code computes the number of pixels from the center of the screen where the label should be placed. A negative number means somewhere to the left and positive to the right.

8. Before we show the final piece of the jigsaw that moves the label on-screen, let's see the code that will approximate to an AR display when the code is run on the simulator. This code will use a slider to emulate a compass. The left of the slider is north (0), and the center is equivalent to south (180). Instead of showing the view as an overlay to the camera, just add the view to the window with a white background so that it covers anything displayed before:

```
function simulatorAR() {
  ARView.backgroundColor = 'white';
  win1.add(ARView);

  // add slider to the window
  var slider = Ti.UI.createSlider({
    backgroundColor:'transparent',
    min: 0,
    max: 10,
    value: theBearing/360*10,
    width: 300,
    top: 10
  });

  slider.addEventListener('change', function(e) {
    updateARView({newBearing: e.value * 36});
  });
```

```
  ARView.add(slider);
  displayBearingOnAR();
};
```

9. Finally, add the code that moves the label across the screen. `updateARView` will accept the new compass bearing as the parameter. The function calls `newPosition`, which determines if the label should be displayed, and if so, where. A description of the movement follows after the code:

```
function updateARView(_args) {
  // update the position of Heading
  var newX = newPosition({heading: _args.newBearing})
  // if the new heading is within -7.5 to +7.5 of the bearing
  then its on the display
  if (newX.onScreen) {
    // its a candidate for display
    ARBearingLbl.show();
    moveLbl = Ti.UI.createAnimation
    ({center:{x:newX.X, y:'50%'},duration:0});
    ARBearingLbl.animate(moveLbl);
  } else
  {
    //Not on the display, hide it
    ARBearingLbl.hide();
  }

};
```

The label is moved to its new place on-screen by an animation that specifies the new placement and the duration of the animation.

Why the animation you might ask?

The compass is only accurate to 1 degree and will send out updates when it moves by a single degree. On a phone with a screen width of 320 pixels that is showing a view of 15 degrees, that is over 21 pixels for every degree of movement. If the label was moved 21 pixels, it would make for very jerky updates so the movement is animated.

10. Run the app!

What just happened?

You added an AR display to the compass app. A user can now press a button that will fix the bearing and then rotate the phone to find the original bearing. A screenshot of the app in action on an Android device is shown next. Note that on an Android device the overlay may be in landscape format, as shown in the next screenshot. This is not the case with iOS.

You will be pleased to know that this is the most complicated (and hardest to explain) example in the book. If you have understood this, the remainder is easy.

Have a go hero - extending the AR example

If you want a challenge, try adding left and right arrows to the screen that are shown when the bearing is off the screen to indicate the way to rotate the phone to get back on the bearing.

There are many more things that you can do to improve the AR experience by adding in inputs from the Accelerometer to determine the phone pitch (y movement).

Maps

Apple Maps, Google maps; it's all the same. This is a cross-platform coding that doesn't need to concern itself with details of the type of map that is installed on your phone. It's one standard call and it works regardless of the device and map provider.

Time for action – adding a map

This short example will create an app that shows a map.

This example is available for download or browse at `https://github.com/myleftboot/Chapter-7-maps`. To add a map, perform the following steps:

1. Create a new blank mobile app by clicking on **File | New | Titanium Project**. Don't use a template as it will just generate code that gets in the way.

2. Create the window for the app:

```
var win1 = Titanium.UI.createWindow({
    backgroundColor:'#fff'
});
```

3. Create a map view. Add the coordinates of the center of the map and the deltas that zoom the maps effectively. The higher the value of the delta, the bigger the area shown:

```
var theMap = Titanium.Map.createView({
      mapType: Ti.Map.SATELLITE_TYPE,
      region: {latitude:      42.909134,
               longitude:      0.145054,
               latitudeDelta: 0.01,
               longitudeDelta:0.01},
      animate:true,
      regionFit:true,
    });
```

4. Add the map view to the window and open the window:

```
win1.add(theMap);
win1.open();
```

5. Run the app!

What just happened?

With only a couple of lines of code, you created an app that shows a hilly region in France, as shown in the following screenshot:

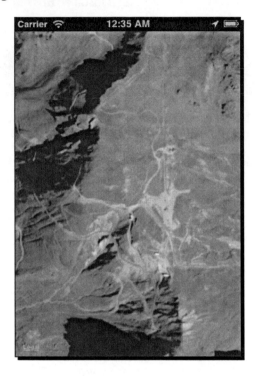

Continuing from the last example, we will now show how easy it is to add a placement marker pin to your map.

Time for action – adding annotations to a map

Perform the following steps to add annotations to a map:

1. Putting a pin bar annotation to a map is simply a case of specifying the coordinates of the pin placement and the properties of the pin such as its color, title, and button:

```
var tourmalet = Titanium.Map.createAnnotation({
    latitude:    42.908655,
    longitude:   0.145054,
    title:       'Col du Tourmalet',
    subtitle:    'France',
    pincolor:    Ti.Map.ANNOTATION_RED,
```

```
    animate:        true
});

    theMap.addAnnotation(tourmalet);
```

2. Run the app!

What just happened

You added code to display a satellite picture of the Tourmalet region of France (it's one of the epic climbs in the Tour De France). You also added a pin showing the rough position of the top of the climb:

Directions

It's very nice showing the top of the epic Tourmalet climb, but it doesn't stand out unless you show the route of the climb. So for the next example, we are going to add directions to the map using the flexible Google Directions API.

Time for action – adding directions to a map

Perform the following steps to add directions to a map:

1. Add code to get the JSON direction data from Google. This will be done using a simple HTTP request. When the data is received from Google, it will be in the form of a string. Convert this string into JSON using the `parse` command and send it to a function to be processed:

```
var url = "http://maps.googleapis.com/maps/api/directions/
json?origin=Luz-Saint-Sauveur,+France&destination=42.908655,0.1450
54&sensor=false";
xhr = Titanium.Network.createHTTPClient();
xhr.open('GET',url);
xhr.onload = function(){
  // Now parse the XML

  var theData = JSON.parse(this.responseText);
  addRouteToMap(theData);
};
xhr.send();
```

2. Create the route processing function `addRouteToMap`. This function will collect the coordinates of the end point of every step and leg on the route. The function will parse the following information from the JSON returned from the call to Google:

```
"routes" : [
    "legs" : [
       "steps" : [
       "end_location" : {
    "lat" : 42.873290,
    "lng" : -0.003290
       },
       "end_location" : {
    "lat" : 42.89015000000001,
    "lng" : 0.04820000000000001
       },
       "end_location" : {
    "lat" : 42.905180,
    "lng" : 0.146620
       },
       "end_location" : {
```

```
      "lat"  :  42.90842000000001,
      "lng"  :  0.145310
         },
         ],
   ],
]
```

The function collates the end coordinates in an array, which are then applied to the map using the `addRoute` method. This method draws the route on the map:

```
function addRouteToMap(_args) {
      var points = [];
      for (var aLeg=0; aLeg < _args.routes[0].
      legs.length; aLeg++) {

         for (var aStep=0; aStep< _args.routes[0].
         legs[aLeg].steps.length; aStep++) {
            // add the end location of every step of the route
            to the array of points
            points.push({latitude: _args.routes[0].
            legs[aLeg].steps[aStep].end_location.lat
                     ,longitude: _args.routes[0].
                     legs[aLeg].steps[aStep].end_location.lng
                     });
         }
      }

      var route = {
            name:"The climb",
            points:points,
            color:"red",
            width:4
         };

      // add a route
      theMap.addRoute(route);
}
```

3. Run the app!

What just happened?

You added directions to a map. For this example, the chosen route is not long and there are not many junctions, so there are not many end points to parse and hence the directions look like a straight line. A longer route with more junctions and changes of road would produce a better looking route. The following screenshot shows the directions when the application is run on the Android emulator:

This is a rough display of the route. It is possible to plot a far more accurate representation of the route by parsing the KML returned from Google. There are instructions on how this can be done on the Appcelerator Q&A site at `http://developer.appcelerator.com/question/74221/mobile-map-route-from-google-server#133781`.

Geolocation

Geolocation allows you to grab the location of the phone. The code can be used in two ways; either as a single call to get the current location, or you can continually track the location of the phone by setting up an event listener. As with the other gadgets, if you do choose to track the location, have a good reason for doing so and only track for as long as you need to, as you will drain the battery.

If you are going to get the phone location or use the phone's compass, the users have to give you permission to grab their location. iOS will show an alert dialog when you first attempt to use location functionality. You should explain the reason why you are interested in the user's location by setting `Ti.Geolocation.purpose` before the code to get the location. The following is an example call to set the purpose:

```
Ti.Geolocation.purpose = 'To display your current co-ordinates';
```

This will result in the following screenshot when the device tries to get the location:

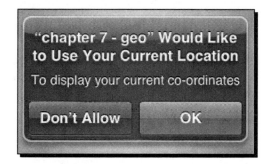

You only need to provide a purpose for iOS apps. If you set the purpose when running on Android, it will be ignored. On Android devices, the users agree to all permissions when they install the app.

Are we allowed to get the location?

Sometimes users may decide that they does not wish to divulge their location details. On all smartphones, the user can switch the location services off for the device so that no apps can get location information. On iOS, they can also disable location services per app. Before you get the user's location you need to include code to check both of these scenarios.

The `Ti.Geolocation.locationServicesEnabled` property is `true` if the location services are enabled for the device. On iOS you have to do a bit more work, as you also have to check if users have allowed your app to get their location. `Ti.Geolocation.locationServicesAuthorization` returns a value that can be one of the following constant values:

Value	Description
`Ti.Geolocation.AUTHORIZATION_AUTHORIZED`	All clear! Location services are enabled and the users have also agreed to let the app find the location.
`Ti.Geolocation.AUTHORIZATION_DENIED`	The user has not allowed the app to get location details or location services are switched off on the device.
`Ti.Geolocation.AUTHORIZATION_RESTRICTED`	The user has not allowed the app to get location details.
`Ti.Geolocation.AUTHORIZATION_UNKNOWN`	This value will always be returned in the rare event of your user still running iOS 4.2 or less (becoming more and more irrelevant).

This is all covered in the following function (that is covered in more detail in an example later in the chapter) that checks if we are allowed to get the user's location. It works on both iOS and Android and will return `true` if we can grab the location:

```
function isLocationAuthorized(_args) {
    //check that we are allowed to use
    var retVal = true;
    if (!Ti.Geolocation.locationServicesEnabled) return false;
// Explain to the user why we are going to use the location services.

        Ti.Geolocation.purpose = _args.purpose;
        var authorization =
        Titanium.Geolocation.locationServicesAuthorization;

        if (authorization == Titanium.Geolocation.AUTHORIZATION_DENIED)
{
          // user has decided to not allow this use of location
          retVal = false;
        }
        else if (authorization ==
        Titanium.Geolocation.AUTHORIZATION_RESTRICTED) {
          // a device restriction prevents us
          from using location services
```

```
            retVal = false;
        } else retVal = true;

    return retVal;

};
```

Accuracy and battery life

Before we start to look at some examples, we need to talk about the accuracy of the location you are going to retrieve and the effect it has on battery life. If you are going to grab the user's location just once, this isn't important, but if you are planning to track the user's location, you need to be aware of the effect it will have. When you ask for the device's location, you can specify how accurate you want the location to be. A low level of accuracy is not hard for the phone to work out as it can derive the location from the phone company operator by checking the details of the mobile signal. Higher levels of accuracy mean the phone has to use GPS to get the location, and that uses more battery power. The following table summarizes the options you have over the accuracy.

The following options are cross-platform. These properties will work on both Android and iOS:

Accuracy Property	Description
ACCURACY_HIGH	High accuracy is computed using GPS. It is accurate to a few meters, but takes extra battery power to achieve this.
ACCURACY_LOW	Low accuracy is computed from the mobile operator. This is accurate to a kilometer, but doesn't take extra battery power.

There are other options that are specific to iOS:

Accuracy Property	Description
ACCURACY_BEST	High accuracy is computed using GPS. It is accurate to a few meters, but takes extra battery power to achieve this.
ACCURACY_NEAREST_TEN_METERS	This is accurate to 10 meters. It has high accuracy, but increased battery usage.
ACCURACY_HUNDRED_METERS	This is accurate to 100 meters from your position. It is good enough for a ZIP code.

Accuracy Property	Description
ACCURACY_KILOMETER	This is accurate to up to a kilometer from your position.
ACCURACY_THREE_KILOMETERS	This has low power usage, but it's not very accurate. It is good enough if you only need a rough idea of the location.

The difference in power usage between each of the five options is beyond the scope of this book. At some point, probably between the 100-meter and 10-meter options, the GPS device has to be engaged, which increases the battery load.

These options should be applied to the `Ti.Geolocation.accuracy` property, which should be set like the `Ti.Geolocation.purpose` property before you try to get the location.

Now that we have covered the warnings and prerequisites, let's get going with the first example, where we get the phone's rough location.

 As with the other gadgets, if you are defining an event listener to the location event, make sure you remove the event listener using the `removeEventListener` method when you have finished with it. If you would like to see an example of how to remove an event listener, you should refer to step 6 of the compass example shown earlier in the chapter.

Time for action – getting the current location

Perform the following steps to get the current location:

1. Create a new blank mobile app by clicking on **File | New | Titanium Project**. Don't use a template as it will just generate code that gets in the way.

2. Create the window for the app:

```
var win1 = Titanium.UI.createWindow({
    backgroundColor:'#fff'
});
```

3. We need to check that we are allowed to grab the location of the phone. Because there are a few platform differences in how you do this; it's best to wrap it all into a function so that the caller of the function isn't troubled with this detail:

```
function isLocationAuthorized(_args) {
    //check that we are allowed to use
```

```
var retVal = true;
if (!Ti.Geolocation.locationServicesEnabled) return false;

    // Explain to the user why we are going to use the
    location services.

    Ti.Geolocation.purpose = _args.purpose;
    var authorization =
    Titanium.Geolocation.locationServicesAuthorization;

    if (authorization ==
    Titanium.Geolocation.AUTHORIZATION_DENIED) {
      // user has decided to not allow this use of location
      retVal = false;
    }
    else if (authorization ==
    Titanium.Geolocation.AUTHORIZATION_RESTRICTED) {
      // a device restriction prevents us from using
      location services
      retVal = false;
    } else retVal = true;
return retVal;

};
```

4. Create the function that will get the current location. We aren't interested in being 100 percent accurate with the location for this, so the accuracy setting is set to low:

```
function getLocation(_args) {
    // we dont need to be any more accurate than this
    // ACCURACY_LOW is one of the settings that work
    with both Android and iOS
    // see the Ti API documentation
    Ti.Geolocation.accuracy =
    Titanium.Geolocation.ACCURACY_LOW;

    Ti.Geolocation.getCurrentPosition(function(e)
    {
      if (!e.success || e.error)
      {
        alert('error ' + JSON.stringify(e.error));
      }
```

```
        if (_args.success) _args.success(e.coords)
    });

};
```

5. Now, create a label that will show the coordinate information and add it to the window:

```
var coords = Ti.UI.createLabel({top:0});
win1.add(coords);
```

6. Add a simple function to update the label with the coordinates:

```
function setLabelText(_args) {
    coords.text = 'Lat: '+_args.latitude+' Lon :'+_args.longitude;
}
```

7. Connect it all together. The following code will check to see if we are allowed to collect the coordinates. If so, then it will get the location and pass the coordinates to the setLabelText function.

```
if (isLocationAuthorized({purpose:'To display your current
co-ordinates'})) {
    getLocation({success : setLabelText});
}
else {alert('Cannot use location services')};
```

8. Run the app!

What just happened?

You created code to get the user's current location and display it on the screen:

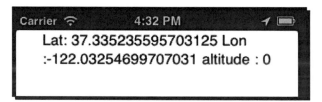

The latitude and longitude were displayed, but other items of information were returned that we could have shown. The following is a list of attributes returned:

Attribute	Description
latitude	The device's latitude
longitude	The device's longitude
altitude	The altitude of the device in meters
speed	The speed of the device in meters per second
accuracy	A meter value indicating the accuracy of the location
altitudeAccuracy	A meter value indicating the accuracy of the altitude

Some of these may not be populated or may contain negative values when the value cannot be computed.

Have a go hero - getting the address of a location using reverse geocoding

Running code to grab the location on a simulator is not very useful. If you are interested in details, for example the device altitude, add code to display the altitude and run the app on a device.

After you have collected the user coordinates, you can use them to determine the street address of the device. This is reverse geocoding and is done by passing coordinates to `Ti.Geolocation.reverseGeocoder` that will return a list of matching addresses. You could try adding this to your code to see how accurate the results are!

Computing the distance from a coordinate

We will now extend the last example by adding in code to compute the distance from the equator. So no matter where you are, you can always use your phone to know how far you are from the equator. Just what you always wanted!

Time for action – getting the distance from a coordinate

This example will compute the distance you would have to travel either south or north to get to the equator. The example is in miles for those of you reading in metric!

This example is available for download or browse at `https://github.com/myleftboot/Chapter-7-Geo`. Perform the following steps to get the distance from a coordinate:

1. Create a new blank mobile app by clicking on **File | New | Titanium Project**. Don't use a template as it will just generate code that gets in the way.

2. Create the window for the app:

```
var win1 = Titanium.UI.createWindow({
    backgroundColor:'#fff'
});
```

3. Add a function that does the hard work of computing the distance across the earth's surface between two coordinates on the surface:

```
function distanceinM(_args) {
    // ---- extend Number object with methods for converting
degrees/radians

    /** Converts numeric degrees to radians */
    if (typeof(Number.prototype.toRad) === "undefined") {
      Number.prototype.toRad = function() {
        return this * Math.PI / 180;
      }
    }

    var R = 3960; // m    ---
    if you want it in KM then use 6371
    var dLat = (_args.toLat-_args.fromLat).toRad();
    var dLon = (_args.toLon-_args.fromLon).toRad();

    var a = Math.sin(dLat/2) * Math.sin(dLat/2) +
            Math.cos(_args.fromLat.toRad()) *
            Math.cos(_args.toLat.toRad()) *
            Math.sin(dLon/2) * Math.sin(dLon/2);
    var c = 2 * Math.atan2(Math.sqrt(a), Math.sqrt(1-a));

    var d = R * c;

    return d;
};
```

This is the JavaScript version of the haversine algorithm grabbed from the Internet. If you would like to know how the algorithm works, there is an excellent reference at `http://www.movable-type.co.uk/scripts/latlong-vincenty.html`.

4. Add a function to compute the distance to the equator. The beauty of this computation is that regardless of your position the latitude of the equator is always zero!

```
function distanceFromTheEquator(_args) {
    return distanceinM({
                fromLon : _args.lon,
                fromLat : _args.lat,
                toLon   : _args.lon,
                toLat   : 0});
};
```

5. Add a function to set the text of the label. This is not strictly necessary but helps to keep the example clean:

```
function setDistanceLabel(_args) {
  coords.text = 'Distance from the equator:
  '+parseInt(_args.distance);
};
```

6. Connect it all together. Update the call to `getLocation` so that it now calls the function to get the distance from the equator, passing the coordinates returned. The computed distance is then passed to the `setDistanceLabel` function:

```
if (isLocationAuthorized({purpose:'To display your current co-
ordinates'})) {
  getLocation(
    {success : function(e)
      {setDistanceLabel(
        {distance : distanceFromTheEquator(
          {lat: e.latitude,
           lon: e.longitude
          })
        })
      }
    }
  );
};
```

7. Run the app!

What just happened?

You added code to the last example to make use of the device location, using it to determine the distance in miles from the equator.

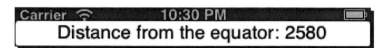

Distance from the equator: 2580

 This screenshot is from iOS Simulator with the location set to the Apple's headquarters in Cupertino, California.

Showing the user's current location on a map

For this last example, we will combine the geolocation functionality with a map. We will add geolocation code to the map example created earlier in this chapter.

Time for action – showing the user's location on the map

This example is available for download or browse at `https://github.com/myleftboot/Chapter-7-maps/tree/CurrentLocation`. Perform the following steps to show the user's location on the map:

1. As we will be asking for the user's location, we need to add the following code to check that we are allowed to do this:

```
function isLocationAuthorized(_args) {
    //check that we are allowed to use
    var retVal = true;
    if (!Ti.Geolocation.locationServicesEnabled) return false;

    if (Ti.Platform.name === 'iPhone OS') {
        // Explain to the user why we are going to use
        the location services.

        Ti.Geolocation.purpose = _args.purpose;
        var authorization =
        Titanium.Geolocation.locationServicesAuthorization;

        if (authorization ==
        Titanium.Geolocation.AUTHORIZATION_DENIED) {
```

```
        // user has decided to not allow this use of location
        retVal = false;
    }
    else if (authorization ==
    Titanium.Geolocation.AUTHORIZATION_RESTRICTED) {
        // a device restriction prevents us
        from using location services
        retVal = false;
    } else retVal = true;
    }
    return retVal;

};
```

2. Add the function that will get the current location. We aren't interested in being 100 percent accurate so the accuracy setting is set to low:

```
function getLocation(_args) {
    // we dont need to be any more accurate than this
    // ACCURACY_LOW is one of the settings that work
    with both Android and iOS
    // see the Ti API documentation
    Ti.Geolocation.accuracy =
    Titanium.Geolocation.ACCURACY_LOW;

    Ti.Geolocation.getCurrentPosition(function(e)
    {
        if (!e.success || e.error)
        {
            alert('error ' + JSON.stringify(e.error));
        }
        if (_args.success) _args.success(e.coords)

    });

};
```

3. Create a function to update the label with the coordinates supplied as parameters:

```
function updateMap(_args) {
    theMap.setLocation({latitude : _args.latitude
                       ,longitude : _args.longitude});
}
```

4. Now connect it all together. This code will check to see if we are allowed to collect the coordinates. If so, then it will get the location and pass the coordinates to the updateMap function:

```
if (isLocationAuthorized({purpose:'To show your location on the
map'})) {
  getLocation({success : updateMap});
};
```

5. Run the app!

What just happened

You added code to the map display function to show your current location. Notice how the map scrolls from the initial point in France to where you currently are.

> If you are running this example on iOS Simulator, you can set your location from the menu to one of the preset locations. The locations are under **Debug | Location**. You may have to reopen the simulator to see the change. You can even enter your own location if you know the coordinates by selecting **Debug | Location | Custom Location....**

Pop quiz - gadgets

Q 1. You want to include a feature in your sports app that computes the directions from the location of user to the stadium. You have the code to get the coordinates of the phone and now you just need to show the directions on a map. What do you use for this?

1. A web view that shows a web-based map with directions
2. `Ti.Map.showDirections`
3. Adding the route to the map object using `addRoute`

Q 2. Which property of the `Ti.Geolocation` object should you set before attempting to grab the user's location? This property will be used to inform the user of the reason why you need to get the user's location.

1. `Ti.Geolocation.purpose`
2. `Ti.Geolocation.reason`
3. `Ti.Geolocation.why`

Q 3. If you wish to get the user's rough location for your cross-platform app, which accuracy should you select that will work on Android and iOS?

1. `ACCURACY_POOR`

2. `ACCURACY_LOW`

3. `ACCURACY_THREE_KILOMETERS`

Q 4. You need to upload a photo from the phone's photo library. You do not want any videos to be selected. Which setting will achieve this?

1. `mediaTypes: ['JPG', 'PNG', 'BMP']`

2. `selectVideo: false`

3. `mediaTypes: [Ti.Media.MEDIA_TYPE_PHOTO]`

Summary

The gadgets packaged with the phones and tablets allow for some really creative uses of the technology. But be warned; if you don't make good use of them by releasing them when you have finished, your app will drain the battery life almost as fast as the users will drain away from your app. Remember, "Power is nothing without control".

All the examples so far have concentrated on the functionality. It's now time to turn our attention to how the app looks. You can have great functionality, but if the app doesn't look good, it isn't going to get very far. The next chapter will concentrate on the methods you need to make your app look great across all platforms.

8
Creating Beautiful Interfaces

Titanium allows you to create native cross-platform apps. You can deploy your app onto devices with screen resolutions that range from 240 x 320, to the latest tablets with resolutions of 2048 x 1536. To make things tougher, there is also a range of display densities (pixels per inch), and some have different aspect ratios. Then there is the matter of orientation. It's enough to make your head spin. While we don't have all the answers, this chapter will attempt to clear a few things up.

This chapter brings together most of the good work that we have done in the rest of the book. If you understand how to program in Titanium, and if you follow the principles laid out in this chapter, you will be off to a flyer. However, a word of caution; if you don't get your layout right, you could end up with an app that looks great on an iPhone but a dog on everything else. Don't expect your layout to look the same across all platforms; you will probably have to make changes to your code to handle different devices as the following note from the Appcelerator documentation says:

Titanium is not a write once, run anywhere framework. It's more aptly referred to as a "write once, adapt everywhere" framework. Your business logic, networking, database, and event handling logic will be close to 100% cross-platform compatible. The user interfaces on iOS and Android differ so significantly that in most cases you'll have to do at least a little platform specific coding. That said, it's not uncommon for cross platform apps to reuse 80, 90, or even 100% of their UI code as well.

Titanium is brilliant for creating cross-platform apps; fact. However, while you are saving yourself a massive amount of time by not having to learn Objective-C, Java, and a bunch of native interfaces in order to have an app that runs on 90 percent of all smartphones, there is some pain. You have to make your UI the hard way by writing it out in code, just like the early days of HTML. There is no nice drag-and-drop interface or design package like there are for website design or for those folks creating apps using Objective-C.

Some of you may say, "You are wrong! There is a UI design tool; look at the `ForgedUI` module in the Appcelerator marketplace. It's one of the most popular modules!"

My answer is this; if `ForgedUI` could be used for all aspects of Titanium UI design and for all platforms, don't you think that the owners of Appcelerator would have invested in the technology or crafted something themselves? I am sure that Appcelerator would love a nice drag-and-drop UI design tool, but largely thanks to the complications of a development tool that can produce apps for such a wide range of devices, it's not going to be easy. Don't waste your time looking for shortcuts.

Once you learn the correct principles of creating Titanium UIs, it's not all that hard. So let's look at the best ways of producing great looking cross-platform apps, as we examine:

- How to size and position items that work cross-platform
- Using views to create flexible layouts
- How to handle orientation
- How to create layouts for both tablets and phones

To start, we will look at how you can create layouts that look good on all platforms.

How to position and size items on a window?

In the compass example shown in *Chapter 7, Putting the Phone Gadgets to Good Use*, the layout generated looked fine on the iPhone, but on Android the text was tiny. Why is that?

The display can often look wrong on Android if you have not coded with this platform in mind, and it depends on the Android device you run your code on. The problem is that there are so many different screen resolutions for Android, and not only that, but there are also different screen densities. This is a by-product of competing manufacturers being allowed to use the same operating system and each seeking their own competitive advantage. When creating a design for Android, you have to consider the following two things:

- **Screen resolutions**: Phone screen resolutions that range from 200 x 320 to 720 x 1280 and beyond. Tablets also vary in resolution.

- **Screen densities**: One manufacturer will want a small phone that crams lots onto the screen (high density), whereas another might be targeted at people who think that less is more and so the density is less. To allow this, Android has the concept of screen density. This is the measure of how many pixels there are in an inch of the screen, referred to as **pixels per inch (PPI)** or **dots per inch (DPI)**, and it can vary a lot between different devices. This is why some things can appear surprisingly small or large on Android devices.

Let's illustrate this Android issue with an example. The following is a simple app that displays a large important notice on the screen. Gridlines have been added for reference:

```
var win1 = Titanium.UI.createWindow({
    backgroundColor:'#fff'
});

// draw the gridlines first so your other elements stack on top of
them
// without requiring you to set the z-index property of each
var grid = require('gridlines');
grid.drawgrid(10,win1);

var theLabel = Ti.UI.createLabel({text: 'Important', top: 20, left:
20, font: {fontSize: 40}});
win1.add(theLabel);

win1.open();
```

 The gridlines script is courtesy of `https://gist.github.com/1187384`.
Thanks to Tim Poulsen (skypanther).

The following two screenshots show the app when run using the Android emulator with the default unit, pixels. The left one shows the app run on a low-resolution/low-density device and the right one shows a higher resolution and higher density:

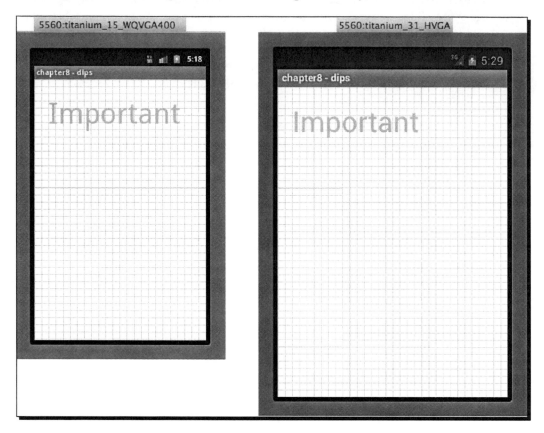

Notice how much more of the screen the message takes up on the lower-density device. It very nearly covers the entire width of the screen. This is not good if you have a layout with something on the right-hand side of this label. For a consistent layout across devices, the label must take up the same amount of space. This is why sizing objects using fixed or absolute size units such as pixels, inches, points, and centimeters, make for hard work when programming cross-platform. A pixel on one phone will be a different physical size on another and depends on how densely packed they are on the screen. You need a uniform measure across devices.

The following two screenshots show the same app when the default unit has been changed to DIPs:

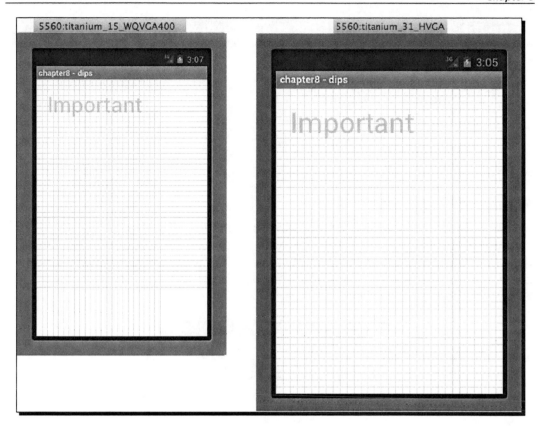

So what is a DIP and what's so good about it?

A **DIP** is a **density independent pixel**. As the name implies, it makes the sizing of an object density independent. When you size objects in DIPs, they are laid out as though the device was a medium density device (160 DPI) regardless of the device's actual density. A DIP takes up the same percentage of the screen regardless of the screen density.

The DIP is the default unit of measurement on iPhone and is the reason why your app looks the same on an old pre-retina phone and a new iPhone. It is also consistent across platforms as Android and iOS both use the same density. So your DIP measurement will take up the same percentage space on iOS and Android. It's consistent.

Time for action - making DIPs the default unit for your app

1. Open `tiapp.xml`.

2. Look for the highlighted line and ensure the property is dp as shown below. If the line does not exist, add it:

```
<analytics>true</analytics>
<property name="ti.ui.defaultunit" type="string">dp</property>
```

3. Run the app!

What just happened?

You have now set the default unit for your app to be DIPs. Unless you override this by specifying a different measure for an item on your layout, DIPs will be used on all platforms. The following screenshot shows the same app when run on an iPhone. Notice that the label takes up roughly the same amount of horizontal width as the Android screenshots, where DIPs was the unit of measurement.

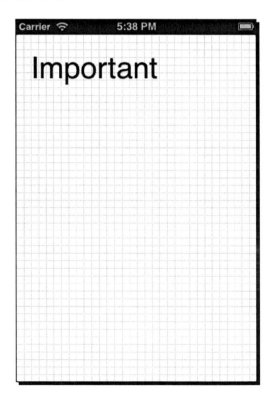

What about percentages?

Like DIPs, percentages also offer relative positioning to the constraints of the device's display that work across platforms and devices. It's very useful for laying out views on a window.

The disadvantage of percentages is that they cannot be specified as a default in `tiapp.xml`. Therefore, to specify a percentage, it has to be indicated with the percent sign (for example, `5%`). The problem with this is that now the measurement of your object is a string and not a number, so while it is possible to change the size of the object, it's not so easy to change the value using mathematical expressions (if for example you wanted to make something slightly larger by adding one percent to it). It's not a major issue, but something to be aware of.

 Make it easy for yourself. Unless you have a specific reason, do not use pixels, points, or inches to create your layout. Use either DIPs or percentages.

Using views to create your layout

If we were to compare an app to a website, an app would be a website, a window would be a webpage, and a view would be a div section (or a block if you are familiar with a CMS). Just in the same way as web pages are built up from a number of div containers, a Titanium window should be built up from a number of views.

But how do you lay out objects in a view?

You can lay out a view in a number of ways. You can position all items yourself with respect to the upper-left corner of the view, or you can let Titanium stack the objects within the view. This is controlled by the view `layout` property that can take one of the following options:

- No layout property specified: You have complete control over position by specifying a combination of the `top`, `bottom`, `left`, `right`, and `center` properties for items.
- `vertical`: All items are stacked vertically within the view. No position properties are required.
- `horizontal`: All items are stacked horizontally within the view. No position properties are required.

An easy way to build up views is to create a stacked layout using a vertical or horizontal layout. You will see examples throughout this book.

```
var vertLayout = Ti.UI.createView({layout:'vertical'});
```

This property stacks the objects within the view either vertically or horizontally. If you want some space before the first object in the view, specify a value for the top of the first object. If you want space between two objects, you can either specify a value for the bottom of the first object or the top of the second. The space will be the sum of these properties. If you are using a horizontal layout, you will use the `left` and `right` properties to add space.

> You can add views to most objects, allowing yourself to build up your layout from a number of smaller views. You can even lay out a table row using a view!

This creates a clean layout that works for most circumstances. If it doesn't, then just create another view without the `layout` property and you will be able to place things wherever you like relative to the upper-left corner of the view.

Orientation

Orientation is frankly a bit of a pain. So let's make it simple. You either handle orientation or you don't. The simple solution is to display your app in portrait unless you really need to display parts of your app in a landscape format.

Restricting the orientation

The problem with allowing orientation for some parts of your app is that you have to handle the transitions. For example, suppose you have two tabs; on one tab is a picture that you need to show in landscape, but on the other tab you have a form in portrait. The users look at the picture and rotate the phone to landscape. They then change tabs, without rotating the phone. What happens now? Should the app show the form in portrait? Or will it show the form in landscape?

Both circumstances are hardly ideal and both could happen; your form could appear in landscape or the app could rotate for portrait, annoying the user.

The simple solution is to create a portrait layout for phones and restrict the orientations in `tiapp.xml`. The user can still rotate the device, but your app will remain in its portrait format. You can always override this at a window level and it makes your layout code simpler.

The method to restricting orientations differs between iOS and Android, so there are two examples of how to do this, one per platform.

Time for action – restricting the orientation of your app (iPhone)

This example shows how you can specify the orientation for an iPhone app. Perform the following steps:

1. Open `tiapp.xml`.

2. Look for the following code:

```
<iphone>
    <orientations device="iphone">
        <orientation>Ti.UI.PORTRAIT</orientation>
    </orientations>
    <orientations device="ipad">
        <orientation>Ti.UI.PORTRAIT</orientation>
        <orientation>Ti.UI.UPSIDE_PORTRAIT</orientation>
        <orientation>Ti.UI.LANDSCAPE_LEFT</orientation>
        <orientation>Ti.UI.LANDSCAPE_RIGHT</orientation>
    </orientations>
</iphone>
```

3. This code restricts your app to portrait mode on an iPhone, but allows other orientations on iPad.

What just happened?

You can change the orientations by making modifications to `tiapp.xml`. The available orientations to choose from are `Ti.UI.PORTRAIT` (home button at the bottom), `Ti.UI.UPSIDE_PORTRAIT` (home button at the top), `Ti.UI.LANDSCAPE_LEFT` (home button to the left), and `Ti.UI.LANDSCAPE_RIGHT` (home button to the right).

You can also restrict orientations on Android, as shown in the next example.

> You should only restrict the orientations of an Android app towards the end of the build lifecycle of your project, when the layout is well defined. If you significantly change your layout by adding in tab groups or other major elements, you will have to redo the example.

Time for action – restricting the orientation of your app (Android)

Perform the following steps to restrict the orientation of your app on Android:

1. Create the layout for your app and build your project; this will create an `AndroidManifest.xml` file. This file can be found in the `build/Android` directory under your project home. This file controls the Android build options of your file. The contents of this file are overwritten with the contents of `tiapp.xml` during the Android build phase. The contents can be any Android customizations need to be made to `tiapp.xml`.

2. Open `tiapp.xml` and look for the line `<android xmlns:android="http://schemas.android.com/apk/res/android"/>`. Modify the file so that the line becomes:

```
<android xmlns:android="http://schemas.android.com/apk/res/
android">
<manifest>
</manifest>
</android>
```

3. We need to copy the existing customizations from `AndroidManifest.xml` so that they are preserved when the app is next built. Open `AndroidManifest.xml`.

4. Copy all of the `<activity>` nodes.

5. Paste the contents into `tiapp.xml` between the manifest `open` and `close` tags.

6. You should now have one or more lines that look similar to the following:

```
<activity android:name="org.appcelerator.titanium.TiActivity"
android:configChanges="keyboardHidden|orientation" android:screenO
rientation="portrait"/>
```

7. Remove the `orientation` label from each copied line.

8. You should now have one or more activity nodes that look as follows:

```
<activity
android:name="org.appcelerator.titanium.TiActivity"
android:configChanges="keyboardHidden"
android:screenOrientation="portrait"/>
```

9. Run the app!

What just happened?

You just modified the orientations of the Android app. You also learned how Android build settings can be added to `tiapp.xml`. This is a useful and advanced skill.

Changing the orientation manually

If you need to force the user to look at something in your app in landscape format, you can do this from the code. It's the same process for both platforms, as shown in the following example, where a button is added to an existing window that forces the window into landscape format when clicked.

Time for action – forcing an orientation change (all platforms)

Perform the following steps to force an orientation change for all platforms:

1. Add a button to the existing layout that will switch the layout to landscape:

```
var switchOrientation = Ti.UI.createButton({title: 'Make
Landscape'});
switchOrientation.addEventListener('click', rotateLayout);
```

2. Add the button to the view. Note the highlighted line:

```
var layout = Ti.UI.createView({layout: 'vertical'});
layout.add(switchOrientation);
```

3. Create the `rotateLayout` function, which will be called when the button is clicked. Note the code hides the button when it is clicked. This is not required; it was added because the button isn't needed when the window is in landscape layout!

```
function rotateLayout() {
  win1.orientationModes = [Ti.UI.LANDSCAPE_LEFT];
  switchOrientation.hide();
}
```

4. Run the app!

What just happened?

You added code to rotate the layout of the screen to landscape. This will happen regardless of the orientation of the device. The following is the preceding code in action on the layout example from an earlier section of this chapter:

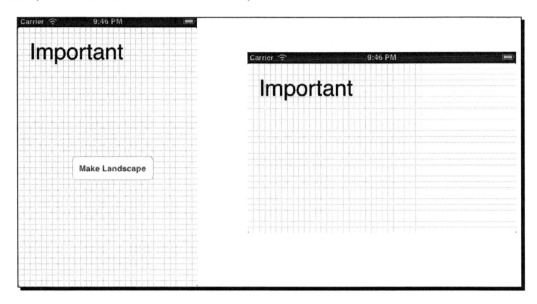

 If you need to respond to a change of orientation, you need to define an event listener for `Ti.Gesture.addEventListener ('orientationchange')`.

Creating layouts for phones and tablets

If you own an iPad or Android tablet, you will know how disappointing it is when you open an app for the first time and it appears with an iPhone layout in the middle of the screen. This doesn't have to be the case. If you get the basics of your layout right, it's not hard to make a layout that works on both tablets and phones.

You need to create layouts built up from views, where each view is a self-contained piece of the layout. For example, a view would be a list of currencies, or a set of text fields where you enter some commentary.

This is why it is important to split your content into files. Give each view its own file. That way you can build your layout by picking the views you require. For your iPhone app, you may need to split your app over several windows due to the constraints on the screen size, but for a tablet you might be able to show several views on the front screen; thanks to the larger screen and landscape orientation. This can be done with minimal changes to your code. The next example shows how the Forex app developed in *Chapter 5, It's All About Data*, can be modified to include both a tablet and phone layout. This example will create a new app, copying the existing code from the previous app.

This project is available for download and browse at `https://github.com/myleftboot/pinbarEntry`.

Time for action – creating a multiplatform interface

Perform the following steps to create a multiplatform interface:

1. Create a new app using the Master/Detail Application template. This template includes the code to distinguish between a phone and tablet layout. A number of directories are created, as described in the following table:

Directory	Contents
`ui/common`	Place files that are not platform specific in here. Views such as the currency listing view shown later in this chapter will be placed in here.
`ui/handheld/android`	This directory contains files that are specific to Android phones. The `ApplicationWindow.js` file is executed when the app starts. This is where you start to create your UI.
`ui/handheld/ios`	This contains files that are specific to iPhones and iPods. The `ApplicationWindow.js` file is executed when the app starts. This is where you start to create your UI.
`ui/handheld/mobileweb`	This contains files where the layout is designed for mobile web. The `ApplicationWindow.js` file is executed when the app starts. This is where you start to create your UI.
`ui/tablet`	This contains files where the layout is designed for iPad and Android tablets. The `ApplicationWindow.js` file is executed when the app starts. This is where you start to create your UI.

You only need to add contents to directories you are going to support. So if you don't plan to release an Android version of your app, you can leave the contents of the Android directory unchanged.

2. When the app starts, code in app.js determines the correct directory to enter. The lines copied out next show the code that determines the correct window layout to load:

```
//considering tablet to have one dimension over 900px - this
is imperfect, so you should feel free to decide
//yourself what you consider a tablet form factor for android
var isTablet = osname === 'ipad' || (osname === 'android' &&
(width > 899 || height > 899));
```

As the preceding comment states, determining the difference between a handheld device and a tablet based on a cutoff point of 900 pixels for the screen width is not perfect. A better solution is shown in an example by Stephen Feather at http://developer.appcelerator.com/question/149572/mater-details-template#answer-258629.

3. Start with the tablet layout. Here are the elements from the file Resources/ui/tablet/ApplicationWindow.js, which creates the layout. We want a layout on the iPad that lists currencies on the left-hand side, then the main panel on the right-hand side, the pin bar view entry view, and below it the currency commentary. The following are the main commands to create this (this is not the entire file):

```
var CurrencyView = require('ui/common/currencyView'),
    pinBarView = require('ui/common/pinbarView');
    commentaryView = require('ui/common/commentaryView');
...
//construct UI
var currencyView = new CurrencyView(),
        pinBarView = new PinBarView();
        commenatryView = new CommentaryView();
...
var masterContainer = Ti.UI.createView({
    top:0,
    bottom:0,
    left:0,
    width:240
});
masterContainer.add(currencyView);
...
// set the height of the top item on the main panel
```

```
pinBarView.height = '60%';
...
var detailContainer = Ti.UI.createView({
  top:0,
  bottom:0,
  right:0,
  left:240,
  layout: "vertical"
});
detailContainer.add(pinBarView);
detailContainer.add(commentaryView);
```

4. Now examine the structure of the `Resources/ui/common/currencyView.js` file (the other two files will be similar). It comprises of a single function that returns a view to the caller:

```
function CurrenciesView() {
  //create vertical layout for the tableview
  var vertLayout = Ti.UI.createView({layout:'vertical'});

  var currencyCommon = require('common/currencycommon');
  var stockList = Ti.UI.createTableView
  ({data: currencyCommon.populateTableWithPairs()});

  vertLayout.add(stockList);

  //add behavior
  stockList.addEventListener('click', function(e) {
    vertLayout.fireEvent('currencySelected', {
      pair:e.rowData.pair,
      rate:e.rowData.rate
    });
  });

  return vertLayout;
};
module.exports = CurrenciesView;
```

> Notice how the event listener on the table just fires an event on the view, passing the information from the selected row. This is good stuff; when the view is created from the call in `ApplicationWindow.js`, it is assigned to a variable. So an event listener can be defined on this view within `ApplicationWindow.js` to process the table event.

5. Run the app on either iPad Simulator or the Android tablet!

What just happened?

This example shows how easy it is to create alternative layouts for tablets when your code is spread over several files with business logic split into logical units, and layouts are created from several independent views. The tablet layout is shown in the following screenshot:

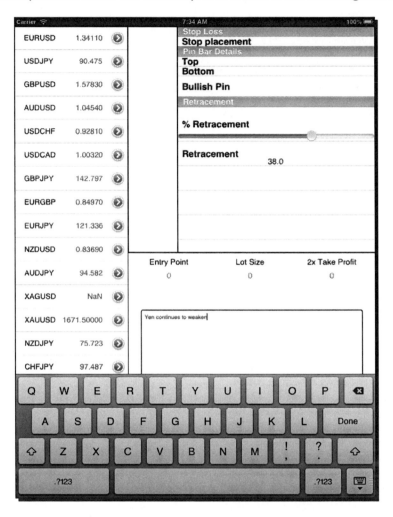

So you have a layout for a tablet. Next we will show the changes that need to be made to create a layout optimized for display on a phone. The example will show files from the iOS branch, but the example works just the same for Android.

Time for action – creating a phone layout for your app

Perform the following steps to create a phone layout for same app:

1. Due to the lower resolution of a phone, we have to make changes to the layout. Gone are the three views on a single window, and in its place are two views on two windows.

2. All of the changes required are in the `/ui/handheld/ios/ApplicationWindow.js` file where the windows and views are defined. The following are the selected code lines that create the two-window layout for the phone:

```
var CurrencyView = require('ui/common/currencyView'),
    pinBarView = require('ui/common/pinbarView');
...
//construct UI
var currencyView = new CurrencyView(),
        pinBarView = new PinBarView();
...
var masterContainerWindow = Ti.UI.createWindow({
  title:'Currencies'
});
masterContainerWindow.add(currencyView);

var pinBarWindow = Ti.UI.createWindow({
  title:'Pin Bar Entry'
});
pinBarWindow.add(pinBarView);
...
//create iOS specific NavGroup UI
var navGroup = Ti.UI.iPhone.createNavigationGroup({
  window:masterContainerWindow
});
self.add(navGroup);
...
currencyView.addEventListener('currencySelected', function(e) {
  pinBarView.fireEvent('currencySelected',e);
  navGroup.open(pinBarWindow);
});
```

The layout for an android phone in `/ui/handheld/android/ApplicationWindow.js` will be very similar. The key difference being that on Android, child windows are opened and not added to a navigation group, as shown in the following code:

```
var commentaryWindow = Ti.UI.createWindow({
    title:'Add Comments',
    navBarHidden:false,
    backgroundColor:'#ffffff'
});
commentaryWindow.open();
```

3. Run the app on a phone simulator!

What just happened?

By making modifications to a single layout file and re-using the existing view components, we created a layout that works on a phone! You now have an app that can be released for phones and tablets; a big bonus. No one with a tablet wants an app with a phone-sized display.

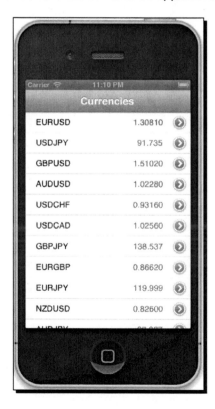

Pop quiz - creating a layout

Q 1. To reuse an analogy where an app was compared to the Web, if a view is a block or a div, and an app is a website, then what is a window?

1. A web page
2. A JavaScript file
3. An iFrame

Q 2. You want to create a view that appears like a sidebar on the left-hand side of the window. The view will contain a number of buttons stacked one below the other. What is the easiest way to do this?

1. Add the buttons to the window, specifying `alignment:"left"` for the window
2. Add the buttons to the view and add the `layout:"vertical"` property to the view
3. Add the buttons to the view, specifying `left:0` for each button

Summary

If there is one chapter in the book that can save you hours of programming effort, it's this one. If you get the basics right of how you put together your app in such a way that it is built up with views as components, you will be flying. It will then be so much easier to modify your layout for any device you need to create a layout for.

Now that you have an app that looks the business on both phones and tablets, it's time to tell people about it. It's time to see how you can embed social networking within your app, and we'll do that in the next chapter.

9
Spread the Word with Social Media

Your app is brilliant, that's why you went to the trouble of making it. It just might be the best app in its class but only you know about it. It's just another app in the store alongside thousands of others. You need to make people aware of your app, and better still you need people to do your work for you by telling other people about your app. You need social media.

The world of social media is dominated by two giants, Facebook and Twitter. So unsurprisingly this chapter is purely about how to incorporate these into your app.

In this chapter you will see:

- How to post Facebook posts from your app
- How to send Tweets from your app
- Sharing and social integration on Android using intents

Facebook

To send Facebook updates from your app you need to register your app with Facebook. Having an app on Facebook allows it to have a presence on the Facebook site and means that the app name is included on any wall posts.

The next two examples show how to set up and create Facebook posts from your app; first the Facebook registration.

Time for action – registering your app with Facebook

To register your app with Facebook, perform the following steps:

1. Log in to Facebook and navigate to `https://developers.facebook.com/apps`.

2. Click on the **New App** button.

3. Enter the name of your app and click on **Continue**.

4. You now have a Facebook app with an App ID. This ID will be used to identify your app on Facebook. You will need this ID later.

5. You now need to register your app with Facebook. Select **Native iOS App**. Add your app bundle ID, which is your app identifier that can be found in `tiapp.xml`.

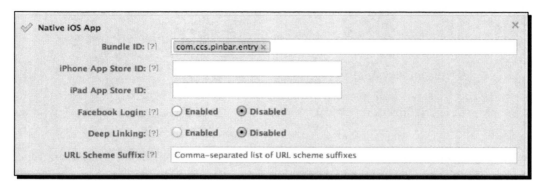

6. Similarly, if you are going to release your app on Android, type in the bundle ID in the **Package Name** field in the **Native Android App** dialog box:

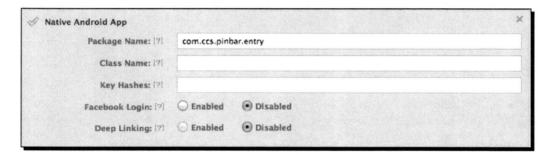

7. Click on **Save Changes**. Your app is now linked to Facebook.

 The bundle ID can contain more than one app ID. So if you have a lite version of your app as well as the full version, or if you have a suite of similar apps, they can all be added here, so when posting to the Facebook it looks as though they were the same app.

What just happened?

You linked your app to Facebook. You can personalize the Facebook app by adding icons, links to your app on iTunes, and so on.

Now that you have completed the setup on Facebook, it's time to start sending posts from your app. In this example we will add a button that will post a screenshot to Facebook.

Time for action – sending a screenshot to Facebook

Perform the following steps to send a screenshot to Facebook:

1. Create a new blank mobile app by selecting **File** | **New** | **Titanium Project**. Don't use a template as it will just generate code that gets in the way.

2. Create the window for the app:

```
var win1 = Titanium.UI.createWindow({
    backgroundColor:'#fff'
});
```

3. Add something to the screen so the screenshot is not just a blank canvas! For this example we will be re-using the code from an earlier section of this book by adding random green blocks to the window. This step is not important for the example; it just adds something to the screen.

```
var height = Ti.Platform.displayCaps.platformHeight,
  width = Ti.Platform.displayCaps.platformWidth;

// add some random boxes on the screen
for (var i=0; i<5; i++) {
  var randomPosView = Ti.UI.createView({
  width:'10%',
  height:'10%',
  backgroundColor:'green',
  borderColor:'black',
  left: Math.random() * width,
  top:Math.random() * height
  });

  win1.add(randomPosView);
}
```

4. To use Facebook you need to add the app ID to your code and to `tiapp.xml`. Open `tiapp.xml` and add the Facebook app ID generated when you registered your app:

```
<property name="ti.facebook.appid">your_facebook_app_id</property>
```

5. Add the app ID and the permissions you require to `app.js`:

```
Ti.Facebook.appid = '<<YOUR APP ID>>';
Ti.Facebook.permissions = ['publish_stream'];
```

The `publish_stream` permission will allow us to create wall posts on Facebook. For a full list of permissions visit `http://developers.facebook.com/docs/reference/api/permissions/`.

6. Add an event listener that will inform the user if the login to Facebook fails. This event listener will be called when Facebook authentication succeeds or fails. In this case we don't need to perform any action when authentication succeeds; we will just output a message if the user cancels or if there is an error.

```
Ti.Facebook.addEventListener('login', function(e) {
    if (e.error) {
        alert(e.error);
    } else if (e.cancelled) {
        alert("Cancelled");
    }
});
```

7. Add the code to log in to Facebook. In this example we will log in as soon as the form opens. For your app you may want to put this call somewhere else, such as when a button is clicked.

```
win1.open();

Ti.Facebook.authorize();
```

 You can add a Facebook-styled button to your app that will log you in to Facebook when clicked. Visit `http://docs.appcelerator.com/titanium/3.0/#!/api/Titanium.Facebook.LoginButton` for details.

8. Create the function that will send the screenshot to Facebook. This function creates the payload that will be sent by combining a caption with the image (the `data` parameter will contain a blob representation of the image). The function then posts the information to the `me/photos` Facebook Graph API. This API call allows you to post images to the logged in user's wall. There are many other Graph calls; for a full list visit `http://developers.facebook.com/docs/reference/api/`. The code will look like the following:

```
function facebookScreenshot(data) {
  // construct the photo object
  var thePhoto = {
```

```
              message: 'My randomly placed squares',
              picture: data
      };
      Ti.Facebook.requestWithGraphPath('me/photos', thePhoto, 'POST',
function(e){
          if (e.success) {
              alert("Success!  From FB: " + e.result);
          } else {
              if (e.error) {
                  alert(e.error);
              } else {
                  alert("Unknown result");
              }
          }
      });
}
```

9. Now add the function that will be called when the user wishes to send the screenshot to Facebook. This function captures the screen and sends the blob representation of the screen to the facebookScreenshot function.

```
function captureScreenForFacebook() {
  Ti.Media.takeScreenshot(function(e)
  {
    // The media property of the object passed in
    contains the screenshot
    facebookScreenshot(e.media);

  });
}
```

10. Join the last few steps together by adding a button to the form that will send the screenshot to Facebook when clicked:

```
var facebookBtn = Ti.UI.createButton({
  title:'Facebook Screen'
});

facebookBtn.addEventListener('click', function(e) {
  //
  captureScreenForFacebook();
});
win1.add(facebookBtn);
```

11. Run the app!

What just happened?

You added a button to your app that when pressed takes a screenshot. When the app first starts a series of pop ups will be displayed, where you will log in and then accept the privileges that are required to post images to the user's wall, as shown in the following screenshot:

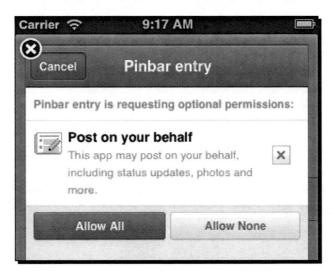

Once the permissions are allowed, the screenshot is taken and the image is posted to Facebook. The end result looks as follows:

Sending tweets

The Twitter functionality has not been built into the core SDK of Titanium, which is surprising given that Facebook is. Nevertheless, thanks to the wide use of JavaScript, there are routines out there that can help. For this example we will make use of the `social.js` script to send Tweets. The script can be downloaded from `https://gist.github.com/myleftboot/5093893`.

> There are many copies of `social.js` out there. Most reference version 1 of the Twitter API. This has now been depreciated. Make sure you use one that references version 1.1 of the Twitter API such as the one listed at the preceding URL.

Before we can send a Tweet from the app, we need to create the app on Twitter.

Time for action – registering your app with Twitter

Perform the following steps to register your app with Twitter:

1. Log in to your Twitter account by going to the site `https://dev.twitter.com`.
2. From the menu bar, select your Twitter account and then **My applications**.
3. Click on the **Create a new application** button.
4. Enter the name of your app and a few other details including the URL of your app, which will be shown when someone clicks on your app name shown on a Tweet. Accept the terms and conditions and click on **Create your Twitter application**.
5. Make a note of your consumer key and secret; you will need them later (or just note the page so you can return to it).
6. The Twitter app is created with read-only permissions by default. This is not good if you want to create Tweets. To modify this to read/write, click on the **Settings** tab and change **Application Type** to **Read and Write**, and click on the **Update** button.

> It can take a few moments for the changes to be applied. Refresh the page after about a minute to ensure the read/write setting has been saved.

What just happened?

You registered your app with Twitter. You will now be able to send Tweets from your app.

In the next example we will modify the existing app created earlier in the chapter by adding a button that when pressed Tweets a message.

Time for action – sending a tweet

Perform the following steps to send a Tweet:

1. Find a working copy of `social.js` (a copy can be found at `https://gist.github.com/myleftboot/5093893`) and copy it into the `Resources` folder of the app.

2. Add a function to `app.js` that will send the Tweet. Notice that most of the Tweet functionality is in the `social.js` file that is referenced using `require` at the start of the function. Nice! Replace the `<<YOUR CONSUMER SECRET>>` and `<<YOUR CONSUMER KEY>>` entries with the values from your Twitter app:

```
function tweetUpdate(_args) {

  var social = require('social');

  var twitter = social.create({
      consumerSecret : '<<YOUR CONSUMER SECRET>>',
      consumerKey : '<<YOUR CONSUMER KEY>>'
  });

    twitter.share({
        message : "More random blocks",
        success : function() {
            alert('Tweeted!');
        },
        error : function(e) {
            alert('ERROR'+e);
        }
    });
}
```

It's important to keep the consumer secret safe. If someone else knew this value, they could send Tweets as though they were from your app. This code is just for an example; you should be more careful with the secret than this in your production code. There is no guaranteed way to keep this value safe if you are going to allow users to Tweet from the app. Some ideas on how to mitigate this risk can be found at `https://dev.twitter.com/discussions/5456`.

3. Add the button to the app:

```
var twitterBtn = Ti.UI.createButton({
  title:'Send Tweet'
});

twitterBtn.addEventListener('click', function(e) {
  tweetUpdate();
});

win1.add(twitterBtn);
```

4. Run the app!

What just happened?

You added a button to your app that when pressed sends a Tweet. When the app first runs, you will be presented with a pop up that authenticates the user of the app with Twitter.

Once authenticated and after the Tweet is successfully sent, the end result looks as follows when viewed on TweetDeck:

Sharing and social media on Android

If you are going to run your app on Android, you can make use of intents to share information between apps. If you have an Android device, you may have seen the following pop up when you click on a link, select a phone number, press a button, or just try to do something that is outside of the functionality for your app. From the following screen you can send Tweets and e-mails, or share your content on Facebook:

A simplification of this sharing process is shown in the following table, which shows the interaction between the user, the app, and Android when a user clicks on a button in your app to share a picture:

User	App	Android
Presses the share picture button.		
	I need to share this picture.	
		No problem, here are the apps on this device that you can use to share this. I'll show this pop up and let the user choose the most appropriate app.
Chooses how the picture is shared.		
		Opens the chosen app and sends a URI of the picture to the app.
		Process completes or is cancelled.
	Control returns to the app.	

Titanium apps, being native apps, can make full use of this functionality. The next example will show how you can code this process in your app.

Time for action – sharing an update using intents

Perform the following steps to share an update using intents:

1. Add a function that shares an item of text (this text could be shared as a message to Tweet or a post to Facebook) . The function creates an Android intent, sets the type of data to be included with the intent as text/plain, and adds the message before launching the intent.

```
function shareUpdate(_args) {
var shareThis = Ti.Android.createIntent({
    action: Ti.Android.ACTION_SEND,
    type: "text/plain"
});
```

```
        shareThis.putExtra(Ti.Android.EXTRA_TEXT, _args.comment);
        shareThis.addCategory(Ti.Android.CATEGORY_DEFAULT);
        Ti.Android.currentActivity.startActivity(shareThis);


    }
```

2. Link this together by creating a button that when pressed calls the
   `shareUpdate` function:

```
var shareThisButton = Ti.UI.createButton({title: 'Share'});

shareThisButton.addEventListener('click', function(e) {
    shareUpdate();
});
layout.add(shareThisButton);
```

3. Run the app!

What just happened?

You added a few lines of code to your app to introduce a method for the user to
share information.

You can share images, telephone numbers, e-mail addresses, sounds, and lots more.
The `type` parameter to the intent specifies the type of content you wish to share and
this influences the applicable options that are presented to the user. You can do far
more than this with intents. The following URL will guide you:

`http://developer.android.com/guide/components/intents-filters.html`

Pop quiz - integrating social media

Q 1. Which permission allows you to send photos to Facebook?

1. `publish_content.`
2. `publish_stream.`
3. `update_stream.`
4. `upload_content.`

Q 2. Which of the following can you use to send Tweets from your app?

1. The Titanium SDK.
2. An Appcelerator marketplace module.
3. `social.js`.
4. Intents.

Summary

Incorporating social media into your app is such a powerful feature when used correctly. Your app can promote itself widely through like-minded people, resulting in great promotion that doesn't cost you a cent.

The next chapter moves the focus away from social networking, where users send messages, to the other side of the coin—push notifications—where you send messages to your users.

10
Sending Notifications

You need to keep your users informed of the fantastic new feature that you have added to your website. Or you want to tell them that their favorite band is appearing in town tonight. Push notifications when used correctly will significantly increase the use of your app and help to retain your user base. This chapter will show you how to make best use of them.

Push notifications were first introduced with iOS 3 as a way to extend battery life of devices. Battery life was being used up by applications which needed to keep checking for new information, such as sports apps checking for the latest scores. Prior to iOS 3 these apps would have to poll a server to check if there was any new information, this would use up battery life and network allowance. Push notifications changed all that.

Now notifications could be sent to devices via **Apple Push Notification Service (APNS)**, which would deliver them to devices. Apps would no longer have to poll for new information. Instead the delivery of new information was centralized within the operating system. Now the device would listen occasionally for messages for all apps on the device, one connection for all apps. It worked beautifully and app developers saw what it could provide and readily incorporated it into their apps.

In this chapter you will see:

- ◆ How push notifications work
- ◆ Setting up push notifications
- ◆ Registering and sending notifications
- ◆ Push notifications using Appcelerator Cloud Services
- ◆ Push notifications using Urban Airship

How push notifications work

Push notifications work as follows:

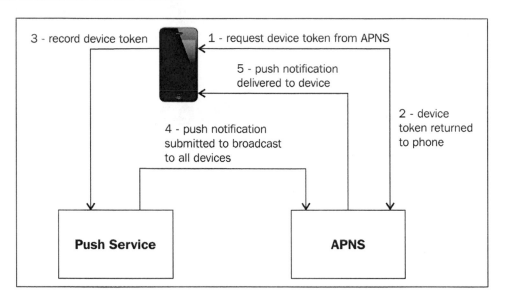

Why do you need to know this?

You need to be aware that there are three components behind a push notification. The device and the push notification server are obvious, but the web service that acts as a register of interested devices is probably not so clear. You could create a web service to do this and there is code out there to guide you, or you could use a third party service. Two popular services for Titanium are Urban Airship and Titanium's own cloud-based push service. We will explore solutions for both of these services in this chapter.

This chapter could include solutions for StackMob and Parse but the implementation of these services is so similar to that for ACS that it would be a waste of space. It should be noted that Parse has excellent documentation that makes implementation far easier.

Setting up notifications - the prerequisites

If you are going to send notifications to iOS devices, then you have to go through the following steps. Regardless of the method you employ to send your messages, whether it be Urban Airship, ACS, or something home-brewed, you will need to register your app with Apple first.

There are various methods for sending Android notifications. Some methods such as GCM are centralized and require some setup, whereas push notifications to Android using ACS need hardly any configuration. We will cover the Android setup in the push notification example later in the chapter.

Setting up iOS notifications

Here is the step-by-step guide to registering for push notifications with Apple. Note that you will need to go through this example twice. Once for development so you can create a certificate for use in testing, and a second time for production for use when your code is live. Production certificates can only be used for apps that are live, and equally, development certificates will not work with live apps.

Time for action – getting a push certificate

Perform the following steps to get a push certificate:

1. You need to register your app with Apple using the iOS provisioning portal before you can register for push notifications. This is described in *Chapter 11, Testing and Deploying* in the section on distributing your app. Assuming your app is registered, you will need to configure your app for push notifications. We can see from the following screenshot that our app is not configured for push notifications at the moment:

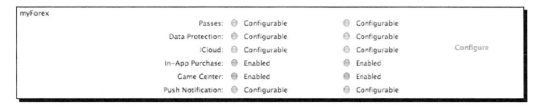

2. Configuring your app for push notifications involves creating a certificate locally which will identify and authenticate you. This is a bit fiddly so bear with me.

3. Launch the keychain application. Open the **Certificate Assistant** by navigating to **Keychain Access | Certificate Assistant | Request a Certificate from a Certificate Authority**. You will a get a screen similar to the following:

4. Click on **Continue** and then on the following screen enter your e-mail address and common name. The common name is your chance to name your certificate. It will be the name of the certificate that is listed in the keychain access. Give it a descriptive name so you can recognize it in a list, and include in your description if it is the development or production key, as shown in the following screenshot:

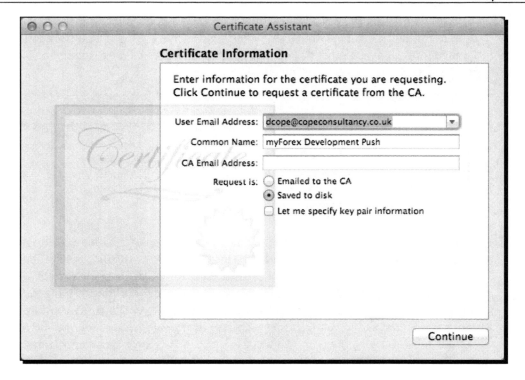

5. Save the certificate request.

 It's a good idea to keep this file so you can use it again when the certificate expires. By doing this you keep the same private key every time you renew and end up with fewer unused keys in your keychain.

6. Exit the assistant.

7. Go back to the iOS provisioning portal, find your app in the list of app IDs, and click on **Configure**.

8. Check **Enable for Apple Push Notification service** and then click on the **Configure** button on either the development or production service.

9. Click on **Continue** and from the following screen upload your certificate request file saved earlier and click on **Generate**.

10. Apple will now generate the push certificate. This is the certificate that will be used to authenticate you with the Apple push notification server when you send notifications. Download the file and run it; your certificate will be loaded into your keychain as shown in the following image:

 Putting the certificate into your keychain allows you to quickly check that all is in order, and you can check locally when the certificate expires. Certificates expire; don't get caught out by letting your production one slip.

11. This step will save you hours of pain if you do it right. If you don't have a development certificate for your app, now is the time to create one. The instructions are in *Chapter 11, Testing and Deploying*. If you do have a development certificate, edit the old one in the provisioning portal, making some token change in order to trigger Apple to regenerate the certificate. Download the new one for use with Titanium. A certificate generated before setting up the push certificate will not allow you to register for push notifications. You will get an error showing **no valid 'aps-environment' entitlement string found for application**.

12. The new development certificate can now be used to authenticate your device with the push notification provider.

13. That completes the certificate steps; you now need to add code to your app to start the push registration process. This needs to be called regardless of the method you will use to send push notifications. You need to add a call to `Ti.Network.registerForPushNotifications` in the `app.js` file. It needs to be called on every application startup. There is a single JSON parameter for the `Ti.Network.registerForPushNotifications` call, and the attributes of this parameter are as follows:

Parameter	Usage
`types`	Specifies an array of types of notification the app can process. Specified as an array of the `Ti.Network` constant values as shown:
	◆ **Badge**: `Ti.Network.NOTIFICATION_TYPE_BADGE`
	◆ **Alert**: `Ti.Network.NOTIFICATION_TYPE_ALERT`
	◆ **Sound**: `Ti.Network.NOTIFICATION_TYPE_SOUND`
	◆ **Newsstand**: `Ti.Network.NOTIFICATION_TYPE_NEWSSTAND`

Parameter	Usage
success	Specifies the code to run when the device successfully registers for push notifications. A device token will be returned. What you do with the device token depends on the service you are going to use to send your push notifications. If it is Urban Airship or ACS then you will need to send it to them so the device can be registered. This device token is a unique identifier that will be used to send the push notification to your device.
error	Specifies the code to run when the registration process fails.
callback	Specifies the code to run when a push notification is received. This code will run even if the application is not active. Typically you will raise an alert showing the message, but you don't have to. This is your chance to process the push notification in the way that suits you best.

14. Here is a sample call. Note the highlighted comment, which indicates the part of the code that needs to change depending on the provider that is storing your device tokens (that is, Urban Airship or ACS):

```
Ti.Network.registerForPushNotifications({
    types: [
    Ti.Network.NOTIFICATION_TYPE_BADGE,
    Ti.Network.NOTIFICATION_TYPE_ALERT,
    Ti.Network.NOTIFICATION_TYPE_SOUND,
    Ti.Network.NOTIFICATION_TYPE_NEWSSTAND
    ],
    success:function(e){
// this is where you send the device token (e.deviceToken) to the
push server

    },
    error:function(e) {
      alert("push notifications disabled: "+e.error);
    },
    callback:function(e) {
      var a = Ti.UI.createAlertDialog({
        title:'myForex',
        message:e.data.alert
        }).show();
    }
```

What just happened?

A push notification certificate was generated from Apple. This certificate will be used to identify and authenticate your app when you wish to send out a push notification. You noticed that there are production and development certificates and that production certificates can only be used for live apps. You also included code within your app to respond to push notifications. In this example an alert box will be shown when a notification is received, but you are free to do something else by modifying the code to suit your needs in the callback property.

This does not complete the setup. The device token needs to be registered with your push provider. The following examples will show how this is done with two providers.

Push notifications using Appcelerator Cloud

Registering for push notifications using Appcelerator Cloud Services gives you a single conduit for receiving notifications to both Android and iOS platforms.

You still need to create the necessary certificates for iOS push notifications if you are using ACS. Push notifications for iOS need a certificate from Apple; there is no getting around this.

Time for action – registering for push notifications with Appcelerator Cloud

This example will show how to process push notifications using Appcelerator Cloud Services (ACS):

1. Check that cloud services have been enabled for your app. Open `tiapp.xml` and check that the `Ti.Cloud` and `Ti.CloudPush` modules are loaded and that cloud services are enabled.

2. You will need to export the push notification key that you imported into keychain in the earlier example. Right-click on the key in keychain and select the **export** option. Save the file for later use.

 You don't have to specify a password for the p12 certificate.

3. Now make the necessary changes on ACS. Go to the Appcelerator Cloud website at `https://my.appcelerator.com/apps`. Find your app and select **Manage ACS**. Select **Development** from the selection buttons at the top.

4. You need to define a user (if you don't have one already) so your app can log in to ACS in order to receive push notifications. From the **App Management** tab, select **Users** from the list on the right. Create a user.

5. If you are going to release your app for iOS, then you need to upload your Apple push certificate. Select **Settings** from the app management screen and upload your p12 file from step 2 into the **Apple Development Push Certificate** field. Save your settings.

6. If you are going to release your app for Android, then you need to enter your application's bundle ID (see `tiapp.xml`) into the **Application Package** field. Save your settings.

7. Add the code to log the user into ACS in `app.js`. The highlighted code is the function we will call when the login is successful.

```
var myCloud = require('ti.cloud');

myCloud.Users.login({
    login:    'pushforex', // replace with your username
    password: 'pushforex'
    },
    function (e) {if (e.success) {
                    registerForACSNotifications();
                } else {
                    alert('Error: ' +((e.error && e.message) ||
JSON.stringify(e)));
                }
    });
```

8. For the purposes of this example the code to register for Android and iOS will be split over different steps so you can see the important bits. First the easy step; define the `registerForACSNotifications` function:

```
function registerForACSNotifications() {
}
```

9. The procedure for registering Android differs to iOS. First the Android registration code; add the following to the `registerForACSNotifications` function:

```
if (Ti.Platform.osname == 'android') {
var CloudPush = require('ti.cloudpush');
CloudPush.retrieveDeviceToken({
    success: function deviceTokenSuccess(e) {
            myCloud.PushNotifications.subscribe({
                    channel: 'forexUpdate',
                    type:'android',
                    device_token: e.deviceToken
        },
```

```
                function (e) {
                    if (e.success) {
                        alert('Success'+((e.error && e.message) ||
JSON.stringify(e)));
                    } else {
                        alert('Error:\\n' + ((e.error &&
e.message) || JSON.stringify(e)));
                    }
                });
            },
            error: function deviceTokenError(e) {
                alert('Failed to register for push! ' + e.error);
            }
        });

    CloudPush.enabled = true;

    CloudPush.addEventListener('callback', function (evt) {
        alert(evt.payload);
    });
}
```

There are three highlighted sections in this example:

- Unlike iOS, we are not using a central device token system for push registration so we have to get the token from ACS. The Android only CloudPush library is used for this.

- The standard ACS cloud push subscription code is used to register the device token.

- A callback event listener is defined to specify what happens when the push notification is received by the device.

In your production code you must ask the user's permission before registering for push notifications. Setting enabled to true without a prompt, which is done in the previous example, is fine for setting up and proving push notifications but is very bad practice in production. If your users switch off notifications for your app, they expect that to be honored. The previous example is purely for development and has been written to keep the code clean and short. For your app, add the code to set the enabled flag behind a button or switch.

10. The iOS registration and notification handling code is as follows. Add this to the registerForACSNotifications function:

```
if (Ti.Platform.name == 'iPhone OS') {

    Ti.Network.registerForPushNotifications({
        types: [
    Ti.Network.NOTIFICATION_TYPE_BADGE,
    Ti.Network.NOTIFICATION_TYPE_ALERT,
    Ti.Network.NOTIFICATION_TYPE_SOUND,
    Ti.Network.NOTIFICATION_TYPE_NEWSSTAND
        ],
        success:function(e){
            myCloud.PushNotifications.subscribe({
                channel: 'forexUpdate',
                device_token: e.deviceToken
                },
                function (e) {
                    if (e.success) {
                        alert('Success'+((e.error &&
e.message) || JSON.stringify(e)));
                    } else {
                        alert('Error:\\n' + ((e.error &&
e.message) || JSON.stringify(e)));
                    }
            });

        },
        error:function(e) {
            alert("push notifications disabled: "+e.error);
        },
        callback:function(e) {
            var a = Ti.UI.createAlertDialog({
                title:'myForex',
                message:e.data.alert
                }).show();
        }
    });
}
```

There are three highlighted sections in this example:

- The `types` array defines the types of notification the app might receive
- The standard ACS cloud subscription code is used to register the device token
- A `callback` code specifies what happens when the push notification is received by the device

11. Run the app on a device!

What just happened?

Quite a lot! You registered for push notifications with Appcelerator Cloud Services and added code to your app that displays an alert box containing the message when the push notification is sent.

Have a go hero - sending push notifications

You have done the hard work, now it is time to reap the rewards. Open your app on a device (not in the simulator), and you should get alerts informing you that the registration is successful. Navigate back to your app on the ACS web page and select **Push Notifications** and **Show Console**. You should have confirmation of a registered device (it may take a few seconds so it might need a refresh).

You have a registered device. Fantastic! Now it's time to send a push notification. Enter your notification text into the **Alert** field and press **Send Push Notification**. Within a few seconds you should receive the notification on your device. Here it is on my Android device:

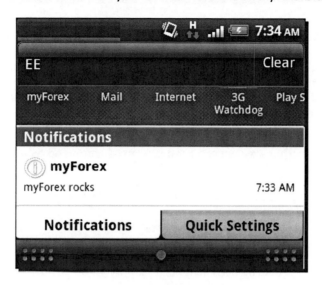

Push notifications using Urban Airship

I have reservations about including a section on push notifications with Urban Airship. It's important to say that my reservations are not with the Urban Airship service, but instead with the availability of interfaces for Titanium apps. When Android was in its infancy and Titanium apps were developed almost purely for iOS with the dream of porting to Android, interfaces were developed from Titanium to Urban Airship. Then as Android matured and went through several different push notification methods, no reliable way of sending push notifications to Android devices using Titanium via Urban Airship were developed. It's still the case now; there are several competing modules on the marketplace which no doubt all work perfectly well and provide good service. However, this book is not about recommending specific modules (especially ones that aren't free), as their reliability cannot be vouched for, and also not in the spirit of the book, which has suggested solutions that mostly work cross platform.

So the next few examples will focus on implementing push notifications to Urban Airship using iOS. If you want to implement a solution using Urban Airship for your Android app, then you should look at some of the solutions in the marketplace (`https://marketplace.appcelerator.com/home`), or, if you are feeling brave, develop your own module as this brave person did: `https://github.com/liccowee/Google-Cloud-Messaging--Titanium-`.

Time for action – registering for push notifications with Urban Airship

This example will show how to register for push notifications using Urban Airship. You can sign up for a free account with basic features at `https://go.urbanairship.com/accounts/register/`.

1. Create a basic (free) Urban Airship account if you have not already done so. Log in to your account. From the menu click on **SELECT AN APPLICATION,** then on **CREATE AN APP**.

2. You should register two apps, one containing your production keys and one development. That way you can keep your production and development keys separate.

> **Why two apps?**
> Apple will only send development push notifications to apps that are signed with the development provisioning profile. This ensures that your development messages cannot be sent to production devices.

3. You will need to export the push notification key that you imported into keychain in the earlier example. Right-click on the key in keychain and select the export option. Save the file for later use.

> You don't have to provide a password for this file.

4. Back to Urban Airship, fill in the **Application Name** field, select the most suitable category, and optionally check the **Debug Mode** checkbox. This checkbox will slow down the speed at which push notifications are sent to multiple devices, but it does give Urban Airship a chance to inspect errors returned from Apple for each device, so it's useful when getting started. You should switch this off before your app goes live or soon after that. Once you have filled in the information, click on the **Add** button.

5. The certificate created earlier now needs to be uploaded. Click on **Configure Now**. You will be presented with a screen, listing the supported operating systems. Click on **Configure** on the **Apple Push Notification Service** tab. Locate the certificate you created in an earlier step (entering the password if you gave it one). Click on **Save** to upload the certificate to Urban Airship.

What just happened?

You registered your app and its push notification key provided by Apple with Urban Airship. This will allow it to keep a register of devices that agree to receive notifications. If you select **API Keys** from the menu bar on the left of the screen, you will see three keys:

Key	Usage
Application Key	This is the key to identify your app.
Application Secret	This key is used in conjunction with the application key by a device to register for push notifications. You can share this key and put it in your app code; it is safe to share as it can only be used to register a device.
Application Master Secret	Take care with this key. This is the key that will be used to authenticate push notifications. If someone knows this and your application key they will be able to send push notifications on your behalf. Don't share it or put it in your application code unless you you want to include functionality where your users send notifications from your app. Be comfortable with the risks.

Coding the interface to Urban Airship

Now that you have registered your app with Urban Airship, you need to add the interface to your app code. This next example will show you how.

Time for action – registering a device for push notifications

You will be pleased to know that you have done almost all of the work for this already.

1. Grab the `urbanairship.js` code from `https://gist.github.com/4438938` and put it into your app code base.

2. Grab your development application key and secret from the app registration. Remember to change these keys prior to going live!

3. Modify the `registerForPushNotifications` call in `app.js`, adding in the highlighted code which calls the Urban Airship registration code:

```
Ti.Network.registerForPushNotifications({
  types: [
```

```
      Ti.Network.NOTIFICATION_TYPE_BADGE,
      Ti.Network.NOTIFICATION_TYPE_ALERT,
      Ti.Network.NOTIFICATION_TYPE_SOUND
   ],
   success:function(e){
     var UrbanAirship = require('urbanairship');
     UrbanAirship.register({token   : e.deviceToken,
                            key      : /* YOUR APPLICATION KEY */,
                            secret   : /* YOUR APPLICATION SECRET
*/,
                            success : function(e) {alert(e.
statusText)},
                            error   : function(e) {alert(e.
responseText)}
      });
   },
   error:function(e) {
     alert('Failed to register with APNS '+e.error);
   },
   callback:function(e) {
     var a = Ti.UI.createAlertDialog({
       title:'myForex',
       message:e.data.alert
     });
     a.show();
   }
});
```

4. Run the app on a device! You should be asked to register for push notifications and then get an alert box with a successful message.

What just happened?

You ran the app that requested and received a device token from APNS. This device token was then sent to Urban Airship so the device could be registered with them and used for any push notifications.

If you log in to your account on the Urban Airship website and navigate to your app you should see the registered device as a device token, as shown in the following screenshot:

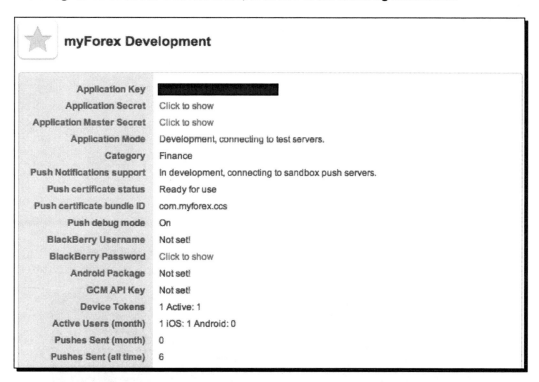

Have a go hero - sending a notification from Urban Airship

Once you have run the app on your device and allowed the app to receive push notifications, you should reap the rewards of this example by going to the Urban Airship site and sending a push notification:

1. Log in to your account on the Urban Airship website. Navigate to your app.

2. Navigate to **Push | Send Broadcast**. Enter your message in the alert box.

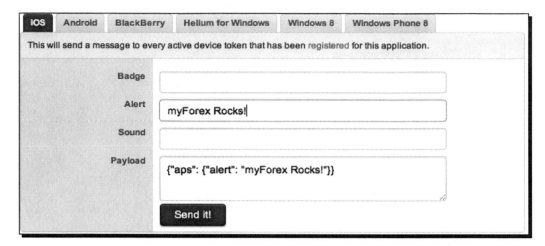

3. Click on the **Send it** button! Wait for about a minute and you will receive the notification.

The notification will appear as an alert box as this is the behavior we requested in the callback code in the last example. You are free to define what you want to do when a notification is received. This is the code that runs when the notification is received in this example:

```
callback:function(e) {
    var a = Ti.UI.createAlertDialog({
        title:'myForex',
        message:e.data.alert
    });
    a.show();
}
```

Pop quiz - push notifications

So you are comfortable with implementing push notifications? Here are a couple of questions to test your knowledge. State whether the following statements are true or false:

Q 1. It is possible to send push notifications from Urban Airship to both Android and iOS devices.

Q 2. You can receive notifications on the iOS Simulator and Android emulator.

Q 3. An app needs to be running to receive notifications sent from Appcelerator Cloud Services.

Summary

This chapter showed you the full process of implementing push notifications in Titanium using ACS or Urban Airship. It also showed that for a cross platform solution, the cloud-based service is the easiest one to implement. But a word of caution these solutions are not free. If your app is a success and gains a large user base, you will have to pay. If you create your own push notification server, then the only on-going cost is the hosting. Which solution is the best for you? It depends on the development time you have available and your plans for your app. It's a competitive marketplace; think about how your app is funded before committing to a solution.

By now you will be able to create apps, and add in extras such as social networking and push notifications. These apps now extend beyond the scope of the simulator. You will need to test the apps on a device before uploading the fully tested app to the app store. The next chapter focuses on this and more as it guides you through the testing and app submission process.

11
Testing and Deploying

While the simulator is a quick way to design and build your app, there are many things that you cannot access such as the camera, accelerometer, or push notifications. More importantly you will need to test your apps on a device before submitting them to the store.

If you plan to release an iOS version of your app, then you need to submit your app through the Apple App Store. On Android the picture is different; the main player and focus of your attention will be Google's own marketplace, but there are alternatives such as Samsung Apps, Amazon, GetJar, and AppBrain.

 If you release your Android app on hosts other than Google Play, then users will have to enable the unknown sources option in the system settings before they can install it. See `http://www.howtogeek.com/howto/41082/install-non-market-apps-on-your-android-device/` for more information.

In this chapter you will see:

- Testing your app on an iOS device
- Testing your app on Android
- Debugging your app in Titanium
- Deploying your app to the iOS store
- Deploying your app on the Android marketplace

Registering your app with Apple

You need to register your app with Apple before you can deploy it to the App Store or test it on a device.

Time for action – registering your app with Apple

Here is a step-by-step guide for registering your app with Apple:

1. Log on to the Apple developer program at `https://developer.apple.com/membercenter/`.

2. Select **iOS Provisioning Portal** from the available options. This is where you configure all elements of your app.

3. From the provisioning portal, select **App IDs** from the menu and click on **New App ID**.

4. Enter the details of your app. Give your app a short description that will be used to identify it in the portal (this will not be the description shown in the App Store). Leave the **Bundle Seed ID** drop down unchanged with the value of **Use Team ID**, and enter your app bundle ID in **Bundle Identifier**. You will find the value for your bundle ID in `tiapp.xml`. Click on **Submit**.

     Apple will add a number to the front of your bundle identifier. When the certificate is generated, it will be something like CX345564. You do not need to add this number to your bundle ID in `tiapp.xml`.

5. You can also configure your app for push notifications or for the game center here. We won't do that now, but if you are interested, *Chapter 10, Sending Notifications*, is all about push notifications.

What just happened?

You have registered an app ID with Apple. The next step is to create a development certificate for your app that will allow you to install your app on development devices.

Installing a development/distribution certificate

If you want to run your Titanium app on your iPhone or iPad, you will need to install a development certificate. This example follows on from the previous step where an app ID was created.

 Creating a distribution certificate is the same as this. You just select distribution instead of development. You will need to create a distribution certificate in order to submit your app to the App Store. More on this later in the chapter.

Time for action – installing a development certificate

Perform the following steps to install a development certificate:

1. Enter the iOS provisioning portal from the Apple developer site.

2. You must register every iPhone and iPad that you wish to test your code on. If you have already done this, proceed to the next step. Otherwise, select **Devices** from the menu. Click on **Add Devices**. You now need to add the **Unique Device ID (UDID)** of the device you wish to register and give it a descriptive name. Press **Submit**.

 If you need to find out the UDID of your device then follow the instructions at https://developer.apple.com/ios/manage/devices/howto.action.

3. Select the **Provisioning** menu option, then the **Development** tab.

4. Click on the **New Profile** button. The entry form for a new development profile will be displayed.

5. Give your development profile a descriptive name, select your development certificate, and select your app ID from the drop-down list. Now select the devices that you would like to run the app on and press **Submit**.

6. You will be returned to the list of development profiles and your new profile will be listed with a status of **Pending**. Refresh the screen; the profile will change from **Pending** to **Active**.

7. Download the certificate.

What just happened?

You created a development certificate and downloaded it to your computer. You can now use this with Titanium to install your app onto a registered device for testing.

Running the app on devices

The next few sections on running your app on devices and debugging will focus on functionality that is accessible from the **Project Explorer** toolbar, as shown in the following image:

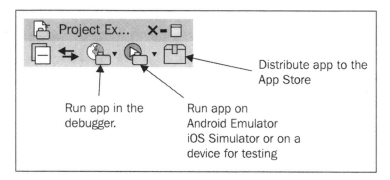

Testing the app on iOS

If you have a Mac then you will be able to test your app on an iOS device.

Time for action – running the app on an iOS device

Before you can run the app on a device you need to tell Titanium about the development certificate you created in the last example:

1. Connect your iOS device to your Mac.

2. From the **Project Explorer** menu, click on the **Run** button and select **iOS Device** from the menu. A pop-up window will appear with three tabs.

3. From the first, **General** tab, select your **SDK Version** and click on **Next**.

4. From the **Certificates** tab, select your development certificate. If it is not listed, download it from the iOS provisioning portal and then execute it to load it into your keychain. Click on **Next**.

5. From the **Provisioning** tab, click on **Browse** and locate your downloaded development certificate if it is not in the list.

6. Select your profile and click on **Finish**.

What just happened?

The Titanium App will be compiled and installed on the connected device via iTunes. You can now run the app from your device!

Testing the app on Android

Installing the test version of an app onto an Android device is far easier as you do not need to create any certificates. However, you do need to make sure your Android device is configured to allow apps to be installed from unknown sources.

You will probably have to install a driver file for the device if you are using Windows.

Time for action – configuring your Android device

Perform the following steps to configure your Android device:

1. From the system settings make sure that **Unknown sources** in **Applications** is checked.

2. If you wish to allow debugging on the device, then you should also check **USB debugging** by navigating to **Applications | Development**.

What just happened?

You configured your Android device so that apps could be installed via the USB cable. You also enabled USB debugging, which means that you can inspect the device using the ddms tool.

Running the app on an Android device is now a matter of connecting the device to the computer via a USB cable and selecting **Android Device** from the drop-down **Run** menu in Titanium Studio. The app will be compiled and installed onto your device ready for you to run.

 You can distribute your module to testers by sending them the apk file. The app .apk file can be found at /build/android/bin/ app.apk.
If the user accesses the e-mail on their Android phone, they can just open the attachment to install the app.

Debug your app

Titanium has a debugger! Some of you will not be excited by that, but to those people who coded in Titanium before the debugger existed, it is a blessing. If your code is well structured and modularized and with small functions, you probably won't use the debugger much, as most of the time inserting a couple of debugging console logs will give you a good idea of what is going on. But if you still cannot see what is going on after trying to output log messages, it's good to know that the debugger is there to help.

Running your app using the debugger is much the same as running the app on a device. The difference is that the debugger is accessed from the debugger icon on the run toolbar.

Publishing your app

Your app is finished and ready to go. It's 2 am in the morning, you have just run it for the last time in the simulator, and it works. The deadline for submission was 5 p.m. the night before. You want to get it uploaded quickly so you can get some sleep... Sounds familiar?

Hopefully it won't be like that this time. While it can be incredibly frustrating having to wait up to a week (and sometimes longer) for Apple to review your app (I do not know of any shortcuts to get your app into the store faster, sorry), it does mean that uploading it in the early hours of the morning when you are strung out on coffee will not have a big effect on the time it takes to release. It's far better to release when you are sure that everything is ok. Do not rush your submission; a rejection can take up to a week, and worse still you could have a silly mistake making it into the store. You don't want to give anyone an excuse to pan your app with one star reviews. You are releasing your app into a world full of the most technically savvy consumers who have high standards, higher still if they pay for your app. Do yourself a favor and make sure you are absolutely happy with your app before you release it.

Make a checklist and go through it before every code submission. Here are a few ideas that you may want to include on one of your own:

Test	Tested
Full code test.	
Orientation check; does you app handle orientation and any transitions?	
Certificates valid for at least six months (iOS) or till October 22, 2033 (Android)?	
Are all debugging logs and development alert box pop ups switched off, commented out, or removed?	
Are all keys for web services, cloud services, and push notifications set to **Production**?	
Have you tested a fresh install onto the device?	
Have you changed all the icons and splash screens? Do they look ok on the device?	
Check your settings in `tiapp.xml`. Is there anything unusual in there?	
Is the release for Android? Create a list of devices the app has been tested on—test it on your friends and colleagues phones. You need to have a good idea what devices your app looks good on. It all helps to avoid those killer one star reviews.	
Check your project directories to make sure all images, databases, icons, html, audio, video content are included.	

Before you publish your app, you need to get your images and promotional material ready. This means creating icons, splash screens, and screenshots of the app in action. You should also put together a couple of punchy sentences that will sell the app. This description is searched, so be SEO aware when writing it.

There are a number of images that you need to gather before you can submit your app. Let's look at the minimum requirements to get your app published and looking good.

iOS

The requirements have been split between iPhone and iPad. Common to both devices is an icon that is shown in iTunes.

All iOS platforms

The details of the icon are as follows:

Purpose	Dimensions	File name
iTunes artwork	512 x 512	`Resources/iphone/iTunesArtwork` (file should be `png` format but remove the file extension)

iPhone

The details of the required icon for iPhone/iPod are as follows:

Model	Purpose	Dimensions	File name
iPhone/iPod non-retina	App icon	57 x 57	`Resources/iphone/appicon.png`
iPhone/iPod retina	App icon	114 x 114	`Resources/iphone/appicon@2x.png`
iPhone non-retina	Splash screen	320 x 460	`Resources/iphone/Default.png`
iPhone 4/4S iPod touch 4th generation	Splash screen	640 x 960	`Resources/iphone/Default@2x.png`
iPhone 5 iPod touch 5th generation	Splash screen	640 x 1136	`Resources/iphone/Default-568h@2x.png`
iPhone/iPod non-retina	Spotlight and settings	29 x 29	`Resources/iphone/appicon-Small.png`
iPhone/iPod retina	Spotlight and settings	58 x 58	`Resources/iphone/appicon-Small@2x.png`

iPad

The details of the required icon for iPad are as follows:

Model	Purpose	Dimensions	File name
iPad 1 and 2	App icon	72 x 72	`Resources/iphone/appicon-72.png`
iPad 3	App icon	144 x 144	`Resources/iphone/appicon-72@2x.png`
iPad 1 and 2 landscape	Splash screen	1024 x 748	`Resources/iphone/Default-Landscape.png`
iPad 1 and 2 portrait	Splash screen	768 x 1044	`Resources/iphone/Default-Portrait.png`
iPad 3 landscape	Splash screen	2048 x 1496	`Resources/iphone/Default-Landscape@2x.png`
iPad 3 portrait	Splash screen	1536 x 2008	`Resources/iphone/Default-Portrait@2x.png`
iPad 1 and 2	Spotlight and settings	50 x 50	`Resources/iphone/appicon-Small-50.png`
iPad 3	Spotlight	100 x 100	`Resources/iphone/appicon-Small-50@2x.png`
iPad 3	Settings	58 x 58	`Resources/iphone/appicon-Small@2x.png`

 Do you want a screenshot of your app running on iOS? Press the *Home* key and the power button at the same time to take a screenshot of your screen that will be saved in the photo gallery.

Android

You have two options to consider when creating splash screens for your Android app. You could create a copy of your splash screen for every combination of screen size, orientation, and density. This means making 12 copies of your splash screen. Even when you do this there will be some devices that have screen sizes that are not a perfect fit and so could be compromised. So given the sheer number of different Android devices, there is an alternative. You can supply a single nine-patch screenshot that will be resized to fit all devices. A nine-patch image is a standard PNG image with regions that have been marked as expandable and others that are marked as fixed. Android takes this information out of the PNG image and uses it to resize and stretch the image to fit all devices. Google recommends the use of a nine-patch image.

For more information, see `http://docs.appcelerator.com/titanium/3.0/#!/guide/Icons_and_Splash_Screens`.

Image	Dimensions	Location
The application icon	128 x 128	`Resources/android/appicon.png`
The application splash screens for all versions of Android and all devices or a nine-patch image	Various	Directories under `Resources/android/`

Do you want a screenshot of your app running on an Android device? You need to use the Android debugger, ddms. It's supplied with the Android SDK. This useful tool will allow you to grab a screenshot by navigating to **Device | Screen Capture** from the menu. It also lists all console messages on the device which is a useful debugging tool.

Deploying the app to the Apple App Store

So if you are truly happy with your app, here is how you deploy it to the App Store.

Time for action – deploying the app to the Apple App Store

Perform the following steps to deploy the app to the Apple App Store:

1. If you have not already done so, create and download a distribution certificate. See the instructions from earlier in the chapter on creating a development certificate if you are unsure on this.

2. Before you can deploy your app, you need to register your app and upload your promotional material in iTunes Connect.

3. To create your app, log in to `https://itunesconnect.apple.com/` using your Apple ID.

4. Select **Manage Your Applications** from the available options, then press **Add New App**.

5. Enter in the details of your app. SKU Number is your own identifier of the app. Continue and provide the promotional material, contact information, icon, and screenshots.

You can edit this information before submission, but you do need at least an icon and a screenshot in order to create the app.

6. Once this is complete, your app will have a status of **Prepare for Upload**. This status needs to be progressed to **Waiting For Upload** in order to submit your app. Select the app once again in iTunes Connect, and from the **Current Version** panel select **View Details**. From the version detail screen click on **Ready to Upload Binary** and complete the legal challenges. You can now submit your app.

7. Once this is complete, return to Titanium Studio. Click on the **Publish** button from the **Project Explorer** window and select **Distribute – Apple iTunes Store**.

8. A series of pop-up dialogs will be presented. The first two should be easy to complete and you may be able to just click on **Next**. On the provisioning pop up you may have to browse to locate the downloaded production distribution certificate if it does not appear in the list. This involves the same process that was shown in the earlier example for development certificates. Confirm the other settings before clicking on **Publish**.

9. Check the console for progress of the build. You cannot run an app packaged for distribution on the simulator or on your device so nothing will happen when the compilation completes. You will get a message as follows on the console if all has gone well:

```
[TRACE] : __ _** BUILD SUCCEEDED **
[INFO] : __ _Finished building the application in 49s 593ms
[INFO] : __ _Packaging for App Store distribution
```

10. Xcode should now be shown on the screen. From here open the organizer (**Window | Organiser**) and click on the **Archives** button.

11. Select your app and click on **Validate**.

12. Did that go well, no issues? Take a deep breath and click on the **Distribute** button. Select **Submit to the iOS App Store** from the options and click on **Next**. Enter your user credentials and then confirm the app you are uploading. Click on **Next**.

13. Your app will now be uploaded to Apple and then queued for review.

What just happened?

Congratulations! You uploaded your app to Apple. You will start to receive e-mails about the progress of the review process of your app, hopefully followed by, after a few days, confirmation that your app is live in the store.

Titanium is cross platform so naturally you will want to release your app on Android also. Here are the instructions on how to submit your app to the Android marketplace.

Deploying the app to Google Play

Deploying your app to Google Play is easy once you have created your certificate. The following example will guide you through the process.

Time for action – deploying the app to Google Play

Perform the following steps to deploy your app to Google Play:

1. If you have not already done so, register yourself as a developer with Google Play.

2. Create your app on Google Play. Enter in the name and description of your app. Enter the details of your app on Google Play and ready yourself for publication by entering your promo text and uploading screenshots and logos.

3. Much like iOS, Android apps are encoded and secured using a certificate. The difference is that with an Android app you generate the certificate. Use the `keytool` command to create yourself a certificate. The parameters to this command are important and are as follows:

Parameter	Meaning
-genkey	Indicates that you wish to create a key.
-v	Provides verbose output throughout the process (reassuring).
-keystore	The location of the local keystore file. This file can be shared by all your Android apps, which is good as it means all your certificates are in one place. Make sure that this file is backed up somewhere safe as you are in a world of pain if you lose it.
-alias	This identifies the key. It's a good idea to name this after your app.

Parameter	Meaning
-keyalg	The algorithm used to encrypt the key. This must be set to RSA. Google enforce this.
-validity	Google will only accept certificates that are valid until October 22, 2033. It seems a lot, but that's the requirement. This parameter is specified in days so a safe setting that clears you with some margin would be 10,000 days.

4. If the keystore file you specify does not already contain a previously generated certificate, that is it's a new file, then you will need to enter a password for the file, so that the keystore file itself can be encrypted. The password you use to encrypt the keystore file must be the same as the password used for all certificates in the file, otherwise Titanium cannot access the certificates.

5. Run the command as shown in the following command line, substituting your keystore location for the keystore parameter (if the keystore doesn't exist it will be created) and alias:

```
keytool -genkey -v -keystore ~/android.keystore -alias pinbarEntry
-keyalg RSA -validity 10000
```

6. You will also be prompted for a password. This will be used to encode your certificate so don't make it too obvious, but equally don't make it something you cannot remember. You are not encoding some vital piece of financial information so it's more important to set a password you can remember than a super secure one that is hard to remember. You do not need to fill in any other details if you don't want to.

 Do not lose this password. If you forget the password to the certificate you will not be able to sign your app with the same certificate when you release an update. This will mean that you will not be able to release an update to your app. You will have to make a new app and leave the old one to stagnate along with the users.

7. Did you remember that password? As the certificate is the critical item that will link your app to its future, just check your details over before we progress by running the following:

```
keytool -list -v -keystore ~/android.keystore
```

8. You are now ready to build your app for publication. Click on the distribute icon and from the menu, click on **Distribute – Android**. The following screenshot will be presented:

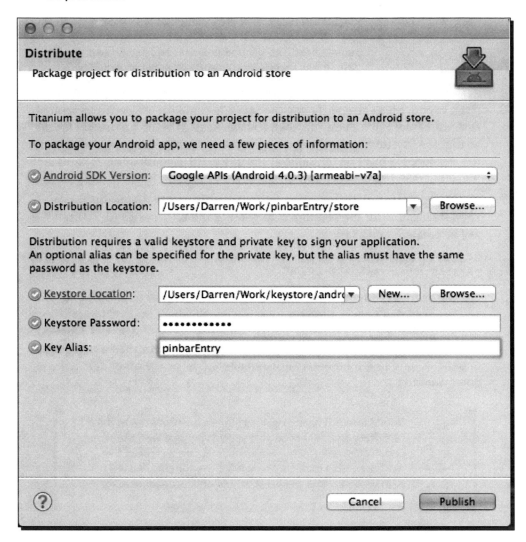

9. Enter the keystore location, keystore password, and alias and click on **Publish**. The console will show many messages indicating the build progress before the following pop up appears indicating the distribution packaging process as completed:

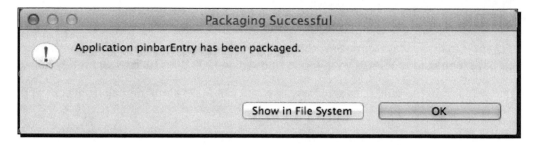

10. You now have an `.apk` file that you can upload to an Android store.

What just happened?

Congratulations! You packaged your app for the Android market. Your app is now ready to be released to the world. You can upload the app to the developer console of Google Play or any of the other Android stores you wish to use to distribute your app.

Pop quiz - deploying your app

Q 1. Why is the Android keystore file important?

1. If you lost it you could not update your existing app.
2. If you lost it your app would no longer run on users' phones.
3. If you lost the password you could not edit your source code.

Q 2. What is the minimum expiry date for an Android certificate?

1. 1 year.
2. 10 years.
3. 22nd October 2033.
4. 1st January 2021.

Q 3. What sort of certificate do you need to generate and download from the iOS Provisioning portal in order to test your app on an iOS device?

1. Distribution certificate.
2. Development certificate.
3. Test certificate.

Summary

This chapter in many ways represents the end of the line, the completion of the process. If you have managed to release your app to Android and iOS then success will surely follow.

All that remains in the book is to show you how you can make some money from your app.

12
Analytics

Your app may be live and you may be gathering great statistics for the number of downloads from iTunes Connect. But that's not even half of the story. How many users are you retaining? How many are using your best feature? Which makes of phone are using your app? If you only rely on iTunes statistics, you will be missing out on vast amounts of important information.

If you are a website owner, you will already appreciate just how useful the analytic tools provided by Google or Bing are. Being able to track visitors to your site and the paths they take is a vital tool. The story should be no different for your apps. You need to know who is using your app and what they are doing with it. When you know this, you can really start to reap the benefits by tailoring your app to the users and targeting your market better.

This chapter will explore the following three analytics providers for Titanium apps:

- ◆ Flurry
- ◆ Google Analytics
- ◆ Appcelerator Analytics

Comparing the providers

How do the preceding three providers compare against each other? What services do they provide and what is the cost? The following table compares the offerings of Flurry, Google Analytics, and Appcelerator Analytics and includes how easy it is to implement an interface on your app:

	Flurry	Google Analytics	Appcelerator Analytics
Cost of service	Free	Free	Free to record up to 1,000,000 events per month
Implementation cost	$5.00 for the marketplace module	Free	Free
Ease of integration	Easy	Easy	Simple
Can it record custom events?	Yes	Yes	Yes
Can it record user information?	Yes	No	No
iOS	Yes	Yes	Yes
Android	Yes	Yes	Yes
Availability	Appcelerator marketplace module.	Third-party JavaScript library with MIT license.	Included in the Titanium SDK.
Why would you choose it?	It's a great user interface for analysis of analytics. It offers unique cross-segment analysis information.	It's free. It makes use of the same Google Analytics web interface that will be familiar to website administrators.	It's the easiest to implement, as it is a part of the Titanium SDK.

There is no clear winner between the three providers; each solution has its merits. Solutions for each of the three providers will be shown in this chapter.

Flurry

Flurry specializes in providing mobile analytic information for apps. Their cross-app analysis is a real bonus for small-time app developers who have a small user base or only a single app. By collecting statistics gathered from other apps on the same device, they can provide analysis about your user base that goes far beyond the information you have gathered. Take a look at the following screenshot of app data from Flurry:

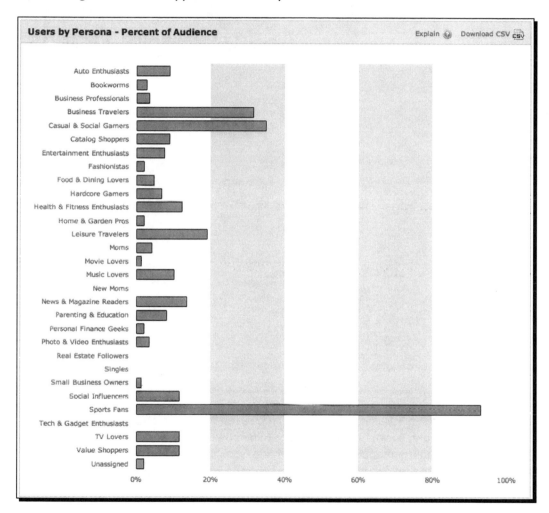

Also, take a look at the following screenshot:

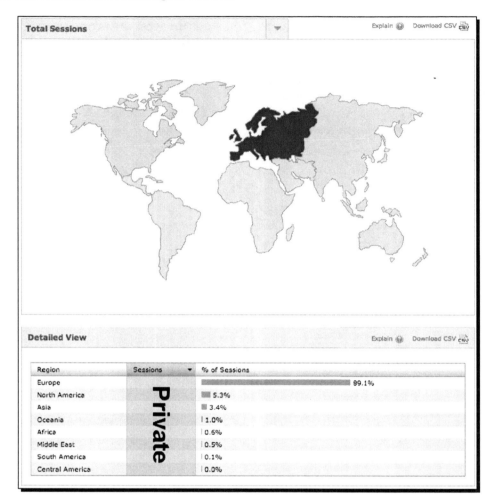

Flurry has not released a JavaScript API that can be used by cross-platform development tools such as Titanium, so we have to interface to a native library. For this you need to either write your own Titanium module or download one from the Appcelerator Marketplace. The example shown at the following link was based on the Flurry module that is compatible with both iOS and Android, developed by One Cow Standing:

```
https://marketplace.appcelerator.com/apps/4116?896634640
```

There is also a free iOS only Flurry module developed by Appcelerator at
```
https://marketplace.appcelerator.com/apps/4971?1612233609.
```

Time for action – setting up Flurry

Perform the following steps to set up Flurry:

1. You need a key to uniquely identify your app. Register your app at Flurry Analytics (`https://dev.flurry.com/secure/login.do`). After registering you will get an application key (also referred to as an API key). This will be the key used to identify your app on Flurry.

2. Install the module into your project home.

3. Open `tiapp.xml` and add the new module to the list of attached modules.

4. Add the following code to `app.js` to initialize the Flurry session, adding your Flurry API key in place of the highlighted code:

   ```
   var flurry = require('com.onecowstanding.flurry');
   ```

5. Run the app!

What just happened?

You created a Flurry account and linked it to the app using the API key. You added code to your app to start a new session when the app is opened and to post analytics updates while the app is open. You should see the statistics within a few hours of running the app on the simulator.

We now need to add calls to the app code to fire the analytics events when something of interest, such as a user clicking an advert, happens in the app.

There are two categories of items we are going to track, as follows:

◆ **Page views**: When someone opens a screen on the app
◆ **Custom events**: When you wish to collect descriptive text for a user-defined event, such as canceling the purchase of a product

Tracking page views

Suppose you wanted to register when a user opened your product catalog. The next example shows how to record the entry into a new window.

Time for action – registering a page view

Add the following code to register your event:

```
var flurry = require('com.onecowstanding.flurry');
flurry.logPageView();
```

What just happened?

You added code to log a page view to Flurry. The module will determine the name of the page. This will be recorded by Flurry, as shown in the following screenshot:

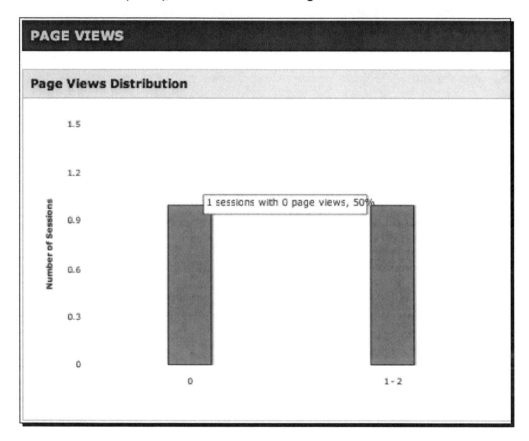

Tracking custom events

If you wanted to record a custom event such as registering when a user selects a currency, you would do the following.

Time for action – registering a custom event

Add the following code to register your event. In this case the event is hardcoded as the selection of the EURUSD currency.

```
var flurry = require('com.onecowstanding.flurry');
flurry.logEvent('Select Currency', {key: 'EURUSD'});
flurry.endSession();
```

 You need to call `endSession` on Android to mark the end of one invocation of the app. This prevents the user from opening the app twice and it being recorded as the same session. This is not required for iOS. See the module documentation for more information and other functions at `http://appcelerator.marketplace.assets.s3.amazonaws.com/downloads/4067/index.html`.

What just happened?

You added code to log a custom event with Flurry. The result of the call can be seen in the following screenshot from Flurry:

Other items you can gather

Flurry allows you to gather other analysis information about your users. There are calls for collecting the users age and gender. You can also send error reports.

Google Analytics

The same powerful features provided by Google Analytics for website administrators and marketing can be used to track your app. The next example shows how to integrate Google Analytics into your app.

This example uses the JavaScript library originally developed by Roger Chapman. The library stores analytics events in a database on the device until a network connection is available when it sends the stored events to Google. The interval between sending events is configurable and should be set to at least half a minute to avoid excessive network consumption.

Time for action – setting up Google Analytics

Perform the following steps to set up Google Analytics:

1. You need a key to uniquely identify your app. Register your app at Google Analytics (`http://www.google.com/analytics`). After registering you will get a tracking ID that will be something like *UA-99999999-9*. This will be the key used in your app.

   > A tracking ID has to be associated with a website and generating data for Google Analytics before Google will accept any data from this example. You cannot just create a new tracking ID for this example and expect it to work. Try using the same tracking ID as used on an existing website.

2. Grab the JavaScript analytics library originally written by Roger Chapman (`https://gist.github.com/4441504`) and put it in your project code base as a new file called `analytics.js`.

3. Include the analytics library in your code. Add the following to `app.js`:

   ```
   Ti.include('analytics.js');
   ```

4. Add the code to set your tracking ID (replace the tracking ID shown next with your own one) and to create a new session when the app starts, so that each app opening is a different session in the analytics results.

   ```
   var analytics = new Analytics('UA-99999999-9');
   analytics.reset();
   ```

5. Each page view or event that you wish to be logged will be recorded by firing an event. Set up the global listener in `app.js`, which will listen for the following events:

```
Ti.App.addEventListener('app:analytics_trackPageview', function(e)
{
  analytics.trackPageview('/' + e.pageUrl);
});

Ti.App.addEventListener('app:analytics_trackEvent', function(e){
  analytics.trackEvent(e.category, e.action, e.label, e.value);
});
```

6. Finally, add the following code to start the new session and set the interval for statistics uploads:

```
analytics.start(30);
```

 The setting for uploads is a delicate balance. You don't want to set it too low as it will fire off lots of network requests that will consume extra resources. However, if you set it to a value that is greater than the time a user ever spends with your app open, it will never fire!

You don't need to call the `close` function when the app completes. A new session will be started when the app is reopened, and any outstanding events from that session will be uploaded then.

What just happened?

You created a Google Analytics account and linked it to the app using the tracking ID. You added code to your app to start a new session when the app is opened and to post analytic updates while the app is open.

We now need to add calls to the app code to fire the analytics events from the app.

There are two categories of items to track, as follows:

- **Page views**: When someone opens a screen on the app
- **Custom events**: Called with descriptive text for a user-defined event

Tracking page views

This example will track when a user enters a new window.

Time for action – registering a page view

Add the following code to register a window opening or a navigation tab changing:

```
Ti.App.fireEvent('app:analytics_trackPageview', {pageUrl: 'Opened
Catalog'});
```

 You can put any text of a reasonable length in the `pageUrl` parameter. Be as descriptive as you want to be.

What just happened?

You added code to fire an event that will be picked up by the corresponding event listener in `app.js`. The text will be recorded and sent to Google Analytics, where it will be recorded as a page view.

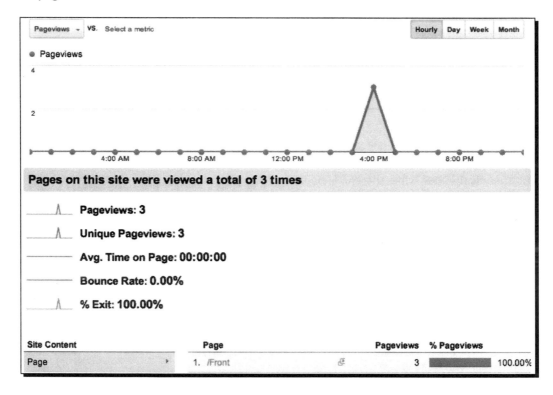

Tracking custom events

If you wanted to record a custom event such as registering when a user selects a currency, you would do the following.

Time for action – registering a custom event

Add the following code next to the action that you wish to capture:

```
Ti.App.fireEvent('app:analytics_trackEvent', {category:'Currency
Selection', action:'Select Currency', value:_args.value});
```

What just happened?

You added code to fire an event that will be picked up by the corresponding event listener in `app.js`. The custom event will be recorded and sent to Google where it can be seen on the analytics console, as shown in the following screenshot:

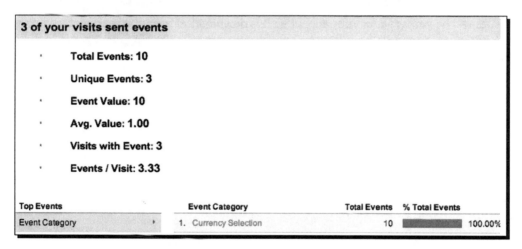

 Don't go rushing off to Google Analytics as soon as you have run the code through the simulator for the first time. You won't find anything! Give it a couple of minutes. Google state that it can take up to 24 hours for your stats to appear.

Analytics using Appcelerator

This example will show how to gather analytics information using the functionality built into the core of Titanium.

Appcelerator gathers usage statistics from your app by default without you having to do anything. So why not make use of them?

Time for action – setting up Appcelerator Analytics

Perform the following steps to set up Appcelerator Analytics:

1. Ensure that the `analytics` setting is enabled in `tiapp.xml`. This setting controls Appcelerator Analytics; if it is set to `false`, no stats will be gathered.

```
<analytics>true</analytics>
```

2. You will need to either deploy the app to the app store, or run the app on a device after it has been packaged for production (by compiling the app with the **Distribute** option). Stats are not sent to Appcelerator unless you run in this configuration.

What just happened?

Statistics will be gathered for your app when it is downloaded from the marketplace or app store. When your app is live, you will be able to view statistics like the ones shown in the following screenshot, which shows your users per country:

Or in a table form:

You can even drill down to city level to see how your app is doing in certain areas:

Catching custom events

If you wanted to record a custom event such as registering when a user selects a currency, you would do the following.

Time for action – registering a custom event

Add the following code next to the action that you wish to capture:

```
Ti.Analytics.featureEvent('EURUSD Currency Selected');
```

You should be specific with the description of the event as the text is used to differentiate events. The preceding example is better than just logging "Currency Selected", as you would have no details on which currency was selected. However, avoid including dates and times, otherwise you will get no grouping at all and far too many single events.

What just happened?

You added code to send a specific piece of analytics information to Appcelerator Analytics.

Other suppliers

You can also store analytics data using StackMob, and can capture events using Parse. Implementing using these cloud solutions will be almost identical to this example so it's not worth repeating. The only real difference will be with the user interface for reviewing the analytics data and the point at which you have to pay money. You can decide what is best for you.

Pop quiz - recording analytics

Q 1. You are using Appcelerator Analytics and want to record when a user clicks a button. So you add the `Ti.Analytics.featureEvent` call to the button event listener. You run the app on the simulator, click the button, and then head off to the Appcelerator Analytics website to check that it has been recorded. What do you find?

1. The event will appear after a few minutes.

2. The event has not been recorded as the code has not been published.

Summary

There is no excuse for not gathering statistics when creating apps using Titanium. You have to do more work to stop gathering Appcelerator statistics than you do to include them, so why not use them? The insight you gain into how your app is used, where it is used, and potentially who is using it, is really powerful.

The segment and cross-app analysis provided by Flurry merit a special mention. Without gathering any information from users of your app, Flurry can make an educated guess at your user's age, sex, and interests. This is powerful information.

If you gather stats for your app, you will know if it is a success. If it's a success, you will be looking for a way to make money from it. This is what we will discuss in the next chapter.

13

Making Money from Your App

If you have developed your own app, you will not be paid for your development time. You may have an app that you can charge for, but if your app is free, you need to consider other ways to make some money from your app.

You will be pleased to know that there are a few ways to make money from your app. The simplest method is to charge for your app. We will not waste your time with an example of how to set this up; instead, we will focus on the other ways to make money, including:

- ♦ Advertising
- ♦ In-app payments

Displaying adverts in your app

Displaying ads in your app can generate significant revenue if your app is a success and if your ads are well targeted. It also fits nicely with the common approach of releasing a free version with trimmed-down functionality and adverts along with full functionality with the paid version.

Three of the major players of mobile advertising have solutions for Titanium. The following table compares them:

	Google AdMob	Millennial Media	InMobi
Ad size	From banner to full screen	From banner to full screen	Banner
iOS	Yes	Yes	Yes
Android	Yes	Yes	Yes
Cost	Free	Free	Free
Availability	Appcelerator Marketplace module	Appcelerator Marketplace module	Appcelerator Marketplace module

The rate of return from each provider cannot be compared, as it changes often and is rarely a flat rate. Most providers pay money based on **CPC** (**cost per click**, whereby money is paid only if the user clicks on the advert) but potentially there are more lucrative **CPM** (**cost per impression**, which pay based on the display of the advert) deals are out there. Do your research to find a solution that best suits your needs.

The next example will add banner adverts provided by Google AdMob.

> You can display adverts from other advertising agencies including iAd, Millennial Media, and InMobi via Google AdMob. Click on the **Configure** button under the **Mediation** section on the AdMob web console to add agencies to your app.

Time for action – configuring Google AdMob

Perform the following steps to configure Google AdMob:

1. If you have not already done so, create a Google AdMob account by visiting `http://www.google.co.uk/ads/admob/`.

2. Log in to your AdMob account and start the registration of your app by selecting **Sites & Apps | Add Site/App**.

3. From the next screen select your platform. If you are making full benefit of Appcelerator and distributing to multiple platforms, you will have to enter the details for all applicable platforms.

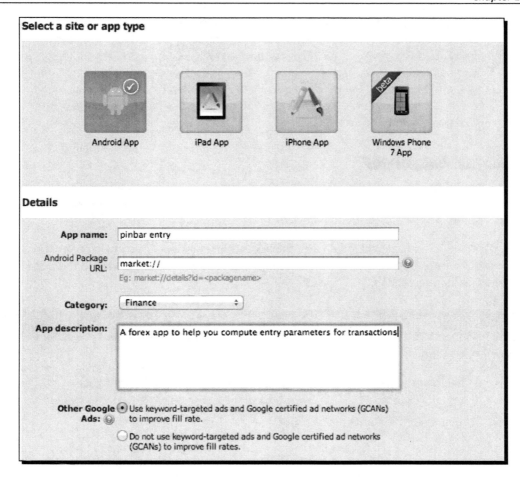

4. Complete the listing details for your chosen platform and click on **Continue**.

> If you have not released your app yet, just enter
> `http://` against the **App Store URL** field.

5. You do not need to download the SDK; the Appcelerator module includes a supported AdMob SDK. Click on **Go To Sites/Apps**.

6. View your app on **Sites/Apps | Sites & Apps**.

7. We now need to configure the adverts that will be served. Press the **Configure** button under the **Mediation** column. Select the size of advert and the refresh rate for the adverts that you would like to be served. Click on **Save & Continue**.

8. Now select the advert providers who can provide adverts for your app. Before you click on **Save**, you should make a note of the publisher ID, (which is the code in brackets) for your app. You will need this ID later. Click on **Save**. Depending on your choice of ad providers you may have to enter more configuration information. When you are finished, return to the app listing on **Sites & Apps**. Did you make a note of the publisher ID? If not, then click on **Manage Settings** under the **Name** column and copy it from the screen.

What just happened?

You have registered your app with Google AdMob and in doing so a publisher ID was generated. This publisher ID will be embedded into your app code to identify your app to Google when your app is run on a device.

We now need to add the code to display the adverts in your app. For this we are going to return to the forex app used in the previous chapters. We will add an advert to the front page of the iPhone version.

Time for action – incorporating AdMob into your app

Perform the following steps to incorporate AdMob into your app:

1. Download the free AdMob module from the Appcelerator Marketplace (`https://marketplace.appcelerator.com/apps/4961?653455394`).

2. Copy the ZIP file to the project root.

> Copying the module into the project creates a local installation of the module for the specific app. Alternatively, you can make the module available to all apps in your workspace by copying the ZIP file to the root of the Titanium installation. For more information visit `http://docs.appcelerator.com/titanium/3.0/#!/guide/Using_a_Module`.

3. Extract the ZIP file, or if you prefer, Appcelerator will extract it for you if you run the app.

> If you already have a `modules` directory, then the extract will create a `modules 2` folder. This will not be spotted by Titanium. Merge the contents into your original `modules` directory.

4. Open `tiapp.xml` and add the `ti.admob` module to the project. Save your changes.

5. The preparations are now complete. It's time to create the view where the adverts will be displayed. The view should have the same dimensions as the adverts configured with AdMob. For this example the changes will be made to `ApplicationWindow.js`, but the same changes can be made to any view.

6. First, request the AdMob module.

```
var ad = require("ti.admob");
```

7. Then create the advert view. Note the height dimension that matches the 50px advert configured with AdMob. Also note the bottom position of 0, as that's where we want the adverts to be shown, at the bottom of the screen. For now we are happy showing test adverts to prove feasibility, so set `testDevices` to `true`. You should replace the publisher ID with your own value.

```
var adView = ad.createView({
     publisherId:"a1111111111eee4",
     testDevices:true,
     bottom: 0,
     height: 50,
     width: Ti.Platform.displayCaps.platformWidth
    });
```

8. Add the new view to the window. Note that the other view has been resized to make room for the new ad view.

```
    var masterContainerWindow = Ti.UI.createWindow({
      title:'Currencies'
    });

    masterContainerWindow.add(currencyView);
    currencyView.top = 0;
    currencyView.bottom = 50;

    masterContainerWindow.add(currencyView);
    masterContainerWindow.add(adView);
```

You need to be explicit with your sizing of the advert view. The view size information is sent to Google so that it can serve up ads of the correct size. So if the window had a vertical layout, and there were no heights specified for the ad view, the display might not work.

9. Run the app!

What just happened?

You created an advert view that will serve up tailored adverts from your AdMob account, as shown in the following screenshot:

Once you are comfortable that everything is as you wish, then you can switch the `testDevices` flag to `false` and begin to serve up real ads that will make some money.

In-app purchases

There are different solutions for in-app payments for iOS and Android. Neither solution works on the other platform, so if you are releasing your app to both platforms, you will have to integrate code for two modules. For iOS you should use StoreKit and for Android, In-App Billing.

> You can also use the free PayPal module for collecting payment. It's available for Android and iOS. However, Apple does not accept payment through any means other than in-app purchases for extensions and subscriptions for your app. You can only make payments for services such as picture postcards or goods via PayPal.

For this example we are going to add an 'exotic currency' purchasable item to the forex app.

Time for action – adding in-app purchases for iOS

Perform the following steps to add in-app purchase for iOS:

1. In-app purchases are defined in iTunes Connect. Log in to your account and select the app.

2. From the **App details** screen select **Manage In-App Purchases** from the buttons on the right-hand side.

3. Click on **Create New**.

4. This will be a non-consumable item. Enter the product name (Exotic Currencies), the product ID (exotic_currency, which is your identifier), and the price tier. For this example we do not need to store any content with Apple that will be unlocked via the purchase, so select **No** for this question. Complete the screen by adding applicable languages and a screenshot, and then click on **Save**.

5. You will be making some test purchases before the in-app purchase goes live, so you need a test user so that your purchases don't cost you money! From the home screen of iTunes Connect, create a test user via **Manage Users**.

6. Return to Titanium Studio to make the code changes. This will be a simple example where the user will be presented with an alert box asking if he/she wishes to purchase the exotic currencies. If the user chooses **Yes**, the purchase will be made.

7. Create a new file, storekit.js, where all the in-app purchase functions will be defined. Add the following function that will request the price of a product given as a parameter:

```javascript
function requestProduct(_args) {
  var Storekit = require('ti.storekit');
  Storekit.requestProducts([_args.PRODUCT], function (e) {

    if (!e.success) {
      _args.ERROR({MSG:'Error'});
    }
    else if (e.invalid) {
      _args.ERROR({MSG:'Invalid'});
    }
    else {
      _args.SUCCESS({PRODUCT:  e.products[0]});
    }
  });
};
exports.requestProduct = requestProduct;
```

8. Create another function to perform the purchase. The function will pop up an alert box asking the user to confirm if he/she wishes to buy, and if so, it will call `purchaseProduct` to complete the sale.

```
function askToBuy() {
  // show alert box asking to user if they wish to purchase
  var alertDialogBox =   Ti.UI.createAlertDialog
  ({
      title:   _product.title,
      message:   'Would you like to buy '+_product.title+'
      which costs '+_product.formattedPrice,
      cancel:  1,
      buttonNames: ['Confirm', 'Cancel'],
  });
  alertDialogBox.show();

  alertDialogBox.addEventListener('click', function(e)
  {
    if (Ti.Platform.osname === 'android' &&
    a.buttonNames === null) {
      null;
    } else {
      if (e.index == 0) {
        // user wishes to buy
        purchaseProduct({PRODUCT:      _product
           ,SUCCESS:      function(e)
           {alert('Product purchased, show content')}
           });
      };
    }
  });
};
exports.askToBuy = askToBuy;
```

9. Now create the `purchaseProduct` function that records the sale.

```
function purchaseProduct(_args) {
  var Storekit = require('ti.storekit');
  Storekit.purchase(_args.PRODUCT, function (e) {

    switch (e.state) {
      case Storekit.FAILED:
        _args.ERROR({CODE:Storekit.FAILED});
```

```
        case Storekit.PURCHASED:
          _args.SUCCESS({CODE:Storekit.PURCHASED});
        case Storekit.RESTORED:
          _args.SUCCESS({CODE:Storekit.RESTORED});
    }
  });
};
exports.purchaseProduct = purchaseProduct;
```

10. Now add the code to `app.js` that loads the `storekit` functionality and requests an in-app purchase.

```
var sk = require('storekit');
// if the content requires a purchase then call the code to
purchase the product
if (sk.canMakePayments()) {
  sk.requestProduct({PRODUCT:'exotic_currency',
        ERROR:function(e) {alert('Error')},
        SUCCESS:function(e) {sk.askToBuy(e.PRODUCT) }
      });
}
```

11. Run the app!

What just happened?

You coded an interface to the iOS in-app payments. When you enter the app, several alert boxes will guide you through the purchase process. The first alert is probably unnecessary. The second is shown in the following screenshot. You may then be asked to enter in your Apple test user ID, before receiving a confirmation alert confirming your purchase.

This was a simple example to prove the functionality. A more complete example would record the purchase to ensure that the user is not asked again to purchase the extra content.

> For a more complete reference see the example app that is provided with the StoreKit module.

Have a go hero - recording a purchase

You could make modifications to the app to record the purchase by setting a property using `Ti.App.Properties`. Then check the property setting when trying to access the paid content.

In-app purchases on Android

The last example in this chapter shows how to implement in-app purchases on Android. You should note that the In-app Billing module can only be implemented in applications that you publish through Google Play. It's a reasonable restriction but it does highlight another fun challenge of developing apps for Android.

Time for action – adding in-app purchases for Android

Perform the following steps to add in-app purchases for Android:

1. You should have the following before you can define in-app purchasing products:

    ❑   A version of your app uploaded to Google Play— although the app does not have to be live to test in-app purchases

    ❑   A test user—you as the publisher cannot purchase your own item, although you can buy Google test products

    ❑   The app must include permission to access in-app products

    We will go through these steps in this example.

2. In-app purchases are defined through the Google Play Developer Console. Log in to your account and select your app.

3. Create a test user by selecting **Settings | Account details** from the navigation bars. Enter a different e-mail address to the one you used to register for the Google Play account under the **Gmail accounts with testing access** text area and click on **Save**. An example entry is shown in the following screenshot:

LICENCE TESTING

In addition to the owner of this console, the following users will get the Licence test response from the application. They can also make in-app purchases from APKs that have been uploaded but not been published yet.

Gmail accounts with testing access

youremail@gmail.com

4. You need a Google Merchant account before you can create products. A Google Merchant account will allow you to receive payments for your apps. Visit www.google.com/merchants for more details.

5. The app needs to have permission to communicate request and response messages to Google Play's billing service. To give your app the necessary permissions, add the line highlighted in the following code fragment to `tiapp.xml`. Note that the position of the line in the XML hierarchy is important. The `uses-permission` element must be a child of the `manifest` list of elements.

```
<android xmlns:android=
"http://schemas.android.com/apk/res/android">
    <manifest android:versionCode="1"
    android:versionName="1.0">
        <uses-permission
        android:name="com.android.vending.BILLING"/>
    </manifest>
    <tool-api-level>14</tool-api-level>
</android>
```

6. Compile and run your app with the revised permissions and then compile the module for distribution. See *Chapter 11, Testing and Deploying*, for instructions on how to distribute an Android app. Upload the app to Google Play.

7. Once your app is uploaded, stay in Google Play and from the menu bar select **In-App Products**. Select **Add New Product**.

8. Enter an identifier of your product and select the appropriate product type. A sample is shown in the following screenshot:

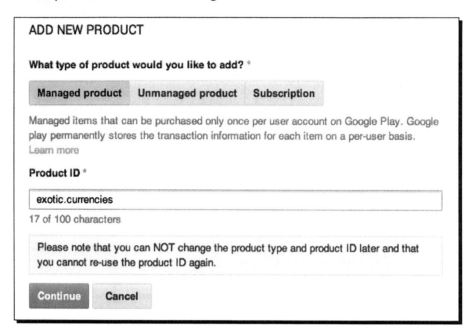

9. Click on **Continue**, and on the next screen complete the product listing by adding in name, description, and pricing information. When you have finished, click on **Save**.

10. The product will be created with a disabled status. In order to test purchasing, make one of your products active. Do this by selecting **Activate** from the drop-down list next to the product name. The product will not be activated until the app is published. Until then, if your app is not published, you will have to purchase Google test products.

 If you do not have access to an Android device with a test account, or if you just want to test in-app billing, you can use one of the Google reserved products, such as `android.test.purchased`. Visit `http://developer.android.com/google/play/billing/billing_testing.html` for more information.

11. Return to Titanium Studio to make the necessary code changes. The first step is to add in the In-App Billing module to your project. Download the module from the Appcelerator Marketplace (`https://marketplace.appcelerator.com/apps/776?642409200`) and then add it to your project. Instructions on how to install a module are shown in the AdMob example earlier in the chapter.

12. Open `tiapp.xml` add the `ti.inappbilling` module to the project. Save your changes.

13. After all that setup, you will be pleased to know that the code changes are simple. Add the following code. The first line accesses the marketplace module functionality. Next, an event listener is defined, which will be fired when a connection is made to Google Play. In this case we will be requesting a product as soon as the connection is made.

```
var inApp = require('ti.inappbilling');

inApp.addEventListener(inApp.ON_CONNECT_EVENT, function(e){
  // we have connected request the product
  inApp.requestPurchase({
    productId: 'exotic.currencies'
  });
});
```

14. Then add code to initiate the connection to the billing service. This line must be run after the event listener that was defined in the last step.

```
inApp.startBillingService();
```

15. You cannot test purchases by running the app on the emulator. Further more, you cannot just run a test version of the app on an Android device (by selecting **Android Device** from the **Run** menu), as doing this compiles the app with a different certificate to the one you used to upload the app to Google Play. You will get a configuration error if you run code this way. You need to package your app for distribution and install it to your device in order to purchase products.

> You can distribute your app to your Android device by e-mailing the `.apk` file created when you packaged for distribution to an e-mail address that can be accessed from the Android device. Open the e-mail and run the `.apk` attachment to install the app.

16. Once you have installed a distribution version of the app on a device, run it to record your purchase.

What just happened?

You coded an interface to the Android in-app payments. When you enter the app, you are presented with the following screen that asks you to confirm your purchase. Note that a test product was used for this screenshot.

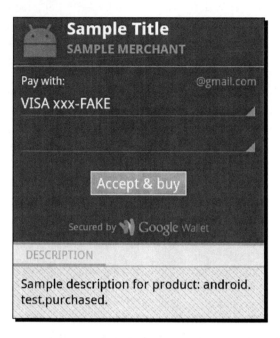

Pop quiz - making money from your app

Q 1. Yes or no, can you test advert code on iOS Simulator or the Android emulator?

Q 2. Yes or no, can you test in-app purchases code on iOS Simulator or the Android emulator?

Summary

Being able to generate income from your apps is an important part of being an independent app developer. Sure, you can get paid writing apps for other people, but if you are able to generate cash from your own ideas, you buy sufficient time to make your own app ideas a reality. Don't be limited in your ideas; the sky is the limit for apps and there is still time to write that killer app that makes a real difference.

I wish you luck with your apps, and congratulate you once again on your choice of tool, and of course on your choice of cookbook!

Git Integration

Titanium Studio is integrated with the cloud-based GitHub source control system. This provides the following benefits:

- **Easy to use**: All source code operations can be performed from within Studio.
- **Indicators**: Project elements that need action are highlighted within Studio.
- **Safe backup of code**: The code is stored off-site in the cloud.
- **Free**: It is free, as long as you are comfortable with your source code being publically viewable. Private repositories cost money. See GitHub for details.
- **Easy collaboration**: The web-based repository makes it easy for disparate teams to collaborate on code.
- **Easier than doing it yourself**: Setting up your own source code repository isn't a simple process.

This appendix outlines the common operations that you are likely to perform with GitHub.

 You can use other Git-based source code repositories such as Bitbucket (`https://bitbucket.org/`) just as easily as GitHub.

Importing a project

If you want to examine or modify an existing project that is hosted on GitHub, you need to be able to import the code into Titanium Studio. The next example will step you through the process.

Time for action – importing an existing GitHub project

Perform the following steps to import an existing GitHub project:

1. Connect to GitHub and find the project you are interested in, for example the one at `https://github.com/myleftboot/stopProgress`.

2. Copy the contents of the box to the right-hand side of **Git Read-Only**; in this case `https://github.com/myleftboot/stopProgress`.
3. In Titanium Studio select **File | Import**.
4. Select **Git/Git Repository as New Project** and click on **Next**.
5. Paste in the URL copied in step 2, and click on **Import**.
6. The project will be copied from GitHub into Titanium Studio.

What just happened?

The project listed on GitHub was downloaded to your workspace and imported into Titanium Studio. The project can be seen in **Project Navigator**. The project is linked with the GitHub repository so any changes you make locally can be committed and pushed as a new version back to GitHub, as shown in the next section.

Time for action – uploading a project to GitHub

Perform the following steps to upload a project to GitHub:

1. Ensure the project is open.

2. Select your project in **Project Explorer** and from the context menu (right-click) select **Team | Share Project**. The following screen will appear:

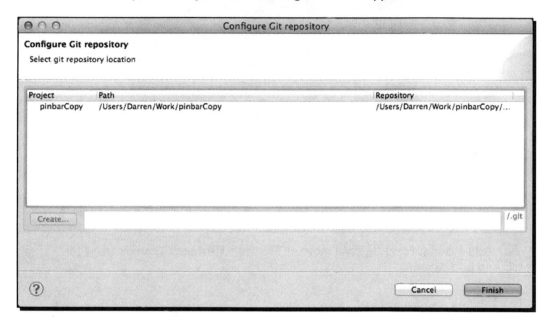

 This and other Git commands are also available by clicking on the cogs icon within **App Explorer**.

3. Select the project and click on **Create**.

4. Dismiss the dialog by clicking on **Finish**. Your empty Git repository is now set up locally and integrated with Titanium Studio. The next screenshot shows the changes that have been made, which are as follows:

   - The name of the branch (master) has been added to the project name
   - The filenames that are not included in the repository have a question mark

□ The stars next to the file and folders indicate that there are outstanding changes

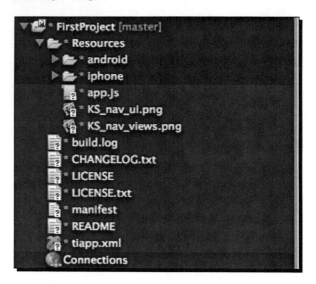

5. To add your project code to the empty repository, right-click on your project in **Project Explorer** and select **Team | Commit**.

6. Add a commit message and move all files from **Unstaged Changes** using the **>>** button.

 Make sure that you include the `.project` file and `.settings` directory in your staged files. These files contain important project configuration, which is used by Titanium Studio. If these files are missing from a project, the code cannot be run.

7. Click on **Commit**. Your changes are now committed locally to the repository. Any new changes will be made to a new version on top of the one just committed.

 The changes are not on GitHub; the code is still on your machine. You still need to push the code to GitHub.

8. Create a repository on GitHub if you have not already done so. Copy the location of the repository that is displayed in the box to the right-hand side of **Git Read-Only**. You will need this for the next step.

9. Add a remote by right-clicking on your project and selecting **Team | Remotes | Add**. Leave the remote name as it is. Add your Git repository URL to the **Remote URI** field.

10. Now push your changes to GitHub by selecting **Team | Push**.

 You do not need to add the contents of the `build` directory to your repository. The contents can be created from the source! Clean your project (**Project | Clean**) before adding any files to it, or better still make sure you ignore the `build` directory by adding it to the `.gitignore` file. The build files significantly increase the size of the project.

What just happened?

Your project code has been uploaded to GitHub and can be seen via the GitHub website. Your code has also been committed so any new changes will be based on this version.

Alternative suppliers

While the examples in this chapter have been based on GitHub, it's not the only player in the field. Titanium should work with any Git-based repository and certainly works with Bitbucket (`https://bitbucket.org/`). Just add the URL of your repository as a remote before you push your committed changes. Choose the supplier that best meets your needs.

Summary

Cloud-based source control software offers the following benefits above just being a source code control system

◆ Multi-developer collaboration

◆ Secure off-site backup of code

The secure off-site backup benefit alone is a no brainer. Why take the risk when integration is so easy?

B
Glossary

This glossary provides the list of the terminologies used in this book:

- **Accelerometer**: This is a component within device that detects movement.
- **Appcelerator Cloud Services (ACS)**: This is the cloud service offering from Appcelerator. This service is integrated into the Titanium SDK.
- **Alloy**: This is a framework designed for rapid development of Titanium apps. Visit `http://docs.appcelerator.com/titanium/3.0/#!/guide/Alloy_Framework` for more details.
- **Android**: This is the mobile phone operating system developed by Google. Its open source nature has led to device manufacturers modifying the code to suit them.
- **Android software development kit (SDK)**: The Android SDK includes a comprehensive set of development tools including a debugger, libraries, and a handset emulator.
- **Apple Push Notification Service (APNS)**: This is the service provided by Apple that controls the sending of push notifications to iOS devices.
- **Appcelerator**: This is the company that created Titanium.
- **app.js**: This is a file that lives in the `Resources` directory. It is the entry point to your app.
- **App Store**: This is an online store where people can download your apps. Apps can be free or paid. There is a single store for iOS controlled by Apple. On Android there are several stores from companies such as Google, Samsung, and Amazon.
- **Augmented reality**: This is the process of adding computer imagery to a real-world image. A mobile device can create an immersive augmented reality experience via the camera and accelerometer.
- **BlackBerry 10**: This is the latest version of the mobile phone operating system developed by BlackBerry. Full support for this platform is planned for 2013.

- **Cross-platform**: This is an app that can be run on different platforms. Titanium allows you to run your app on both Android, iOS, and BlackBerry.

- **Foreign exchange market (Forex)**: This is a market for the trading of international currencies.

- **GCM**: This is a push notification system for Android that is more akin to APNS.

- **Geolocation**: A component in the mobile device that can determine the phone's location to a configurable accuracy.

- **iOS**: This is the mobile phone operating system developed by Apple. iPhones and iPads use iOS.

- **JavaScript**: This is an interpreted computer language that is implemented with almost all modern browsers. It is included with all modern smartphones. Titanium uses the JavaScript interpreter to run your app. If you need to learn more about JavaScript, visit `http://javascript.crockford.com`.

- **JavaScript Object Notation (JSON)**: This is a text-based format for data interchange. It is an alternative to XML. It can be used to transmit information from the Web to your app and can also be used to transmit and store information within your app. It is used extensively throughout the book.

- **Model-View-Controller (MVC)**: This is a design methodology that promotes the separation of the solution between model, view, and controller elements. See `http://en.wikipedia.org/wiki/Model%E2%80%93view%E2%80%93 controller`.

- **Platform as a Service (PaaS)**: PaaS is a service model of cloud computing. In this model, the consumer creates the software using tools and/or libraries from the provider. The consumer also controls software deployment and configuration settings. The PaaS provider provides the hardware including the networks, servers, storage, and other services.

- **RSS**: This is a standardized XML format for publishing content. It is often seen on blogs and news sites where the user can subscribe to the RSS feed to keep abreast of the latest content.

- **Software development kit (SDK)**: This contains the libraries and emulators that allow you to compile your app and deploy it to a device. You will need the SDK of every platform you want your application to release to; iOS, Android, and Windows 8 all have their own SDKs.

- **SQLite**: This is a database system that is installed on most smartphones and tablets. It is ideally suited to these devices due to its small size.

- **Tiapp.xml**: This is the file that contains all of your compilation settings for the app. It lives in the root directory of your Titanium project.

- **Titanium**: This is the cross-platform language used to create apps for phones and tablets.

- **Unique device identifier (UDID)**: For iOS this is a 40-digit code unique to the device. Android devices don't have the same concept.

- **Windows 8**: This is the mobile phone operating system developed by Microsoft. Appcelerator plan to support this platform from mid 2013.

- **YQL**: This Is a service from Yahoo!, which allows users to query web content as though they were querying a database. If you wished to get the weather forecast for Sunnyvale, California, you could enter the query `select * from weather. forecast where woeid=2502265`. You can test queries and see examples by accessing the YQL developer console at `http://developer.yahoo.com/yql/ console/`.

C
Pop Quiz Answers

Chapter 1, How to Get Up and Running with Titanium

Pop quiz - Titanium installation and configuration

Q 1.	2
Q 2.	3
Q 3.	2

Chapter 3, How to Design Titanium Apps

Pop quiz - Titanium design

Q 1.	1
Q 2.	3
Q 3.	1

Chapter 4, Gluing Your App Together with Events, Variables, and Callbacks

Pop quiz - adding callbacks

Q 1.	2
Q 2.	1
Q 3.	3

Chapter 5, It's All About Data

Pop quiz - data handling

Q 1.	b

Chapter 6, Cloud-enabling Your Apps

Pop quiz - cloud services

Q 1.	Yes
Q 2.	No

Chapter 7, Putting the Phone Gadgets to Good Use

Pop quiz - gadgets

Q 1.	3
Q 2.	1
Q 3.	2
Q 4.	3

Chapter 8, Creating Beautiful Interfaces

Pop quiz - creating a layout

Q 1.	1
Q 2.	2

Chapter 9, Spread the Word with Social Media

Pop quiz - integrating social media

Q 1.	2
Q 2.	3
	4, if developing for Android

Chapter 10, Sending Notifications

Pop quiz - push notifications

Q 1.	True
Q 2.	False
Q 3.	False

Chapter 11, Testing and Deploying

Pop quiz - deploying your app

Q 1.	1
Q 2.	3
Q 3.	1

Chapter 12, Analytics

Pop quiz - recording analytics

Q 1.	2

Chapter 13, Making Money from Your App

Pop quiz - making money from your app

Q 1.	Yes
Q 2.	No

Index

color attribute 36
commentary entries
  showing, by creating panel 144-147
commonJS compliant code
  prompting 63
compass
  about 163
  heading, displaying 163-165
controller function 65
coordinate
  distance, computing from 185-187
CPC (cost per click) 278
CPM (cost per impression) 278
Create a new application button 220
current location
  getting 182, 183, 184
custom event, Appcelerator Analytics
  registering 275
custom events, Flurry
  registering 269
  tracking 268
custom events, Google Analytics
  registering 273
custom objects
  storing, parse used 148, 149

D

data
  execution context 80
  sharing, between windows 80
  sharing, ways for 81
  storing, in database 114, 115
  storing, in files 114
  storing, on device 111
data property 123
debug messages
  capturing 51
density independent pixel. *See* DIP
detail window 75
development certificate
  installing 249
devices
  app, running 250
DIP
  about 197

making, default unit for app 198
direction property 89
directions
  about 175
  adding, to map 176-178
displaybearingOnAR function 169
distance
  computing, from coordinate 185-187
Distribute option 274

E

error parameter 155, 233
events
  about 81, 85, 87
  properties 88
  scope 87
execution context 80
external data 102

F

Facebook
  about 213
  app, registering with 214, 215
  screenshot, sending to 216-219
fetchRSSFeed 110
filesystem 81
fireEvent 89, 90
Flurry
  about 265, 266
  custom events, registering 269
  custom events, tracking 268
  page views, registering 268
  page views, tracking 267
  setting up 267
  URL 267
foreign exchange list
  creating 124, 125, 126, 127
forexCommentary object 144
ForgedUI 194

G

garbage collection
  and global event listener 95, 96
geolocation 179

Thank you for buying
Appcelerator Titanium Application Development
by Example Beginner's Guide

About Packt Publishing

Packt, pronounced 'packed', published its first book "Mastering phpMyAdmin for Effective MySQL Management" in April 2004 and subsequently continued to specialize in publishing highly focused books on specific technologies and solutions.

Our books and publications share the experiences of your fellow IT professionals in adapting and customizing today's systems, applications, and frameworks. Our solution-based books give you the knowledge and power to customize the software and technologies you're using to get the job done. Packt books are more specific and less general than the IT books you have seen in the past. Our unique business model allows us to bring you more focused information, giving you more of what you need to know, and less of what you don't.

Packt is a modern, yet unique publishing company, which focuses on producing quality, cutting-edge books for communities of developers, administrators, and newbies alike. For more information, please visit our website: www.PacktPub.com.

Writing for Packt

We welcome all inquiries from people who are interested in authoring. Book proposals should be sent to author@packtpub.com. If your book idea is still at an early stage and you would like to discuss it first before writing a formal book proposal, contact us; one of our commissioning editors will get in touch with you.

We're not just looking for published authors; if you have strong technical skills but no writing experience, our experienced editors can help you develop a writing career, or simply get some additional reward for your expertise.

PUBLISHING

Appcelerator Titanium:
Patterns and Best Practices

Take your Titanium development experience to the next level,
and build your Titanium knowledge on CommonJS structuring,
MVC model implementation, memory management, and
much more

Boydlee Pollentine
Trevor Ward

[PACKT]

Appcelerator Titanium: Patterns and Best Practices

ISBN: 978-1-849693-48-6   Paperback: 110 pages

Take your Titanium development experience to the next
level, and build your Titanium knowledge on CommonJS
structuring, MVC model implementation, memory
management, and much more

1. Full step-by-step approach to help structure your
   apps in an MVC style that will make them more
   maintainable, easier to code and more stable

2. Learn best practices and optimizations both
   related directly to JavaScript and Titanium itself

3. Learn solutions to create cross-compatible
   layouts that work across both Android and
   the iPhone

Quick answers to common problems

PhoneGap Mobile Application
Development Cookbook

Over 40 recipes to create mobile applications using the
PhoneGap API with examples and clear instructions

Foreword by Brian Leroux, Senior Product Manager, PhoneGap Lead and
SPACELORD1!! at Adobe Systems Ltd

Matt Gifford   [   ] open source

PhoneGap Mobile Application Development Cookbook

ISBN: 978-1-849518-58-1   Paperback: 320 pages

Over 40 recipes to create mobile applications using the
PhoneGap API with examples and clear instructions

1. Use the PhoneGap API to create native mobile
   applications that work on a wide range of mobile
   devices

2. Discover the native device features and functions
   you can access and include within your applications

3. Packed with clear and concise examples to show
   you how to easily build native mobile applications

Please check **www.PacktPub.com** for information on our titles

iOS 5 Essentials

ISBN: 978-1-849692-26-7   Paperback: 252 pages

Harness iOS 5's new powerful features to create stunning applications

1. Integrate iCloud, Twitter and AirPlay into your applications.

2. Lots of step-by-step examples, images and diagrams to get you up to speed in no time with helpful hints along the way.

3. Each chapter explains iOS 5's new features in-depth, whilst providing you with enough practical examples to help incorporate these features in your apps

WordPress Mobile Applications with PhoneGap

ISBN: 978-1-849519-86-1   Paperback: 96 pages

A straightforward, example-based guide to leveraging your web development skills to build mobile applications using WordPress, jQuery, jQuery Mobile, and PhoneGap

1. Discover how we can leverage on Wordpress as a content management system and serve content to mobile apps by exposing its API

2. Learn how to build geolocation mobile applications using Wordpress and PhoneGap

3. Step-by-step instructions on how you can make use of jQuery and jQuery mobile to provide an interface between Wordpress and your PhoneGap app

Please check **www.PacktPub.com** for information on our titles

CPSIA information can be obtained at www.ICGtesting.com
Printed in the USA
LVOW10s0717310814

401703LV00002B/4/P